1875 310
$34·00

# Computer Communications:
## A BUSINESS PERSPECTIVE

# Computer Communications:
## A BUSINESS PERSPECTIVE

Keith Bearpark

Peter J. Beevor

McGRAW-HILL BOOK COMPANY

**London** · New York · St Louis · San Francisco · Auckland · Bogotá · Caracas
Lisbon · Madrid · Mexico · Milan · Montreal · New Delhi · Panama · Paris
San Juan · São Paulo · Singapore · Sydney · Tokyo · Toronto

Published by
McGRAW-HILL Book Company Europe
SHOPPENHANGERS ROAD · MAIDENHEAD · BERKSHIRE · ENGLAND
TEL 0628 23432   FAX 0628 770224

**British Library Cataloguing in Publication Data**
Bearpark, Keith.
  Computer Communications: Business
  Perspective
  I. Title II. Beevor, Peter J.
  004.6

  ISBN 0-07-707794-6

**Library of Congress Cataloging-in-Publication Data**
Bearpark, Keith.
  Computer communications: a business perspective / Keith Bearpark,
  Peter J. Beevor.
      p.    cm.
  Includes bibliographical references and index.
  ISBN 0-07-707794-6
  1. Business—Communication systems.   2. Computer networks.
  3. Computer architecture.   4. Telecommunication systems.
  I. Beevor, Peter J.   II. Title.
  HD30.335.B43   1993
  650'.0285'46—dc20                                          92-44974
                                                                  CIP

Copyright © 1993 McGraw-Hill International (UK) Limited.
All rights reserved. No part of this publication may be
reproduced, stored in a retrieval system, or transmitted,
in any form or by any means, electronic, mechanical,
photocopying, recording, or otherwise, without the prior
permission of McGraw-Hill International (UK) Limited, with
the exception of material entered and executed on a
computer system for the reader's own use.

1234 CUP 9543

Typeset by Goodfellow & Egan, Cambridge
and printed and bound in Great Britain at the University Press, Cambridge

# Contents

Preface   ix

**1**  A case study   1
   1.1 The Wessex and Northern Bank   1
   1.2 Information flows in the WNB   3
   1.3 Analysis of information flows   9

**2**  Basic telecommunications   12
   2.1 Introduction   12
   2.2 Information encoding   13
   2.3 Data transmission   16
   2.4 Communications media   24
   2.5 Summary   25

**3**  Network components and topologies   27
   3.1 Introduction   27
   3.2 Network nodes and addressing   28
   3.3 Network links   32
   3.4 Other networking equipment   32
   3.5 Network types   33
   3.6 Network design   34
   3.7 Summary   37

**4**  Introduction to communications architectures   42
   4.1 Introduction   42
   4.2 The nature of a communications architecture   42
   4.3 The development of communications architectures   46
   4.4 Standards organizations   48
   4.5 The structure of a network   49
   4.6 The ISO's reference model for Open Systems Interconnection (OSI)   50
   4.7 Systems Network Architecture (SNA)   53
   4.8 Local Area Networks (LANs)   58
   4.9 TCP/IP   61
   4.10 Summary   62

5 X.25  64
  5.1 Introduction  64
  5.2 The packet layer  65
  5.3 Layer 2  76
  5.4 The X.25 physical layer  82
  5.5 Packet Assembler/Disassembler (PAD)  84
  5.6 Summary  88

6 The OSI reference model  90
  6.1 Introduction  90
  6.2 Fundamentals of the reference model  91
  6.3 The layers of the reference model  94
  6.4 The OSI network service  96
  6.5 The upper layers of the OSI model  99
  6.6 Summary  111

7 Systems Network Architecture (SNA)  113
  7.1 Introduction  113
  7.2 SNA terminology  113
  7.3 LUs and LU-LU session types  116
  7.4 Control sessions  117
  7.5 Session establishment  118
  7.6 Some more terminology  119
  7.7 The path control network  121
  7.8 SNA messages  125
  7.9 The upper layers of an SNA node  128
  7.10 Application-to-application communication and LU6.2  135
  7.11 Peer-to-peer networking in SNA  138
  7.12 Summary  139

8 Local Area Networks (LANs)  141
  8.1 Introduction  141
  8.2 Medium Access Control (MAC) layer  143
  8.3 Logical Link Control (LLC) layer  152
  8.4 The network layer and above  154
  8.5 Bridges, routers and gateways  154
  8.6 Summary  158

## 9 Transmission Control Protocol/Internet Protocol (TCP/IP) 159

9.1 Introduction 159
9.2 The Internet Protocol (IP) 160
9.3 The Transmission Control Protocol (TCP) 164
9.4 The User Datagram Protocol (UDP) 167
9.5 Upper Layer Protocols (ULPs) 168
9.6 The TCP/IP standards process 172
9.7 Summary 172

## 10 Integrated Services Digital Network (ISDN) 173

10.1 Introduction 173
10.2 Lines and customer premises equipment 174
10.3 ISDN services 176
10.4 ISDN protocols 177
10.5 Broadband ISDN 181
10.6 Fast packet switching 182
10.7 Summary 185

## 11 Network security 186

11.1 Introduction 186
11.2 Attacks and countermeasures 186
11.3 Cryptography 190
11.4 Cryptography and security functions 196
11.5 Key management 200
11.6 The practical use of cryptography 201
11.7 Summary 203

## 12 Network management 205

12.1 Introduction 205
12.2 The OSI management framework 207
12.3 Management in the TCP/IP environment 209
12.4 Management of an SNA network 214
12.5 Integrated network management systems 216
12.6 Summary 217

## 13 Conclusion 219

Bibliography 220
Index 221

# Preface

There are many books on communications networks and their architectures. Some address the subject in a general sense while others concentrate on specific areas. There are also a number of books on various aspects of the use of communications by a business enterprise. A technical manager responsible for deciding on, or implementing, a communications strategy needs technical information presented within the context of the business. In our view, available technical literature does not provide this context, while business literature has insufficient technical content. This book seeks to bridge the gap by providing a technical work with a business orientation.

The need for such a book has become apparent to the authors through their experience in recruiting and training communications professionals. Graduates in a scientific discipline enter the world of business with a sound technical foundation but with little awareness of the nature and needs of business. Graduates in a business discipline enter with a sound business awareness but with inadequate technical knowledge. Many workers in the field of communications have acquired their knowledge through practical experience and lack awareness of those parts of the field that lie outside that experience. Managers often lack the technical background to support their decisions but not the ability to acquire it given appropriate material.

The book is aimed at all these groups of people. Undergraduates contemplating a career in business will find it useful general reading. Computer scientists will find it beneficial both as an introduction to the use of communications in business and as an overview of communications architectures. Technical professionals already employed, but asked to work in an area in which they have no experience, will find it a useful guide. It should be valuable in providing technical information to managers to aid their decision making. Developers and suppliers of communications products may find the book useful in assessing their customers' needs.

The opening chapter describes the fictitious Wessex and Northern Bank, a typical large information technology (IT) user. The chapter discusses the nature of the Bank's business and its data communication requirements. Each subsequent chapter describes a particular aspect of communication technology and ends with a summary, including a short section that relates the content of the chapter to the way in which the Wessex and Northern met its requirements in the past and the options open to it in the future. Chapter 1, and these sections, may be read consecutively as the story of a typical IT user. Each chapter may be read as an introduction to the more specialized works on its particular subject that are listed in the bibliography.

We are deeply indebted to the many colleagues, too numerous to mention, with whom we have worked and from whom we have learned. If they read this book, they will recognize their contributions. The credit is theirs; the mistakes are ours. We are also indebted to many people who have read and commented on different sections of the book, in particular to Les Blott. George Bearpark proofread the manuscript as only a professional can. We are also most grateful for the advice and encouragement from the staff of McGraw-Hill.

# CHAPTER 1

# A case study

## 1.1 The Wessex and Northern Bank

The Wessex and Northern Bank (WNB) is a thriving UK retail bank. Its origins can be traced back to the coffee houses of eighteenth-century London where the earliest forms of bank clearing systems were organized. WNB is a conglomeration of a number of small banks, but its main constituents, involved in a merger in 1968, were the Wessex Bank and the Northern Counties Bank. Both these banks had emerging computer departments, but there was little major investment in the information technology (IT) area until after the merger. In the UK clearing bank sector, WNB operates as a small clearer, but with a number of specialized, related banking businesses.

WNB has 1000 branches in England and Wales, and a number of representative offices in Scotland, Ireland and mainland Europe. Its international interests are not extensive, although it owns a retail banking operation in New England and another in Portugal. It has investment banking interests in the UK and in Europe. In the UK it runs a large foreign exchange operation.

The structure of WNB has undergone a number of changes since the merger of the Wessex and Northern Counties Banks in 1968. The current structure comprises four main business divisions and a support unit that is dominated by the IT Group. The business divisions concern themselves with UK retail businesses, international businesses, treasury and investment banking. In its last accounting year, WNB made a pre-tax profit of £250m, of which the UK Retail Division contributed some £200m. Other contributions were from the Treasury Division (£20m), International Division (£20m) and Investment Banking (£10m).

The bank's IT Group provides services to all the business units and its costs are allocated by a transfer charging mechanism to the separate units. In the accounting year for which the above profit contributions were made, the IT Group spent a total of £100m, of which £60m was spent on communications, including wide area and local area networks (WAN and LAN).

WNB employs 25 000 staff world-wide. Most of its staff are employed in the UK Retail Division (20 000). There are 3000 employees in the International Division, 600 in the Treasury Division, 600 in the Investment Banking Division and 800 in the IT Group and other support groups.

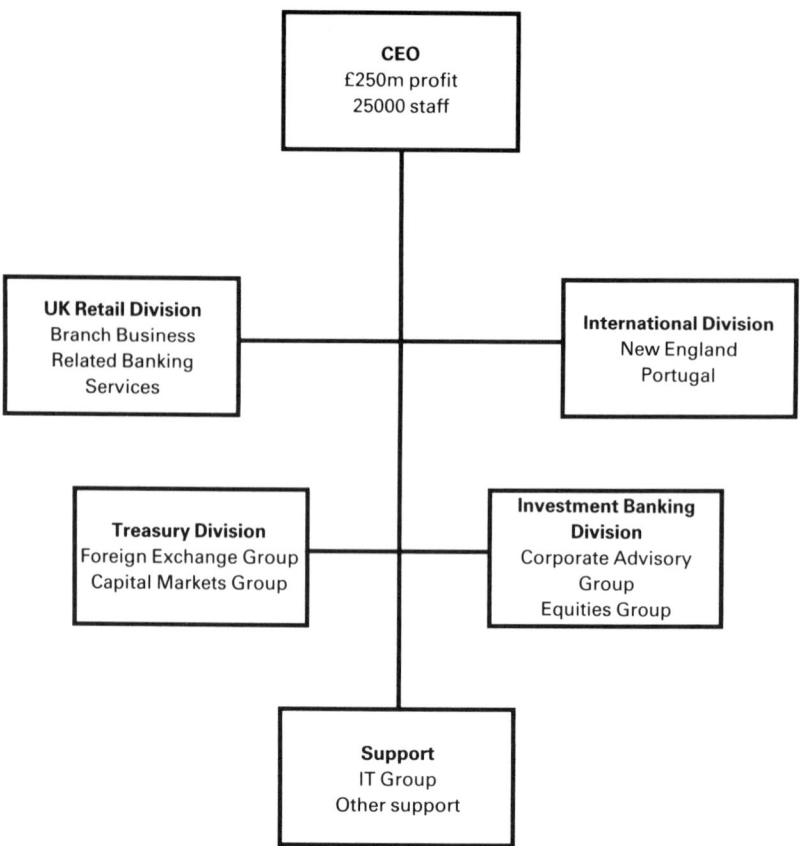

*Figure 1.1   The structure of the WNB*

The organization of the bank is illustrated in Figures 1.1 and 1.2. The UK Retail Division is split between the branch business in the High Street and the specialized, related services. The Investment Banking Division contains a Corporate Advisory Group and a large Equities Group. The Treasury Division includes a large Foreign Exchange Group, but also deals in capital markets. The IT Group consists of three main components: Data Centre Operations, Network and Branch Operations and Software Development.

The Data Centre Operations Team in the IT Group concerns itself with the operation of two data centres. Its responsibilities include the operation and security of the two main sites and the provision of technical support for hardware and systems software. Similarly, the Network and Branch Operations Team concerns itself with operations in these areas and with technical support for the related hardware and systems software. However, in addition to these responsibilities, it has a direct link with the users of the IT Group's services and has a major responsibility for ensuring that overall service levels are met. The

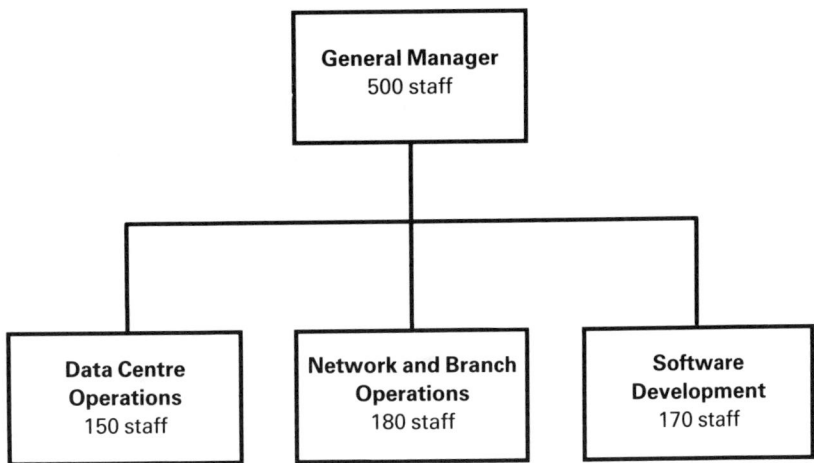

*Figure 1.2   The WNB's IT group*

Software Development Team was originally one of the largest teams in the IT Group, but has shrunk in recent years as more use has been made of packaged software for banking services.

The communications requirements of the four divisions are described in the following section and analysed in Section 1.3.

## 1.2 Information flows in the WNB

This section considers the information flows, both voice and data, that exist in the four divisions of the WNB. The information flows represent the communications requirements that must be satisfied by the WNB's network designers in its IT Group.

The requirements of the UK Retail Division are strongly influenced by the requirements of its 1000 branches. Similarly, the requirements of its International Division are influenced by the retail banks under its control, although there is a world-wide communications requirement for other representative offices. The communications requirements of the Treasury and Investment Banking Divisions are mainly determined by the dealing operations in foreign exchange and equities. The communications requirements of the four divisions are considered in turn below, while Section 1.3 discusses the implications of these requirements.

**UK Retail Division (branch business)**

The branch communications requirements are illustrated in Figure 1.3 and fall under the following main headings:

- telephone
- interaction with the branch accounting system
- access to same-day value payment systems
- access to the corporate database

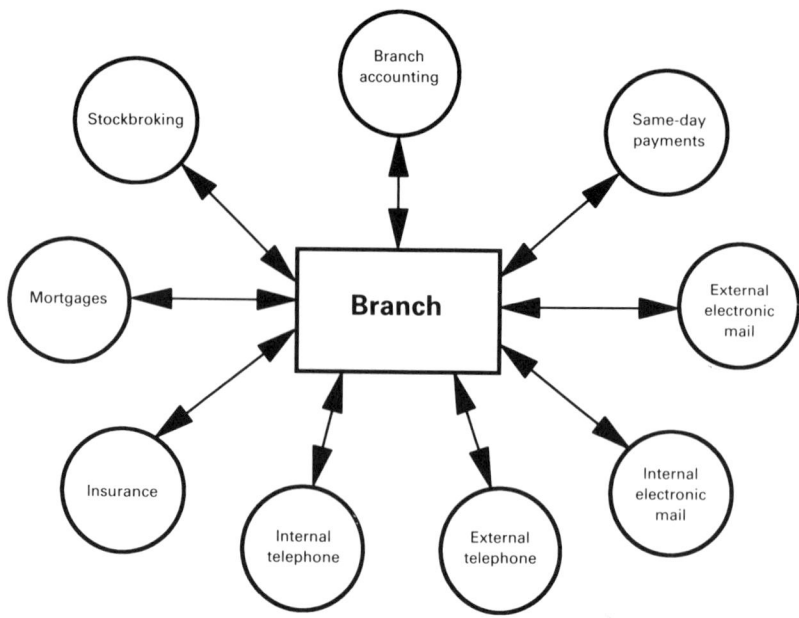

*Figure 1.3   The WNB's branch information flows*

- access to special financial services
- office automation services.

**Telephone**

The telephone requirements in a branch of the WNB are relatively simple: branch staff need to make and receive calls to and from customers and other bank staff. In addition to these simple requirements, there is some demand for a voice messaging service in which callers to a branch can leave messages for particular branch staff and branch staff can leave messages for other branches and Head Office units. There is a requirement to transfer calls from customers to other parts of the bank and also to allow incoming callers, particularly from within the bank, to book calls on engaged extensions.

**Access to branch accounting system**

The branch accounting system in the WNB was the first element of computerization. Prior to the introduction of computers, each branch maintained the accounts of its customers and presented the WNB's Head Office with details as required. The branch ledgers, containing details of the accounts, were maintained by ledger clerks. Cash, credits and debits passed over the counter were entered directly and cheques presented elsewhere were returned to that branch for payment and entered into the bookkeeping records. Cheques written by a customer were collected in the branch and sent to the customer at a later date. All the details of a customer's account were kept within the branch and the mechanics of maintaining the account were confined to the branch.

Maintenance of accounts in this way was costly and, as the growth of the banked population increased, it was clear that a degree of automation would provide significant gains in productivity. Branch accounting was therefore seen as the first choice for computerization in the late 1960s.

The initial branch accounting system collected items (debits, credits, cheques and so on) from branches, which were then keyed into the accounting program. Items were sorted according to the requirements of the program, which was operated from late in the evening until early on the following morning when printouts showing details of balances and transactions posted were sent to the branches. Some years later, a data network was installed and branches were then able to enter details of paper transactions in the branch to allow processing to start earlier and to allow later reconciliation with the paper clearing system.

The branch accounting system is at the heart of the WNB's banking operation. Not only does it provide a record of debits and credits, it also allows for standing orders and direct debits to be maintained and bank charges and/or interest to be posted. Accounts that require the attention of the branch are collected in a report, which is printed on the branch printer.

Branch staff in a branch of the WNB use the branch accounting system for presenting details of transactions collected at the branch and for making amendments to standing order and direct debit instructions and customer details. Enquiries may be made regarding customers' accounts during the day, either as a result of a direct request from a customer or an enquiry made from within the branch.

**Access to same-day value payment systems**

Items presented in the normal way into the WNB's branch accounting system are processed according to the three-day cycle of the British clearing system. A cheque presented at a branch on day 1 will be credited to the customer's account on day 3. This allows time for the cheque to be sent to the WNB's clearing centre, to be sorted and possibly sent to another bank's clearing centre and, finally, to the payee's branch for presentation. If the cheque is honoured on day 3, then the sum will be credited to the receiving account.

Occasionally, customers of the WNB's branches require money to be transmitted on the day in which the instruction is made. UK payments above £10 000 may be transmitted through the Clearing House Automated Payment System (CHAPS) and international payments may be sent through the network of the Society of World-wide International Financial Transactions (SWIFT). Payments presented into the CHAPS and SWIFT systems are normally substantial and, as their transfer is immediate, this presents a difficult security problem for the WNB.

**Access to the corporate database**

The WNB holds a large corporate database containing records of customers at all its branches. Branches require access to this database to extract information that is held centrally for the purposes of dealing with an individual account or customer. In addition, they also need to target groups of customers for direct marketing purposes.

## Computer Communications

**Access to specialized services**

As a major retail bank, the WNB's activities are significant in both the money transmission and lending businesses. In order to decide whether to sanction or refuse a personal loan application, a branch requires details of the customers and their financial records. In many instances, this information is held within the corporate database and so a simple automated process will yield a decision on whether to sanction or refuse the loan. In certain circumstances and, in particular, for new customers, the branch requires access to external credit agencies before making a decision. In all cases, decisions must be made quickly.

Traditionally, the WNB was happy to leave home loans to building societies, but, in the mid 1980s, it set up its own mortgage business as a subsidiary to the main UK Retail Division. In order to develop this system quickly and efficiently, it was decided to install a proven software package on a computer that was not of the type traditionally used by the WNB. This computer was installed in the Head Office of the mortgage business rather than in one of the WNB's main data centres.

Branches of the WNB are required to market the services of the mortgage company and, in so doing, require access to the computer system sited at the mortgage company's Head Office. A simple automated system combined information held on the corporate database with information provided by the mortgage company and this enables mortgages to be granted or refused, subject to certain legal conditions, very quickly.

In the early 1980s, the WNB acquired a medium-sized insurance broker that had developed its own computer system but used different techniques to those of the WNB's IT Group. Branches of the WNB were required to market the services of the insurance broker and, in order to do this, needed access to the insurance broker's computer system.

The WNB had traditionally provided good foreign exchange services for personal and corporate customers. When the service was first provided as a general branch service, the demand was slight and branch staff were able to telephone the foreign exchange specialists at the WNB's Head Office to ensure that foreign currency was bought or sold at the correct rates. As demand increased, however, the Foreign Exchange Group was unable to handle requests from branches and so developed a simple computer system to provide help and to log details of transactions. Branches, therefore, required access to this computer system to provide an efficient service to their customers.

In the 1980s, the WNB also acquired an investment bank and decided to offer certain stockbroking facilities through its general branch network. Stockbroking services were entirely new to the branches and, in order to provide a basic service for buying and selling UK equities quickly and efficiently, the investment bank developed a computer system to provide information and accept transactions from branches. Branches also require access to this computer system.

*A case study*

**Office automation services**  Branches of the WNB need the normal office automation services that now exist in most businesses. In particular, word processing of a number of standard letters to customers is required, together with means of communicating electronically with customers using fax or electronic messaging systems. In addition, branches of the WNB need to send standard documents to regional offices and to Head Office. These are used, for example, when a loan application requires the sanction of a regional office or when the branch orders stationery from a Head Office unit.

Branches and offices of the WNB use these services with the following special requirements:

- accessibility at all desks in the office
- no more than one four-hour outage per annum for each general system
- security of data for both internal and external communications
- ability to recover by the following working day from a major disaster at any site connected with the delivery of services
- ability to access automated services from the branch without requiring specialized IT skills from branch employees
- availability of a single help desk to provide assistance as necessary for all of the above services.

In the early days of automation in the WNB branches, computer facilities were contained within a 'machine room'. Certain junior staff within the branch were given the responsibility of handling the machines and any information about the systems required by other members of the branch was obtained by direct communication with the machine staff. As the demand for information grew, however, it became clear to the UK Retail Division that information should be presented at the point where it was required—namely, at each desk in the office.

Branches of the WNB were able to survive major faults with the communications and computer systems provided service was restored within an hour or two. If the outage became longer than two hours, the branch manager could decide to transfer work, which required the interaction of the computer and communications systems, to a nearby branch. This was very inconvenient and one such outage a year was considered to be the minimum acceptable standard of service.

Prior to the introduction of computers, branches of the WNB could realistically continue a banking business without the assistance of major units within the Head Office of the WNB. However, the introduction of computers had a centralizing effect and so branches of the WNB were unable to continue their business if major systems were unavailable for more than one working day. Quick recovery is, therefore, required in order to counter the effects of any major disaster affecting a data centre of a major communications centre in the bank.

It has been a tradition in the WNB for the IT Group to provide a complete service to the branches and, therefore, to provide all expert assistance directly to them. Although computer skills within the bank have increased considerably over the years, it remains a requirement that management of computer and communications systems is the responsibility of the IT Group.

As the branch is not expected to undertake any diagnosis of faults within systems, a single help desk is required to provide assistance at all times.

## UK Retail Division (Head Office and regional offices)

The communications requirements of Head Office and regional offices in the WNB largely mirror those of the branches. In addition, these sites have found that videoconferencing is of considerable use to them in conducting difficult business. The Insurance Broker is developing a mobile sales force requiring voice and data communications.

## International Division

The two retail banks run by the International Division in New England and Portugal have similar requirements to those of the UK Retail Division, including a requirement for videoconferencing between the two overseas Head Offices and the Head Office of the WNB in the UK. It should be noted that the retail banks in Portugal and New England are considerably smaller than the UK bank and there are fewer special services that are available to individual branches. However, the requirement to provide access to external sources of information and to services that could be marketed through the branch outlets is important to the development of the two overseas banks.

The communication requirements of the numerous, small representative offices of the WNB around the world are comparatively undemanding. However, in many of these offices, small accountancy systems are provided within the building and a variety of reports are required by the WNB's Head Office. These reports are required on a daily basis.

The representative offices frequently provide banking services to international subsidiaries of major UK corporates and there is a requirement for access to the corporate database to be made available to the representative offices. In addition, details of the local accounts are frequently required in report form by the Head Office of the WNB in order to provide an overall picture of the accounts to the corporate customer.

## Treasury Division

Although the Treasury Division is a small part of the WNB's overall organization, it is a major profit earner and a considerable user of communications services. Many of these are associated with its very successful Foreign Exchange Group. The key to its success is an efficient dealer board as this allows dealers to have instant access to their opposite numbers in other Foreign Exchange Groups in the UK and overseas. Deals are struck by verbal agreement on calls set up by the dealer board, but information systems and decision support systems advise the dealer on the best strategy at any particular time. Deals are entered into the dealer's terminal, that links to a settlement system on which all transactions are recorded and for which settlement is made. In addition to screens containing information on foreign exchange rates, the dealers are presented with broadcast commentary, giving details of market movements. In addition, an intercom system allows dealers in different parts of the dealing room to communicate effectively.

It has been traditional to provide dealers at the WNB with a large number of separate screens and terminals to provide suitable back-up for the efficient transaction of business. In recent years, there has been a requirement for decision support systems, office automation systems and special purpose information systems (giving foreign exchange rates and so on), to be provided by means of a single screen, using windowing techniques to separate the various services that may be required simultaneously.

The Capital Markets Group has similar requirements to those of the Foreign Exchange Group, although it is somewhat smaller and the information sources available are more limited.

**Investment Banking Division**

The Investment Banking Division's communications requirements are dominated by those of its Equities Group. This Group has similar requirements to those of the Foreign Exchange Group in the Treasury Division and, like the Foreign Exchange Group, requires links between dealer boards and information systems in its small overseas units. Full communications with the overseas trading units are required in order to present an overall picture of the WNB's exposure and to ensure that, at all times, the WNB complies with UK law with regard to the acquisition of UK equities.

The Corporate Advisory Group in the Investment Banking Division has requirements for information services, office automation and general telephone and videoconferencing services.

## 1.3 Analysis of information flows

The WNB's telecommunications planners conducted a study of the use of the telephones within the bank, which revealed that 50 per cent of all calls were internal to the bank. For these calls, the ability to book a call when the called party was engaged was considered to be a major benefit. However, they were unable to place a value on this facility and believed that it would be desirable but not essential to the work of the bank.

In investigating the telephone requirements of the dealing, foreign exchange and equities areas, it was found that there was no substitute for dedicated circuits between important dealing locations. It was clear, therefore, that the dealer boards in London would need a substantial number of dedicated private circuits in addition to public network access.

The requirements of dealers for voice quality was investigated with particular reference to the need for expensive, long-distance circuits to connect international dealing operations in New York, Paris, Zurich and Frankfurt. It was found that dealers could operate effectively with a data rate of 8 kbits/second for digitally encoded speech. The special requirements of certain staff in the Foreign Exchange and Equities Groups to make calls from their homes to dealing operations in different time zones was examined and it was found that there was a considerable demand for low-cost transatlantic communications.

In examining the data requirements, the WNB's planners classified the data according to the following system:

- point-to-point or any-to-any
- interactive or bulk transfer
- security requirements
- data integrity.

In considering the data requirements of the UK Retail Division, it was clear that branches would need to communicate with a number of separate locations. Computing services would be required by the WNB's main data centres and, additionally, by data centres operated by the related banking businesses (for example, the insurance broker and mortgage company). The electronic mail requirements of the branches included branch-to-branch, branch-to-regional office and branch-to-Head Office traffic. A switched network would be required to satisfy all the data flow needs of the branches in an efficient manner.

Due to the large number of parties in the bank's data communications systems, the WNB's planners carefully considered the need for standardized and open systems. It was appreciated that it would be possible to run special-purpose priority systems for the main banking communications between the data centres and the branches, but that this would create difficulties in communicating with computers operated by the related banking business and those operated by external agencies.

An examination of branch data requirements revealed that much of the traffic associated with the banking business was of an interactive nature. This traffic had a characteristic daily profile and a peak requirement in the busiest half-hour period of the day. This information, together with the response times associated with various services, was used to size the network capacity required in a wide area network (WAN) and in local area networks (LAN) specific to a branch or group of nearby branches.

The profile of the interactive traffic was compared with the demand for file transfer. It became clear that much of the file transfer traffic would be associated with access to the corporate database and, in addition, there would be some file transfer following recovery from a failure of the branch system. The total volumes were assessed, together with the transmission requirements. In the case of branches, it was clear that there were no stringent requirements for the duration of the file transfer, except in cases where the file transfer was associated with recovery from failure.

An examination of the security requirements for the branch traffic revealed a strong need for data authentication. It was clear that authentication was required for same-day value payments and, in addition, a method to prevent repeating or deleting payments properly made would be required.

In assessing the network capacity required to allow efficient data transfer from the branches to the main data centres, the planners made use of their calculations for response times and traffic volumes. It became clear that response time would be the result of contributions from a number of separate processes, of which the WAN was one. Of particular importance was the response time of the central computer systems and the response time from a station on a LAN to the communications gateway.

The response times of the WAN could be related easily to the utilization of circuits and switching elements; the response times in the LAN were more complicated as they depended on the utilization of intelligent work station capacity in terms both of applications and systems software. To this end, planners relied on empirical results taken from a prototype branch system and compared these with the results of a computer modelling process. In general, the planners designed the systems so the major part of a system's response time was related to processor utilization in the branch and the data centre, with the network adding only a small component to the overall performance.

The requirements of international business were examined and it was clear that the substantial and varied communications from representative offices to the WNB's Head Office would give rise to a networking requirement. The volumes were not great and the security requirements were similar to those of the branch network.

In considering the data requirements of the dealing operations in the Treasury Division and Equities Group, the greatest problem was to assess the capacity required for the internal information services network. This involved a complex modelling exercise that stemmed from an understanding of the capacity requirements of local network communications software, windowing software (for the presentation of information) and decision support software (for the processing of that information). These aspects were modelled carefully and linked to the bank's LAN's transmission capacity and the capacity of bridges and routers.

The communication requirements of the WNB are typical of those of a large, distributed business. They have developed as the business has grown and diversified. At the same time, IT has grown and diversified. The following chapters describe various aspects of the technology and the way in which they have enabled the WNB to meet its needs.

# CHAPTER 2

# Basic telecommunications

## 2.1 Introduction

Communication may be defined as the science and practice of transmitting information. Information may be represented in many forms. It may, for example, be expressed in spoken words, in written text or in pictures. The oldest form of information transfer is its expression as sounds, which, over time, became formalized as spoken languages where particular sequences of sounds convey information. Ways of representing sounds as a set of characters (an alphabet) resulted in written languages in which particular sequences of characters also convey information. In the absence of a common language, people convey information by pictures (conscious sign language or unconscious body language). Ironically, computers have only recently learned sign language—they call it a Graphical User Interface!

The word *telecommunications* means the transmission of information over large distances. When information transfer was limited to audible means, telecommunications were limited to primitive people cupping their hands over their mouths. Drums and trumpets extended the limit. Then, pictorial methods, such as smoke signals, further extended the range. The information that a new Pope has been elected still relies on smoke signals, while native Americans now rely on cellular radio to communicate. Written (and preferably common) language was needed to enable true telecommunications, although the response time may have left something to be desired.

Telecommunications relied on the written word, or more primitive means, until the nineteenth century when electricity began to be exploited for this purpose. The representation of information by electrical signals and its use in the telegraph and telephone, marks the beginning of modern telecommunications. The invention of the digital computer marks the beginning of modern information processing. The convergence of telecommunications and information processing towards the science of IT is one of the more significant developments of the late twentieth century.

Information may be expressed, as we have seen, in sounds, words or pictures. Digital computers process information expressed in numbers and, in particular, binary numbers. Processing of information by a digital computer requires information to be represented as a set of binary digits, or, *bits*. Communication of information over a distance requires information to be represented in the form of electrical signals. The convergence of information processing and information transmission into the science of IT, in essence, requires a means of expressing information in bits and a means of transmitting bits as electrical signals. Both techniques are called *coding*. In the following section some coding systems are described.

## 2.2 Information encoding

**Transmission of text**

Text is written using characters (letters, numbers, punctuation marks and other special symbols like % and &) from a character set or alphabet. A *character code* assigns a binary number to each character to facilitate the processing and transmission of text. In addition to the printable characters, coding schemes usually incorporate special characters for control purposes. The number of bits needed depends on the size of the character set including its control characters.

The use of codes to represent characters originated in telegraphy. An important early example is the *International Alphabet number 2 (IA2)*, adopted as a standard in 1932. It uses 5 bits to represent characters. This would normally allow for 32 characters, but the code is extended by using two *shift* characters (*figure shift* and *letter shift*) that change the meaning of the following characters until another shift character is transmitted. This effectively divides the character set into two subsets – a *primary set* (letters) and a *secondary set* (figures and punctuation). A similar early code is the *Baudot code*.

Both are limited in the number of printable and control characters that they define. An additional disadvantage is that these codes do not follow the normal collating sequence for letters and numbers—the code representing 'A' being higher than the code representing 'Z' and the code representing '1' being higher than the code representing '9'. This makes these codes much more suitable for data *transmission* than for data *processing*.

As telegraphy devices became more widely used and more sophisticated, IA2 was superseded by *IA5*, a 7-bit code. IA5 resulted from a 1962 proposal by what is now the *American National Standards Institute (ANSI)* and is based on the *American Standard Code for Information Interchange (ASCII)*. This code is standardized by both the Comité Consultatif International Télégraphique et Téléphonique (CCITT) (Recommendation T.50) and ISO (ISO 646). IA5 differs slightly from ASCII in that the basic IA5 does not assign characters to some bit combinations that are assigned in ASCII. The standards do, however, define an international reference version of IA5 that allocates these optional combinations. This differs from ASCII only in replacing the $ character with an international currency character. IA5/ASCII is probably the most widely used character code.

Text consisting entirely of decimal numbers requires a code of only 4 bits. An example of such a code is the *Binary Coded Decimal (BCD)* code. An extended version of BCD, using an 8-bit code, is the *Extended Binary Coded Decimal Interchange Code (EBCDIC)* used in some larger processors, particularly IBM machines, for both processing *and* transmitting information.

## Transmission of pictures

The most common form of information transmission after the telephone is the ubiquitous fax machine, which transmits a picture rather than a character string. A page to be transmitted is converted to a bit map by scanning at 3.85 or 7.7 lines per millimetre. Each line is scanned at 8.05 picture elements (pixels) per millimetre. A black pixel is represented as a 1 bit and a white pixel as a 0 bit. An A4 page consequently produces around 2 megabits. A compression process reduces this and, hence, the time taken to transmit the page, by factors of about 10:1. Group 3 fax machines transmit the bit string by modulation of an analog telephone line. Group 4 machines use a digital line. Group 1 and group 2 are largely obsolete.

The process of representing a picture by a bit map is also used to display text and graphics on a display screen. Manipulating the bit map enables the appearance of the display (size, orientation, font and so on) to be changed. Sophisticated printers enable the picture to be printed as it appears on the screen.

## Transmission of voice

The appearance of a section on voice transmission in a discussion on expressing information in bits may seem surprising. It is not difficult to appreciate that computers handle information numerically. The coding schemes discussed so far are designed to reduce other forms of information to numbers. Numbers handled by computers are particularly simple—they consist only of 0s and 1s. The whole world is apparently reduced to these two, discrete values. Sound does not obviously lend itself to expression in numerical form, particularly when there are only two numbers available.

The basic parameters of a sound are its frequency and amplitude. Each of these parameters may take one of a continuous range of values. One determines the pitch of the sound; the other its loudness. The human voice, or any other complex sound, may be analysed into a superimposition of pure sounds with different frequencies and amplitudes. Physically, a sound results in a variation in pressure at a point in the medium through which the sound passes. This is conventionally represented as a graph of pressure against time. In the case of a pure note it is a simple, sinusoidal graph. In the case of a complex of sounds, such as the human voice, it is a complicated wave pattern of continuously varying frequency and amplitude. The frequency and amplitude of this pattern are equivalent, respectively, to the pitch and loudness of the sound; it is an analog process.

The transmission of sound has, of course, been the most common form of telecommunications since 1876 and still is. It was made possible by the invention of the telephone—an instrument for converting continuous (analog) variations in air pressure to continuous (analog) variations in electrical current and vice versa. For the century or so following Bell's invention, the world-wide telephone network developed to provide analog transmission of sound between its subscribers.

Towards the end of this period, digital computers were developed and gradually came into common use. At about the centenary of the telephone, computer communication was born. Initially, the merging of the data processing (computer) world and the telecommunications (telephone) world was dominated by the latter. Digital information, produced by computers, needed to be transformed into analog form for transmission by means of the world's telephone networks. Digital-to-analog converters and analog-to-digital converters were needed to enable computer-to-computer communication.

The provision of a connection between two telephone subscribers requires action on the part of the telephone company, the provider of the service. In the early days, this action was taken by a human operator making a manual connection. A Kansas City undertaker, Almon Brown Strowger, claimed that calls to him were being diverted to a competitor and so invented the first automatic circuit switch to overcome this problem. The *Strowger exchange* is part of the history of telecommunications.

An automatic telephone exchange needs to make a decision based on information provided by the calling subscriber. This information was initially provided verbally by the caller to the operator and later by dialling codes. Computers are good at making decisions based on input information and can be programmed to cope with a variety of circumstances. They can even approach the intelligence of a human operator! Telephone companies quickly realized the potential benefits of a computer as a switch and the *Stored Program Control* exchange was developed. The worlds of data processing and data transmission began to overlap.

Computers handle information in digital form and telephones handle information in analog form. The introduction of computers as telephone exchanges has developed in two phases. The first, largely complete in many countries, was the use of digital circuits between exchanges. The second, still being introduced, is the use of digital circuits between the subscriber and the local exchange. This second phase requires a telephone that transmits *and* receives sound as numbers.

The technique for converting sound to numbers is called *Pulse Code Modulation (PCM)*. The amplitude of the sound wave is measured at regular intervals and converted to a number. This number can then be transmitted as a digital signal. When it is received at its destination, a close approximation to the original waveform can be recreated from the stream of incoming numbers. The closeness of the approximation and, hence, the quality of the received sound, depends on the frequency at which the original sound is sampled and the number of bits used to represent the sample.

PCM normally samples human speech at 8000 times per second and represents each sample as an 8-bit number. Consequently, a transmission line operating at 64 kbits/second is needed to achieve high-quality reproduction. Compression techniques may be used to reduce the line speed requirement. If lower quality is acceptable, digital voice transmissions may be intelligible at line speeds as low as 2.4 kbits/second.

In this section we have seen that information—spoken, written or drawn—may be expressed as binary digital numbers for transmission via a telecommunications line. Now let us look at the way in which bits are represented as electrical signals.

## 2.3 Data transmission

**Analog and digital**

A complex waveform, such as speech or music, may be represented as a superimposition of many simple waveforms of different frequencies and amplitudes. The same is true of the analogous current flow from a telephone. The mathematical foundation lies in *Fourier analysis*.

A voice circuit provided by the telephone company will carry a range of frequencies between 300 Hz and 3400 Hz, which is adequate for intelligible speech. It has a bandwidth of 3100 Hz—the range of frequencies that it will transmit. Is it suitable for digital transmissions? If not, why not, and is there anything we can do about it?

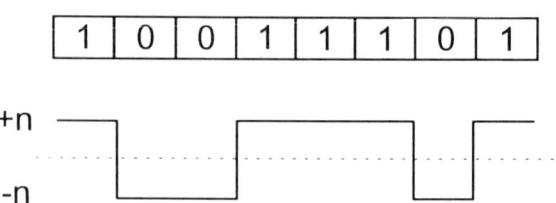

Figure 2.1   Digital signal

Digital information, as we have seen, is encoded as binary numbers. Such information may be passed to a telecommunications line as voltage changes at regular intervals, say + n volts for a '1' and −n volts for a '0'. The corresponding waveform is the square wave shown in Figure 2.1. Fourier analysis of this waveform indicates that it contains frequencies extending over a range much greater than the bandwidth of a voice-grade circuit. Attempts to transmit this waveform over a voice circuit would result in distortion and unintelligible information.

In order to transmit such a signal over a telephone line, therefore, it must be converted to an analog signal, which may be transmitted within the 3100 Hz bandwidth, and converted back to digital form at the receiving end. The digital signal is carried by modifying (modulating) some parameter of the waveform. The modulation and demodulation is performed by a *modem*, which takes its name from these two words. The modified parameter is the amplitude, the frequency or the phase of a carrier signal transmitted between the modems.

In all cases, the digital signal is fed to the modem as a square wave representing a string of binary digits that in turn represent text or pictures. In *amplitude modulation*, '0' and '1' bits result in different carrier amplitudes. In *frequency modulation*, the frequency of the carrier is different for the two binary values. The abrupt change in frequency, resulting from a binary modulation, is sometimes called *Frequency Shift Keying (FSK)*. In phase modulation, or *Phase Shift Keying (PSK)*, the phase of the carrier changes by 180 degrees when the modulation signal changes from '0' to '1'.

In Section 2.2 the gradual movement of public telephone networks towards the use of digital exchanges and transmission lines was mentioned. As this digital network is extended to the private and business subscriber, with sufficient bandwidth to carry digital signals, conversion of these signals to analog form is no longer needed. Voice digitization enables the same line, without modems, to be used for voice and data. Addition of a *multiplexer* (see below) enables the same line to be used simultaneously for several services. This is an *Integrated Services Digital Network (ISDN)*, the subject of Chapter 10.

## Asynchronous and synchronous transmission

On both analog and digital lines, data is transmitted and received by a computer as binary digits with different voltage levels representing '0' and '1'. Bits are transmitted (that is, the signal level is changed) at regular intervals determined by a clock at the transmitter. The signal level then stays constant, for a period known as a *bit cell*, until the next bit is transmitted. The same signal pattern, representing the same bit pattern, is received at the other end but may no longer be a square wave as the edges may have been rounded off due to the limited bandwidth of the transmission medium. The receiver samples the signal level at regular intervals determined by its own clock. It is important that the sample is taken well into the bit cell, preferably at its centre. If it were to be measured when it is changing from the '0' level to the '1' level, particularly if the transition is not sharp, the receiver may interpret a '0' as a '1' or vice versa.

In order to interpret the incoming bit stream correctly, the receiver's clock needs to be synchronized with the bit stream. It may, or may not, be synchronized with the transmitter's clock. If it is, the transmission is called *synchronous*; if not, the transmission is *asynchronous*. We will examine the latter first.

The original purpose of asynchronous transmission was to handle data streams in which characters are generated at random intervals, such as when an operator enters characters at a keyboard that are transmitted directly to the line. Characters appear at the receiver at random times; in between characters, the line is idle. A technique known as *start/stop* is used to achieve synchronization at the receiver. When a character is to be transmitted, an additional '0' bit (the *start bit*) is added at the start of the character and one or more '1' bits (the *stop bit* or *bits*) at the end of the character. The start bit is used by the receiver to start its clock, which runs at some multiple n of the incoming bit rate (n is commonly 16). Following detection of the start bit, the incoming signal is sampled after n/2 clock cycles and thereafter every n cycles. This ensures that the sample is taken near the centre of each bit cell. The stop bit, which is of opposite polarity to the start bit, is used to ensure that a transition always occurs at the start of a character. Although used mainly for intermittent transmission, start/stop data streams are also used to transmit regular streams of characters.

Bit stream

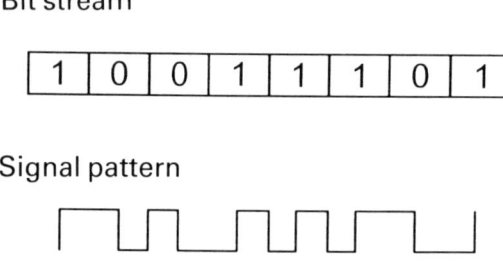

Signal pattern

*Figure 2.2   Manchester encoding*

In synchronous transmission, the transmitter and receiver clocks are synchronized by timing information carried by the data stream. This information is contained in the way the bits are represented as signal changes on the line. Figure 2.2 shows a common bit encoding scheme known as *Manchester encoding*. A '0' bit is encoded as a high-to-low transmission and a '1' bit as a low-to-high transition. These transitions occur at the centre of each bit cell and are used by the receiver to generate clock pulses to indicate the points, in the second half of the bit cell, at which the incoming signal is sampled and decoded. Synchronization is initially established, and maintained when the line is idle between blocks of data, by the transmission of *synchronous idle (SYN)* characters.

*Basic telecommunications*

We have now seen how a receiver determines when to sample the incoming signal to decode it into a bit stream. This is called *bit synchronization*. The receiver also needs to know when a character starts and the next one begins (*character synchronization*) and when a block of data starts and ends (*block synchronization*). In asynchronous transmission, character synchronization is achieved by the start/stop mechanism that also establishes bit synchronization. Character synchronization on synchronous lines and block synchronization on both types of link is established by the use of special demarcation characters or, bit patterns. These special bit patterns are generated and used by the *link level protocol* controlling the exchange of data on the link.

**Data transmission rates**

In the transmission systems that have so far been considered, individual bits have been encoded as one of two voltage levels or signal transitions. A change in the signal takes place every bit cell. Signalling systems are also used in which more than two signal conditions are used. Figure 2.3 shows a scheme in which four voltage levels are used, each representing 2 bits.

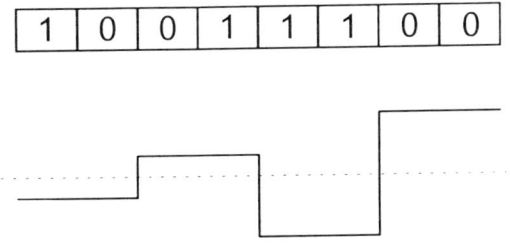

*Figure 2.3   Multilevel signalling*

The rate at which the signal changes (the reciprocal of the bit cell length) is measured in *Bauds*. The rate at which bits are transmitted is measured in bits per second (bits/s or bps) or some multiple (kbits/s or Mbits/s). These rates are not always the same, but are the same if each change in signal conveys one bit of information. In Figure 2.3, 2 bits are transmitted for each signal change. With a bit cell of 20 milliseconds, the signalling rate is 50 Baud, while the bit rate is 100 bits per second. In general, if the bit cell is T seconds and the number of signalling levels is n, the bit rate is:

$$1/T \log_2 n \text{ bits/s}$$

The signal presented to a transmission line can be represented, as we have indicated, by a square waveform that in turn, may be analysed into its component frequencies. Data rates are ultimately determined by the range of frequencies the channel can carry, that is its bandwidth. A paper by Nyquist in 1924 on factors affecting telegraph speed showed that the maximum theoretical capacity (C) of a noise-free channel of bandwidth W is given by:

$$C = 2W$$

assuming two signalling levels. If n signalling levels are used, the capacity is increased to:

$$C = 2W\log_2 n$$

The use of, say, 8 signalling levels (3 bits per Baud) on a 3 kHz voice line enables a data rate of 18 kbits/second to be sustained on a noise-free channel, although such rates are rarely achieved in practice. The generally accepted limit for data transmission on a telephone line is 9.6 kbits/second. There is also a limit to the number of signalling levels that may be used. As the number increases, the difference in voltage between levels decreases, making it more difficult to detect and more susceptible to noise.

No communication channel is completely immune to noise. The effect of noise on the capacity of the channel was studied by Shannon and published in a famous paper in 1948, which showed that the capacity of the channel is given by:

$$C = W \log_2(1 + S/N)$$

where S/N is the signal to noise ratio.

## Multiplexing

A multiplexer enables the capacity of a communication channel to be shared between a number of devices. Two multiplexing techniques are in common use. *Frequency Division Multiplexing (FDM)* divides the bandwidth of the channel into several ranges and allocates each range to one of the devices attached to the multiplexer. The circuit becomes a set of independent channels, each with a lower bandwidth and, hence, a lower data capacity, than the bearer (parent) circuit. To prevent overlapping of signals in adjacent channels, resulting in cross talk, the frequency bands in which data is transmitted are separated by guard bands. Consequently, some of the bearer bandwidth is wasted. Another disadvantage of FDM is that the channels may vary in quality as higher frequencies are attenuated to a greater extent than lower frequencies.

*Time Division Multiplexing (TDM)* allocates the whole bandwidth to each attached device, but only for part of the time. Each device is periodically given a time slot in which it can transmit a number of bits. Some devices may be given more slots than others. The contents of the various slots are assembled into a single bit stream (a *frame*) for synchronous transmission through the bearer circuit. The frame is de-multiplexed at the receiver. *Pulse Code Modulation (PCM)* enables digital voice channels to be multiplexed with data channels.

# Basic telecommunications

A basic TDM system allocates a slot to a device whether or not it has data to send. *Statistical Time Division Multiplexers (STDM)* allocate bandwidth only when it is needed. A TDM system often has other facilities to improve utilization of the bearer bandwidth. For example, if an asynchronous device is connected to one of the channels, the start and stop bits are not transmitted. Instead, they are removed by the multiplexer and replaced by the de-multiplexer as bit and character synchronization are provided by the synchronous data stream. Some multiplexers also incorporate compression facilities.

## Error detection and correction

Distortion of the signal on a transmission line can be controlled but not entirely avoided. The effect of excessive distortion is that the receiver will interpret a '1' bit as a '0' bit or vice versa. More than one bit in a block of data may be affected. In addition to individual bit changes, strings of bits or whole messages may be lost. The detection and correction of errors are mainly provided by hardware and software functions in communicating devices, whereas in this chapter we are concerned with the physical aspects of data transmission. The subject is introduced here and will be returned to in later chapters when relevant.

Errors are detected, if at all, by the receiver of a message. Error detection depends on the presence of extra information added to the message by the sender. This information is redundant as far as the content of the message is concerned, but vital if the information is to be understood and used with confidence.

Two techniques are used to correct errors, depending on whether correction is applied by the sender or the receiver. It is most commonly applied by the sender by retransmitting the message and is referred to by various names—*Automatic Repeat Request (ARQ), feedback error control* or *backward error control*. It is accomplished by using a data link control protocol and an example of this is given in Chapter 5.

A simple form of error correction, applied by the receiver, is *forward error control*. Redundant bits are inserted into a data stream that enables the receiver to detect and correct some errors. As a simple example of the use of redundant information for forward error control, the *Hamming Code* is now described.

Figure 2.4 (a) shows a string of 16 bits to be transmitted. The transmitter inserts additional bits in positions given by $2^n$ (positions 1, 2, 4, 8 and so on). The result is the 21-bit string shown in part (b) of the figure, where the 'h' bits are *Hamming bits*. The values of these bits are determined as follows.

The positions in which '1' bits occur are noted. They are positions 21, 19, 18, 17, 13, 10, 9, 6 and 3. These numbers are expressed in binary form and added modulo 2 (no carry). This is shown in part (c) of the figure. The result of the addition gives the values to be assigned to the

(a)         1011100100110101
(b)    1011h0010011h010h1hh

(c)    10101    21
       10011    19
       10010    18
       10001    17
       01101    13
       01010    10
       01001     9
       00110     6
       00011     3

       01110    Σ

(d)    10110001001110101110

(e)    01110    from (c)
       01000     8
       00100     4
       00010     2

       00000    Σ

(f)    10110011001110101110

*Figure 2.4   Error detection by Hamming Code*

Hamming bits ('0' to bit 16, '1' to bit 8, '1' to bit 4, '1' to bit 2 and '0' to bit 1). The transmitted bit string is shown in part (d).

The receiver performs a similar function, noting the '1'-bit positions and adding them modulo 2, as shown in part (e). Because of the values given to the Hamming bits, the result of this addition is zero, provided no bit has changed. The final part of the figure, (f), shows an error resulting in a change of bit 14 from '0' to '1'. The addition now includes the binary value for 14 and results in the non-zero value 01101—the position of the bit in error that is corrected by the receiver.

The Hamming technique enables single-bit errors to be detected and corrected. Errors affecting 2 bits are detected but cannot be corrected by the receiver as their positions cannot be determined. Errors affecting several bits may, or may not, be detected depending on their position in the bit string and cannot be corrected. The technique is most useful if the message is divided into relatively small blocks, to reduce the probability of multiple-bit errors, with Hamming bits added to each block.

Adding redundant information, such as Hamming bits, is the technique used in all communication systems, at all levels, to control the exchange of data between the sending device and the receiving device. Although called 'redundant', this information is vital to the provision of a reliable delivery system. It does, however, reduce the capacity of the channel for user data by an extent determined by the nature of the control information. The control information depends on the protocols defined by the network architecture. In assessing the useful capacity of a network, these protocols need to be taken into account. This is particularly the case in asynchronous transmission, where the addition of at least two extra bits (the start and stop bits) to each character reduces the capacity of the circuit for user data.

## Data compression

Having noted the expansion of a data stream that occurs as a result of the insertion of control information, now let us look at techniques for compressing the data to make better use of the bandwidth. In fact, one compression technique has been described already—the use of the 4-bit *Binary Coded Decimal (BCD)* code to encode numerical data (see Section 2.2). In many data streams, long sequences of the same character occur, such as runs of space characters in a document. Rather than transmit each repeated character, a sequence is transmitted consisting of a special *control character*—the character itself and a count of the number of occurrences of the character. In some other data streams, numbers in the data stream differ slightly from the preceding number, such as a series of measurements from a process control device. *Relative encoding* may then be used in which each number is coded as the difference between it and the preceding number.

More sophisticated techniques are based on the relative frequency at which characters occur. The more common characters are encoded using fewer bits than the less common characters. Consequently, the number of bits per character is no longer constant and bit-oriented transmission, rather than character-oriented, is necessary. The most common technique based on the frequency distribution of characters is *Huffman compression*. The allocation of codes to characters is made by analysing the character string to be transmitted and building a binary 'tree' structure, with the characters to be encoded as the 'leaves' of the tree. The tree may be pre-built or may be built dynamically by the transmitter and receiver (*dynamic Huffman compression*).

The tree starts at the 'root', which is connected by branches, each of which divides into two other branches until a leaf is reached. At a division point, the two branches are assigned binary numbers 0 and 1. Common characters are nearer to the root than less common characters. The code to be used to represent a given character is determined by following the tree from leaf to root and noting the number (0 or 1) of each branch on the path. The set of numbers representing the branches traversed is the code to be used. This results in numbers near to the root being given smaller codes than those further from the root. The receiver recreates the original character string by repeating the analysis.

Huffman compression takes time but is widely used in such situations as file transfer, where large amounts of data are to be transmitted and time is relatively unimportant. Compression ratios of 2:1 are typical. A modified version of Huffman compression is used in most fax machines where codes are preassigned (by the CCITT Group 3 and Group 4 Recommendations) to different length runs of black or white pixels. Compression ratios of up to 10:1 for fax transmissions are common.

## 2.4 Communications media

In Section 2.2, the encoding of various types of information into digital form was described. In Section 2.3, the way in which digital signals are coded for transmission was analysed, including the encoding of control information and compression information. Note that the word 'encoding' is used in several different contexts, always meaning the transformation from one form of representing information into another form. Various other words have also been used to refer to the connection between the sender and receiver of a data stream—channel, link, circuit and so on. In this section, the effect of the physical nature of the circuit on information transmission is examined.

Telecommunications is about transmitting information over a distance. Information is represented by some form of signal and a means of transmitting the signal from sender to receiver is fundamental to telecommunications. The encoding of information as electrical signals, in the early days of telegraphy and telephony, required the use of conducting physial media for transmission. Such media still dominate the telecommunications world for both voice and data.

A pair of copper wires, twisted together and twisted round other pairs to reduce cross talk, is the most common means of providing a user with a network connection for both voice and data. Such a circuit will carry either analog or digital signals. It normally carries analog signals and uses modems for data communication. Digital lines are, however, becoming increasingly common.

The bandwidth of a copper wire depends on its resistance, which in turn depends on its diameter and length. Standard telephone lines are restricted to a bandwidth of 3.1 kHz, although twisted pairs intrinsically have a higher bandwidth. Coaxial cables are used where higher bandwidth is needed over longer distances and are capable of carrying many thousands of voice-grade circuits.

The use of light to transmit signals has a long history. Its use in modern communication systems is relatively recent, but is rapidly taking over from electrically based systems. Optical fibres have bandwidths of hundreds of MHz with correspondingly very large information-carrying capacity. Digital information is carried on an optical fibre as on/off light pulses that are generated when a voltage is applied to a *Light Emitting*

*Diode (LED)* or an *Injection Laser Diode (ILD)* and converted by the receiver into electrical pulses by a *photodetector*. The pulses are generated in the infra-red part of the electromagnetic spectrum.

Light pulses are confined to the cable by total internal reflection at the boundary between the optical core of the fibre and its optical cladding, which have different refractive indices. There are several types of fibre. In a *multimode stepped index fibre*, the core and cladding have uniform refractive indices. Light takes different amounts of time to travel along the cable, depending on its angle of emission from the source. This results in a dispersion of the pulse and limits the bit rate. *Multimode graded index fibre* uses a core with a variable refractive index, which causes light emitted at different angles to take approximately the same time to travel to the receiver, thus reducing dispersion. The maximum data rate is achieved using *single mode* (or *monomode*) *fibre* in which the core is reduced in diameter to a single wavelength (a few μm), effectively providing a single path through the cable.

*Metallic* and *optical cables* may be compared by quoting a bandwidth/distance parameter. This parameter is in the range of 1 MHz/km for wire pairs, 20 MHz/km for coaxial cable and 400 MHz/km for optical fibre. Repeaters are used at regular intervals on all types of medium to regenerate the signal as it becomes attenuated.

Transmission of information does not require a physical medium between source and destination. Electromagnetic radiation is also used to carry signals representing various forms of information. Modulated transmission in the microwave range (several GHz) is used for both terrestrial microwave systems and satellite systems. Lower frequency radio waves and infra-red radiation are also used in special circumstances over limited distances.

## 2.5 Summary

In this chapter the basic techniques for encoding and transmission of information on a circuit between sender and receiver have been examined. Such circuits are important components of a communications network. In the next chapter, other components and the ways in which they are assembled to provide any-to-any connections between users are considered.

*As nations develop their economies, a shift occurs away from the manufacturing sector towards the services sector. Service-sector industries are characterized by having a large number of outlets at which their services are provided and, hence, a particularly demanding communications requirement. They often need rapid access to information held either centrally within their own organization or by other related organizations. A large clearing bank, such as the WNB, typifies this trend. Banks have* been at the forefront of this trend in their use of IT in support of their business.

Despite the growing tendency to transmit information in textual or pictorial form, voice is, and will remain for many years, the primary means of telecommunication. The ability to represent all types of information in digital form, however, has eroded the traditional distinction between voice and data to the extent that it is legitimate to ignore it and consider all information as bit streams. The methods of encoding the information into bits distinguish the types of information.

The WNB recognized this trend when it decided to integrate voice and data transmission to the extent that 1980s technology allowed. Integration was limited to the trunk circuits between switching centres, which housed separate data and voice switches. Compression of voice signals into a data rate of 8 kilobits per second was considered to provide acceptable voice quality. Multiplexers enabled sharing of the trunk bandwidth between voice and data circuits. The availability and cost of digital tail circuits dictated that the network would use analog transmission between switching centre and end-points for both voice and data, using separate private circuits.

The availability of digital circuits on local loops, as the Integrated Digital Network and its services are extended to the customer, will enable the WNB to extend its digital network to its branches and other offices. Increased bandwidth will be available and separate circuits for voice and data will not be required. The impact of ISDN is considered in Chapter 10.

# CHAPTER 3

# Network components and topologies

## 3.1 Introduction

The word *network* is in common use in such phrases as 'the telephone network', 'the postal network' or 'the airlines network'. These examples have a number of things in common. They are all concerned with moving something from one place to another. Telephone and postal networks move information while airline networks move people. They all have entry and exit points—telephones, mail boxes and airports. They all have intermediate processing points—telephone exchanges, sorting offices and intermediate airports. They all have transmission channels—telephone lines, a postal transport mechanism and the world's flight paths.

There are, of course, differences. Telephone connections provide a single circuit between sender and receiver by physically connecting a number of individual circuits to and between exchanges. Postal networks provide a series of links, often with different transport mechanisms. Airline networks sometimes provide a direct connection (a direct flight) and sometimes require a passenger to change at an intermediate airport.

This book is concerned with information networks. A network may be defined as *a set of interconnected operations*. Information processing operations take place at discrete points in the network, where information is entered, forwarded or delivered. Many names are used for these points—node, switch, box and others. They are connected by network components that transmit signals, into which information is encoded, according to methods outlined in the previous chapter. Many names are also used for these components—line, link, channel, circuit and so on.

From the point of view of a network user—such as a telephone subscriber or a data terminal operator—the network exists to provide connections to other users for the exchange of information. The user is not concerned with, and may well not know, the internal workings of the network. Networks are commonly represented graphically as clouds to emphasize this lack of concern or knowledge. The network designer and builder, on the other hand, are very much concerned with what happens inside the cloud. The choice and positioning of network nodes and the choice and capacity of links critically affect the service provided to users. In this chapter, some of the fundamental decisions to be made in building a network are considered.

## 3.2 Network nodes and addressing

The *nodes* of a network are the data processing machines that cooperate to provide an information channel between users. The channel may be a *physical connection*—a continuous circuit between the users, passing through a number of nodes, established at the request of one user, maintained for the duration of the connection and released when no longer required. Alternatively, the channel may be a *logical connection* that is discontinuous in that it consists of a sequence of links between nodes. The sequence may well change during the connection and the 'outbound' sequence may differ from the 'inbound' sequence. The channel may well be *multiplexed*, along with other channels for other users, on to physical media of high bandwidth.

Network nodes may be divided into two types—those that provide the user with a means of sending and receiving information and those that determine the route along which information will flow. We will call them, for the moment, *end nodes* and *intermediate nodes*. The distinction may be illustrated by returning to the examples of networks that were used above. In the telephone network, the end nodes are telephone handsets and the intermediate nodes are exchange switches. In the postal system, the end nodes are letter boxes and the intermediate nodes are sorting offices. The distinction is less clear in the case of the airline system where an airport may be an end node for some users but an intermediate node for others. Most airports are intermediate nodes in that they provide a choice of routes. Perhaps the best way to maintain the analogy is to treat the city airline terminal as an end node.

The end nodes of a data network are computers. The users of a data network, which generate and receive data, are people or programs. Data networking is still dominated by interactive communication between a terminal operator and an application, although application-to-application communication is increasing rapidly. A terminal operator requires, as a minimum, a means of entering information (such as a keyboard), a means of receiving information (such as a video display) and a means of selecting a partner for communication. These correspond respectively to the mouthpiece, the earpiece and the dial or keypad of a telephone.

The end node normally plays no part in deciding the route that data will take, other than to identify the destination, although some networks provide a source routeing facility. Routeing decisions are made in the intermediate nodes of the network, based on the identity of the destination as provided by the source user. Each end node is connected to an intermediate node where the first routeing decision is made. The decision may be to forward the message, or extend the connection, to another intermediate node and repeat the process until the intermediate node is reached to which the destination end node is attached. The process is familiar from the establishment of a telephone connection via

*Network components and topologies*

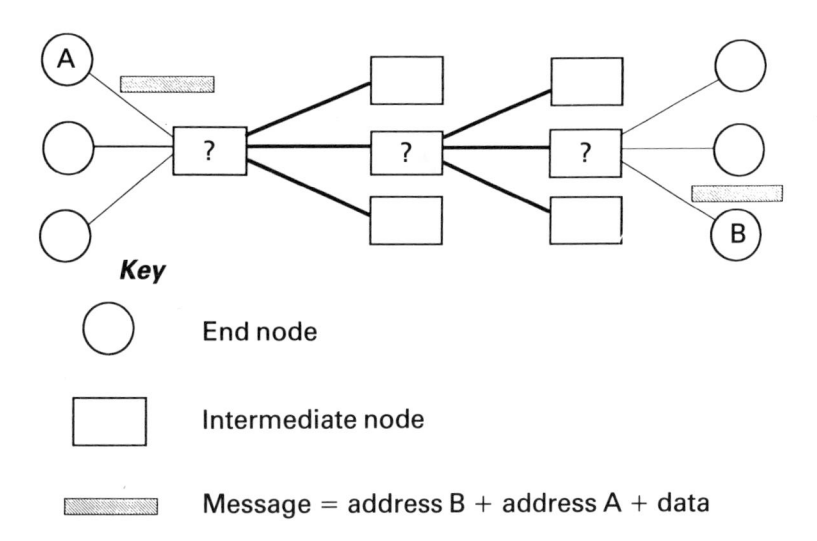

*Figure 3.1 Message routeing*

a number of exchanges or the delivery of a letter as a result of it passing through a number of sorting offices. The process is illustrated in Figure 3.1.

The role of a network, providing any-to-any connections between users, means that it can be thought of as a switch. The 'switching' function may be provided by a single intermediate node, by a number of interconnected intermediate nodes, each making part of the routeing decision, or by sending all messages to all users, relying on each user to pick out its own messages and forward the others. The spatial arrangement of switches (routeing points) determines the topology of the network.

Figure 3.2 shows various network topologies. The simplest form is the *star network* (a) in which all users are connected to a single, intermediate switching node. The *mesh network* (b) has a number of nodes, each connected to some of the others (*partial mesh*) or all of the others (*full mesh*). The star and mesh arrangements may be combined into a *snowflake* topology (c) in which subsets of users are connected in a star configuration to an intermediate node, forming a peripheral network, and intermediate nodes are connected in a mesh configuration, forming a backbone network. The telephone network and many data networks conform to this hybrid topology. A *hierarchical tree* topology is shown in (d).

Parts (e) and (f) of the figure show, respectively, a *ring* topology and a *bus* topology, in which a message generated by one user is available to, and examined by, all other users. The user for which it is destined copies the message. Note that in these arrangements a single link connects all end nodes and the concept of an intermediate node has little meaning. Networks with different topologies, and different routeing techniques, may be connected together to form so-called *internets*.

(a)

(b)

(c)

(d)

(e)

(f)

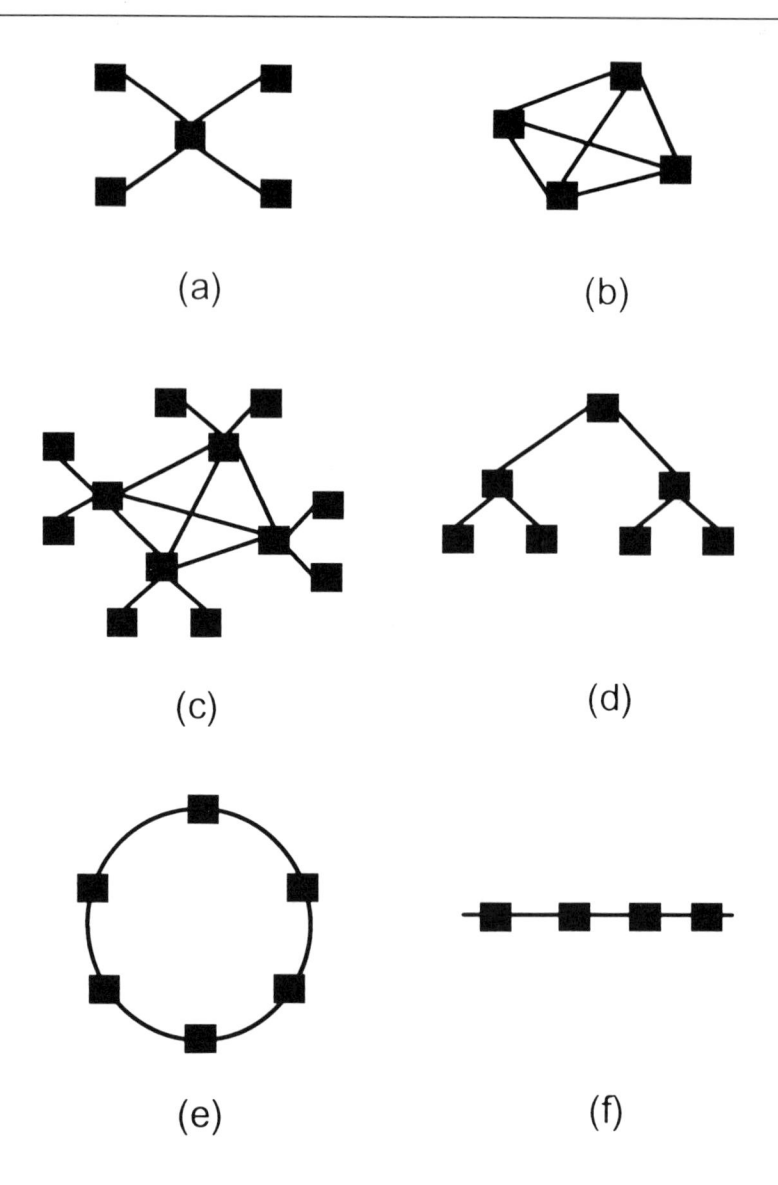

*Figure 3.2   Network topologies*

Each of these topologies has advantages and disadvantages. The star topology reduces the number of 'hops' between end nodes to two, but has a single point of failure—if the intermediate node fails, no connections can be made. In busy periods, the performance of the network is likely to be impaired. The mesh and snowflake topologies distribute the routeing function across a number of machines. Alternative routes may be defined between nodes and traffic flow balanced across the network. The penalty, though, is an increase in the number of network hops and in the complexity of the network. In the hierarchical tree topology, the root node is involved in routeing only between widely separated end nodes, but is a single point of failure for these routes. The ring and bus topologies have minimal routeing functions but require special functions to handle simultaneous attempts to send messages by two or more end nodes.

A network user, wishing to make a call to another user, needs to identify the destination end node to the network. End nodes of the telephone network are identified by a number, divided into groups to indicate country, area and individual subscriber. End nodes of the postal network are identified by an address incorporating, in many countries, a post code or its equivalent. This information is used by *network switches* (exchanges or sorting offices) to determine the route between source and destination.

Note that the important information as far as the network is concerned is the address of an end node rather than the name of the user for whom the information is destined. Telephone callers may know the name of someone they wish to call but not the number of the telephone connection point. Directories of names and numbers are provided, either on paper or through the network, to resolve a name to a number. Data networks also provide directory services.

A network end node may be shared by several users just as different members of a family share a telephone and an address. The identification of the user to whom information is sent is not a network function but is provided by the end node or by the user.

*Network addresses* need to be unique for information to be delivered correctly. A common technique to ensure uniqueness is to structure the addressing information into groups, each representing a subset of end nodes. A telephone number consists of a country code, an area code and a local number. An address consists of a house number or name, a street name or number, the name of a town, a county, state or province and a country. Data networks use a similar addressing mechanism although different network architectures use different addressing structures. *Network switches* use different parts of the addressing structure to determine a route. For public networks, names and numbers are allocated by the relevant operating agency or by international agreement.

In the case of private networks, operated by different companies, it may not be possible to ensure that names or addresses in one network are not repeated in another. For example an end node may be called TERM1, and given address 1, by network A and a quite different end node may be called TERM1, and given address 1, by network B. This is not a problem while traffic is confined to one network. However, if the companies decide to connect their networks together to allow inter-company traffic, an extension to the addressing mechanism will be needed in order to restore uniqueness. Equally, if the networks each have a different addressing structure, translation is required, not only of the names and addresses, but also of the structure of the addresses. Different techniques are used in different network architectures to resolve the problem. Some of them are described once the discussion of network architectures has been developed.

## 3.3 Network links

*Network links* carry messages from end nodes to intermediate nodes and between intermediate nodes. An intermediate node acts as a concentrator as well as a switch. Consequently, *backbone circuits* generally have higher capacity than *peripheral circuits*. The former are often called *trunk circuits* and the latter *tail circuits* or *local loops*. Any of the transmission media described in Chapter 2 may be used.

A tail circuit connecting an end node to an intermediate node may be permanently in place or it may be established only when required. A permanent or leased line is leased from the local telecommunications company. A switched or dialled line is established when needed by making a telephone call to or from the intermediate node. The use of a permanent line backed up by a dialled line, often to a different intermediate node, is common and allows for failure of an intermediate node or of the leased line. A tail circuit may have one end node (a *point-to-point line*) or it may have several (a *multipoint* or *multidrop line*). In the latter case, precautions need to be taken against simultaneous attemps by more than one end node to use the line.

A *route* is a path through the network between two end nodes. It has a tail circuit at each end. In between, it consists of a number of intermediate links between intermediate nodes. The term 'route' is often restricted to this intermediate, and potentially variable, section. Using the term in this restricted sense, the switching role of the network is to determine the route. Some networks allow the user to specify certain qualities of the route (capacity, security, reliability or transit delay). Some allow the user to specify the actual route.

## 3.4 Other networking equipment

In Section 3.2 the network nodes were described. End nodes enable users to send and receive information. Intermediate nodes provide attachment points for end nodes and route information through the network. Each of these nodes is identified by a unique network address to which messages can be sent. Many other types of equipment are used in networks to assist in the movement of information through the network.

Modems are used to enable digital signals to be carried on circuits designed for analog traffic. Some have autoanswer facilities to enable dialled lines to be used. Some have multiple input ports allowing several devices to be connected to a multidrop line. The modem is then acting as a concentrator. Concentration is also provided by other devices that have several input channels and one output channel, such as the controllers that support a number of video displays and printers. Multiplexers have several input channels and may have several output channels. A multiplexer apportions the bandwidth of its physical output channels between a number of logically distinct circuits.

*Protocol converters* cater for situations in which the control characters in a data stream conform to different rules (different architectures). The converter accepts data in one form and converts the control information to another form without changing the user data, if any. *Bridges, routers* and *gateways* are particular examples of protocol converters that will be discussed in detail later.

## 3.5 Network types

Two types of network may be distinguished in terms of their approach to routeing. *Circuit Switched Data Networks (CSDN)* provide a continuous physical circuit through the network. The circuit is established by reference to information provided by the caller. The telephone network is an example of such an approach in which routeing information is provided by dialled digits. Some data networks are also based on circuit switching. Once the circuit is established, all traffic follows the same route.

Most data networks, however, adopt a different approach. User data is split into units each of which carries the address of the destination end node. At each intermediate node, the address is examined and used to determine the next section of the route to the next intermediate node. The route may be predefined or determined dynamically to make it possible to adapt to traffic conditions on the network. These techniques are referred to respectively as *static routeing* and *dynamic adaptive routeing*. The postal network, appropriately, is an example of a network that routes information in packets. Data networks using the same principle are called *Packet Switched Data Networks (PSDN)*.

Networks may, in addition, be *public* or *private*. Public networks are built and operated by a government body or by private companies licensed by government (*Recognized Private Operating Agencies*). The *Public Switched Telephone Networks (PSTNs)* and *Public Data Networks (PDNs)* are examples. The latter are normally PSDNs.

Private networks are built and operated by private companies. They may provide communication services to many other companies or to a single company. In the latter case, they are *owned* by the single company (although lines are leased from a public carrier) but may be *operated* by an outside company—so-called facilities management. Both public and private networks may carry voice and data traffic, multiplexing both types of traffic on the same circuits.

A further distinction may be made based on the geographic scope of the network. Some networks are country-wide or world-wide in their scope while others are confined to a smaller area—a room, a building or a site. Networks with wide geographical coverage are termed *Wide Area Networks (WANs)* while those with more localized coverage are termed *Local Area Networks (LANs)*. *Metropolitan Area Networks (MANs)*—networks with intermediate coverage, serving a whole city—are being developed. Networks of all three types may be connected together to form complicated internets.

## 3.6 Network design

This section looks at some of the many factors affecting the design of a network. The first thing to be considered is the *use* of the network. Is it for voice, interactive computing, electronic mail, file transfer, electronic data interchange, process control or one of the many other uses for which networks are provided? A network for one specific service may be tailored to provide that service with attendant high quality. On the other hand, networks are expensive and most users demand a multipurpose network that is able to support a number of value-added services, so such a network will be assumed in this brief overview of design principles.

The second thing to be considered is the network *architecture*. Network architectures are fully defined and discussed in Chapter 4, but for the purpose of this section, a network architecture defines the rules for the interoperation of the components of the network and the way in which users interact with the network. The architecture does not define the way in which components should be designed, nor does it define rules for putting components together to form a network. There are a number of network architectures to choose from. Many of them have been developed by individual computer manufacturers and incorporated in their products. Some manufacturers implement other manufacturers' architectures in addition to their own, so that the choice of a proprietary architecture does not necessarily limit the designer to a choice of the proprietor's products. A smaller number of architectures have been developed by international organizations and may be implemented by any manufacturer. These are said to be *open* in the sense that a network based on such an architecture is open for communication to systems that obey the rules, that is, implement the architecture. The use of an open architecture gives the network designer a greater degree of vendor independence, provided sufficient vendors of network components determine that there is a business case for developing open systems.

Many designers try to achieve the best of both worlds by building hybrid networks using both open *and* proprietary architectures, converting from one to the other when necessary.

A network architecture must meet the requirements of the network by providing the communication functions necessary to support the services the network will offer. A general purpose network therefore requires a general purpose architecture. In this book, a number of general-purpose architectures are described, one proprietary (to IBM) and the remainder open. The designer must also be sure that components are available from which to build a network of the chosen architecture.

What about the physical design of the network? For the purposes of this discussion, let us assume the most demanding problem of a WAN with snowflake topology. The nature of network traffic, and its distribution over geography and time, must first be considered as they determine the capacity of network nodes and links and their spatial distribution—the network's topology.

A general-purpose network is expected to carry data of various types. The performance of the network, in terms of the capacity and transit delay of routes through the network, must meet users' requirements for each type of data. Interactive connections between two users require small transit delays. Transfer of bulk data requires circuits and nodes able to handle the large throughput. Electronic mail needs to be stored by the network until the recipient is able to receive it. Traffic volumes vary with time of day, week or year and end nodes are unevenly distributed.

The specification of a network topology and its capacity is not a precise process. Traffic volumes (type and rate of messages) are rarely known with any precision and cost constraints are always placed on the designer. The placing of intermediate nodes may be governed by the availability of suitable premises. Links of the desired capacity may not be available. Technological limitations are generally in force.

A designer must produce a network capable of handling the estimated maximum traffic volume while maintaining the service levels required by users. A prudent designer will not allow *any* component to exceed a certain percentage of its maximum capacity when operating under peak traffic conditions. A commonly used rule of thumb is 70 per cent utilization. For example, a 9600 bits per second circuit should not be expected to carry more than about 6800 bits per second of information. Messages will not necessarily be lost if the component utilization exceeds this maximum, but queues of messages waiting to be processed develop, response time suffers and demands are imposed on the capacity of components to store messages. A computerized model of the network, which simulates its behaviour under different conditions, may be employed.

An approach to estimating network traffic may be made by first examining the population distribution of potential users. Many networks provide services to, or on behalf of, the general public. The volume of traffic generated in a particular town may be assumed to be proportional to the population. The designer acquires an initial feel for where to place the intermediate nodes.

The volume of data originating from, or destined for, a particular end node depends not only on the number of users that the node serves, but also on the services for which the node is used. More attention is normally given to interactive services that affect the user in real time. A knowledge of the interaction between a user and an application enables the number and length of messages exchanged to be determined. Input messages (to the application) are commonly shorter than output messages (from the application). The work pattern of a user needs to be examined to determine if, as is often the case, use of the networks peaks at certain times.

By combining knowledge of the number of end nodes on each peripheral line, the interactive message flows and the user work patterns, the designer is able to estimate the maximum number of bits per second the line is expected to handle, also taking into account the introduction of redundant bits for control purposes. He or she now has a feel, not only for the placing of intermediate peripheral nodes, but also for the capacity of lines connecting them to the end nodes. Dialled connections may be introduced for infrequently used lines and multipoint lines to share capacity between low-volume end nodes. The designer then focuses on the backbone network of intermediate nodes.

The peripheral intermediate nodes (those to which end nodes are directly connected) act as concentrators and switches. These components have a finite capacity for handling messages, usually expressed in *characters per second* or *given-sized packets per second*. Attached to each node are a number of low-capacity links to end nodes and a number of high-capacity links to other intermediate nodes. The number and capacity of lines that may be connected to an intermediate node are also limited. The designer must next ensure that the proposed nodes and connections do not exceed this capacity. If so, additional nodes are introduced to distribute the load.

Processing of a message by an intermediate node takes time and adds to the message transit delay. A fully meshed backbone network, in which each peripheral node is connected to all others ensures three network hops—one from the source end node to an intermediate node, one between intermediate nodes and one to the destination node. Such a topology requires a large number of intermediate links, some of which may be underutilized due to an uneven distribution of traffic. The intermediate nodes may be incapable of supporting the required number of circuits. Many networks, by the nature of the services they offer, concentrate traffic on to a small number of end nodes. This is particularly true of networks that provide access by a large number of user terminals to a small number (sometimes one only) of mainframe computers.

To alleviate these problems, many networks introduce a hierarchical structure into the backbone network. Figure 3.3 shows a topology in which the backbone network consists of two tiers, neither of which is fully meshed. The lower tier provides attachment for low-capacity end nodes. The upper tier consists of a small number of high-capacity switches to which are attached high-capacity end nodes—mainframe computers. Each intermediate node in the lower tier is connected to one or more nodes of the upper tier. Under normal circumstances, a route between end nodes is routed through one intermediate node in each tier. Connections between low-capacity end nodes are made through the lower tier. Such a topology provides a flexible system for balancing traffic and providing alternative routes without seriously impacting response time.

A network should be available to users when needed and should be reliable in use. Facilities should be incorporated to enable the network operator to observe and change the state of the network to enable faults to be detected and corrected. Facilities should also be incorporated to account for use of the network by individual users. These facilities fall under the heading of network management, which is covered in Chapter 12. A particular aspect of managing a network is to restrict its use and the use of the services it provides to authorized users. The security aspects of networking are considered in Chapter 11.

## 3.7 Summary

In this chapter, some of the components used in building networks and some basic design principles for putting them together to provide services of an acceptable quality to users have been described. An early decision when building a network is to select the architecture to which it will conform. The next chapter describes a number of network architectures.

*Figure 3.3 shows two data centres (D) connected to the network providing a means of disaster recovery. One data centre is normally used as the live or production centre, while the other is used for development and to provide contingency cover. High-speed circuits between the two data centres allow the data from core applications to be sent from the production centre to the contingency centre so that, in the event of a major disaster, the contingency centre is able to take over from the production centre without loss of data. The network would direct all interactive traffic to the contingency centre in the event of a major disaster at the production centre.*

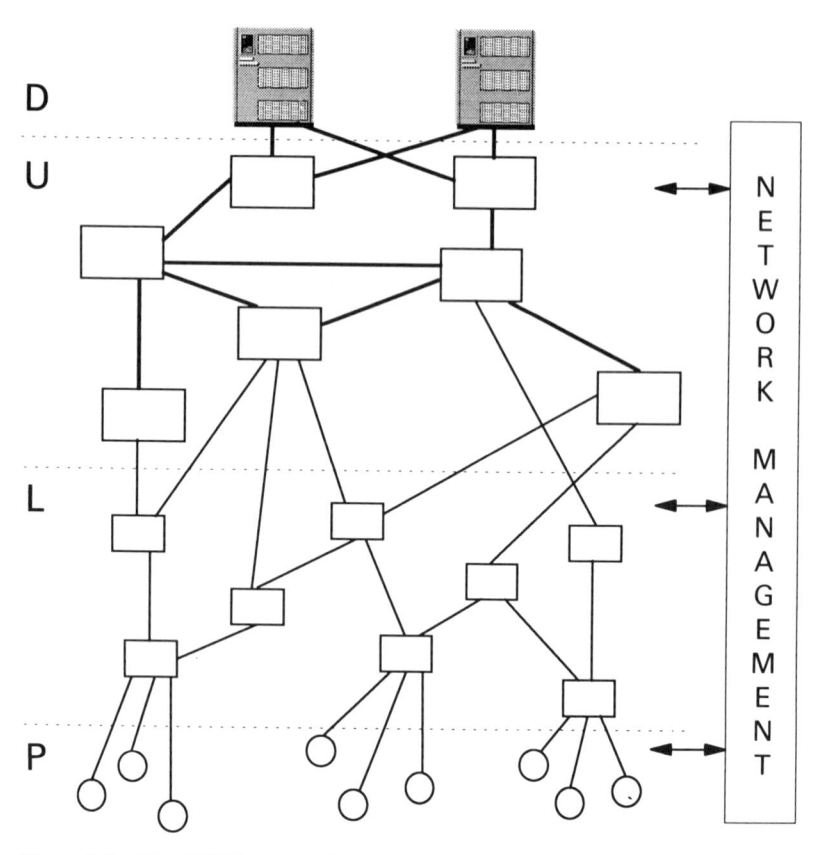

Figure 3.3  The WNB's network

The ability of the network to direct interactive traffic to the surviving centre depends on the provision of a network management centre. In order to protect the network management centre, it was decided to install it at a location remote from either data centre and to provide a back-up network management centre to take over in the event of a disaster at the live network management centre.

Switching centres are connected in a mesh topology with some elements of a tree structure in that the nearer traffic gets to the root of the tree (the data centre), the thicker are the trunks. This backbone network consists of two tiers. The lower tier (L) supports the peripheral network (P) and is partially meshed with 64 kbits/second multiplexes between switches. It acts as a concentrator to the upper tier (U), which consists of larger capacity switches with 128 kbits/second multiplexes and multiple connections to the data centres. Peak utilization of switches and circuits is low to meet the requirement that the network transit delay should not substantially increase the interactive response time to the user.

Each end point in the peripheral network (branch, regional office or head office) supports multiple users who need simultaneous access to the network. They also need to communicate with each other and with local servers within the branch. The WNB's solution is to implement a LAN in the branch with a communications gateway to the WAN. The LANs have a bus topology supporting work stations of various types, together with on-site ATMs and other customer-operated devices. Off-site ATMs are connected to the communications gateway by leased external circuits. The overall topology of the WNB's network is an early example of an internet — a set of networks connected by gateways or routers.

The WNB has upwards of 1000 end points, all of which have one or more telephones and most of which have multiple data terminals. These include terminals operated by its staff and terminals, such as ATMs, operated by customers. Much of the data flow is between branches and a data processing centre, while much of the voice flow is branch-to-branch in nature. Data flow is largely interactive with a half-hour peak period in the middle of the day. Branches must have access to the network throughout the working day.

The telecommunications planners in the WNB, in considering the telephone requirements, compared the cost of telephone traffic carried through public networks with the cost of a private network. They concluded that it would be economical to build a private network to take most of the in-bank traffic. However, it was clear that this private network could not be extended to all offices of the WNB. Detailed calculations showed that some 300 offices (including the large Head Office sites) should be included in the private telephone network and that such a network would be able to carry over half of the in-bank traffic.

Turning to the requirements for a private data network, it became clear that there would be considerable advantages in planning both networks together in order to provide a combined voice and data service. The plan that was proposed by the WNB is illustrated in Figure 3.4, which shows that voice and data integration is provided on the long-distance trunk routes between switching centres. Each switching centre contains a digital circuit switch and a data switch. The switching centres are themselves connected through 2 Mbits/second trunk circuits that terminate on the voice circuit switches. In order to allow voice and data integration on the 2 Mbits/second routes, a multiplexer is inserted in the circuit and 64 kbits/second data feeds are slotted into available channels on the 2 Mbits/second trunks. The planners at the WNB calculated that, after taking all capital and running costs into account, this method of voice and data integration gave them a saving of £100 000 per annum.

The section of the voice network shown in Figure 3.4 shows two digital circuit switches connected via a 2 Mbits/second trunk. The total network contains a number of circuit switches, each of which exchanges information according to an ISDN-type of protocol known as the Digital Private Network Signalling System (DPNSS). In addition, digital links to the public networks were made with 2 Mbits/second circuits carrying the Digital Access Signalling System (DASS) protocol that is compatible

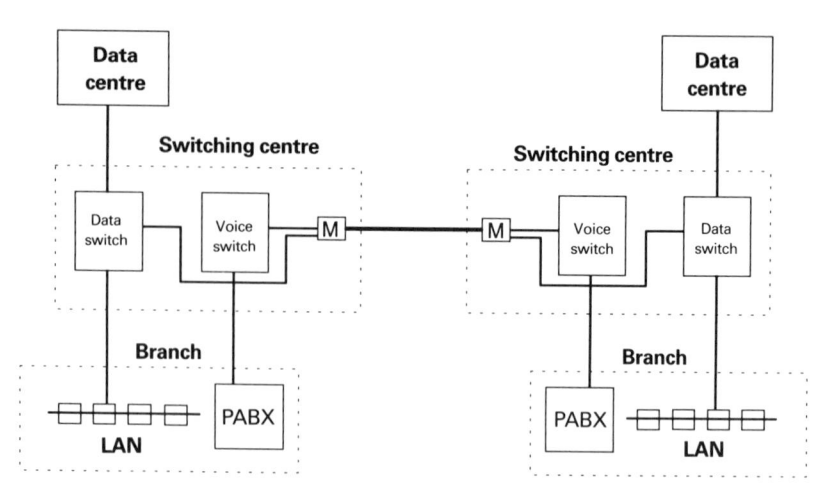

*Figure 3.4  Voice and data integration*

with DPNSS. *The use of these protocols allowed calls to be set up very quickly within the network and certain special facilities to be provided to in-bank users of telephone services. In particular, telephone users served by a digital* Private Automatic Branch Exchange (PABX) *provided with DPNSS signalling were able to book calls on similarly connected extensions. In addition, they were able to make trunk calls cheaply and efficiently through a combination of the private network and the public network. In order to achieve this, the serving PABX would translate a trunk telephone number in a way that allowed the call to be routed to a switch in the private network close to the called party. The connection over the public network would then be made from the private network via a local call. The planners in the WNB calculated that the use of this facility, known as PSTN breakout, would give them a saving of some £50 000 per annum.*

*Full facilities on the digital private telephone network would be available to any PABX user on a digital DPNSS switch. However, the smaller branches of the WNB could not be economically supplied with such switches and, in this case, connection was made through analog circuits. Calls can be set up through the private telephone network, but no special facilities are available.*

*The nature and volume of the WNB's information flow determined the topology and capacity of the network. The planners in the WNB calculated that the interactive traffic required for the main banking applications and the file transfer traffic associated with customer records could be carried with adequate performance on a 9.6 Kbits/second circuit. At the time that the design was proposed, the WNB found that this connection to the switching centre could be made most economically through a standard analog circuit and modems. In considering the service requirements of branches, it was clear that the combination of the PABX and a branch LAN would allow accessibility of services to all desks in the office. As regards the maximum four-hour outage, it was realized that, with the failure rates that could be expected of both circuit and packet switches, it would be essential to provide contingency against normal, single-element failures. In the case of the data network, this was achieved by providing a dial back-up facility to allow a branch to be reconnected to the network at a different switching centre. This, therefore, allowed for failure of the leased line, of the packet switch, of the switching centre and of certain trunk routes connected to the switching centre. In order to improve the contingency services, the switching centres are themselves connected by separate 64 kbits/second circuits as well as through the standard digital trunk framework.*

# CHAPTER 4

# Introduction to communications architectures

## 4.1 Introduction

Communication is a complicated and, at times, subtle process. Consider the transfer of information between two people in a face-to-face conversation. Many processes are involved, ranging from the mental formulation of a statement to the production of sound waves. The conversation is subject to rules established by convention—both participants do not speak at the same time, for example. Body language (facial expressions or gestures) is used both to control the flow of information and to indicate failures in reception or understanding. A conversation may take place through a third party if the participants do not share a common language.

Consider now a telephone conversation. The necessary processes still range from the cognitive to the physical—from the formulation of an idea to the production of sound. Rules for dialogue control, flow control and error recovery are still required, but visual contact between the participants is removed. Body language is no longer appropriate, although it is still employed—observe the gestures and expressions of a person on the telephone. Phrases such as 'Are you still there?' or 'We got cut off—where were we up to?' are introduced. Conversion of sound waves to electrical signals becomes necessary. Contact between the participants relies on switches to establish an electrical circuit. Despite these differences, the conversation still relies heavily on human knowledge and experience.

Consider finally the situation in which both participants are represented by data processing machines. As an example, take the withdrawal of cash from a cash dispenser—an Automatic Teller Machine (ATM). The transaction is between the account holder and the bank. Each is represented by a machine—the ATM in the case of the account holder and a mainframe computer in the case of the bank. The rules that govern the 'conversation' must be programmed into these machines, with minimal human intervention. These rules are embodied in a communications architecture.

## 4.2 The nature of a communications architecture

The term 'architecture' is overused and misused in the field of information technology. Statements such as 'the architecture of an OSI system' or 'the architecture of an SNA system' are common and, in both cases, misuse the word 'architecture'.

A communications architecture defines the *rules for communication between data processing systems*. It defines both the rules for the behaviour of each system and the rules for the exchange of information between systems. It does *not* define the means by which these systems should be designed. Consequently the terms 'the *architecture* of an OSI/SNA system' should be replaced by 'the *design* of an OSI/SNA system'. In each case the architecture is predefined as OSI *or* SNA.

In the introduction to this chapter it was noted that many different processes are involved in communication between people or machines. In the case of machine-to-machine communication, each machine must contain the necessary communications functions, provided by either hardware or software. In the absence of any guiding principles, the designer of a machine may implement these functions in many different ways. The implementation of the same function by another designer, or by the same designer on another machine, is likely to be very different.

In these circumstances reliable communication is unlikely to result. Communication relies on cooperation between machines. To achieve reliable communication, each machine must be able to indicate to the other conditions such as a change in the direction of flow of information, an inability to handle the rate of incoming data or failure to receive a message—the processes provided in person-to-person conversations by conventional human experience. A communications architecture seeks to introduce order into this potentially chaotic world—hence the use of the term 'architecture'. It addresses two areas: the structure of the communications functions in a data processing machine and the exchange of control information between machines.

In addressing the communications functions in a particular machine, the architecture recognizes that they span a wide range but that they may be divided into a relatively small number of subsets. A possible subdivision might be:

- the process of constructing a message
- the translation of that message into a syntax recognizable to the receiver
- the establishment of a logical connection between sender and receiver
- the control of the direction and flow of information
- the establishment of a physical connection between sender and receiver.

The division of communications functions into subsets, or layers, is a feature common to all architectures. The term *layer* implies a hierarchical relationship between the functional subsets. In the above example each layer depends on the functions performed by the layers below in order for a message to be sent and received successfully. This book is very much about layered communications architectures.

Although it may seem reasonable to divide the processes involved in communication into subsets, the usefulness of such a division needs further justification. Some of the reasons are fairly obvious. The reduction of a large and complicated set of functions into a number of subsets is, in itself, an aid to understanding. It is particularly helpful if the functions in a given subset are closely related to each other and manifestly different from those in other subsets. While maintaining the validity of such distinction, a small number of subsets is preferable to a large number. It seems reasonable to base the choice of subsets on observation of real communications systems.

In order to develop this intuitive approach into an architecture, it is necessary to examine the way in which functional subsets cooperate—both within and between systems—to provide the complete set of required communications functions. It is here that layering is introduced. It is conventional to represent the communication functions within a data processing system as being divided horizontally with the functions that interface to the physical medium at the bottom and the functions that interface to the user at the top. This is illustrated in Figure 4.1. The use of the term 'layer' should now seem more appropriate and a means of defining rigorously the rules for cooperation between and within layers (that is, the architecture) begins to emerge. This layered structure is often called a *stack*. The stack is a conceptual device enabling the logical structure of a communications system to be analysed. It does not, in any way, represent the physical structure of the system.

The purpose of any communications system is to support the exchange of information between its users via some physical medium. A number of points should be noted here. A communications architecture does not specify *how* to design or build a system; it defines rules to be observed *in the design process*. Furthermore, these rules do not apply to the user or to the physical medium, but only to the communications stack.

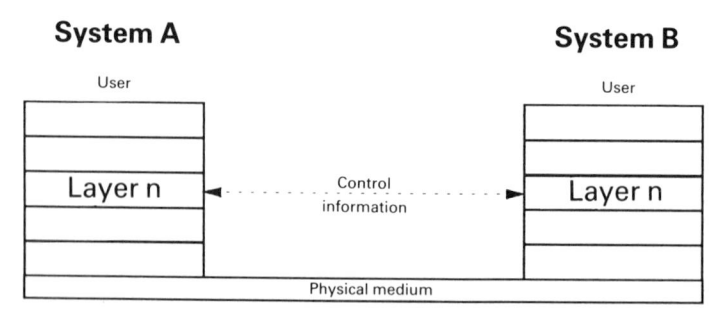

*Figure 4.1   Layered communications functions*

Let us examine more closely the role of a particular layer in the stack—layer n of Figure 4.1. The layer contains functions that play a particular role in the process of communication between system A and system B. The position of layer n in the stack implies that other functions are provided both below and above it. The layer therefore relies on functions performed by layers below, adds its contribution and is then available for use by the layers above. This concept of a layered stack, with each layer adding value to the layers below and providing a service to the layers above, is one of two concepts that are fundamental to a communications architecture. We now turn to the second of these concepts.

Layer n functions appear in both systems and their role within each system has been indicated. It is more rigorous, if rather more abstracted and perhaps pedantic, to consider the layer n functions in system A and the layer n functions in system B as two instances of a single entity—layer n. An analogy with the telephone system here may be useful. A telephone handset contains functions that generate dialling signals off-hook and respond to dialling signals on-hook. These functions are part of the 'establish a connection between two telephones' layer of the telephone system and the two handsets cooperate to perform that role. This concept of cooperation between two instances of a particular layer, as part of the overall process of providing user-to-user communication, is the second, and perhaps more important, property of a communications architecture.

Let us assume that we have identified control of the rate of flow of information between users (flow control) as a layer n function. Layers below layer n do not provide it; layers above layer n assume that it is provided. It is layer n's job. It should be apparent that the layer n functions in system A cannot provide this function unaided. In particular, they need help from system B—specifically, the layer n functions in system B. Flow control is a cooperative process within layer n. A mechanism is required, within layer n, to detect and resolve flow control problems.

It is now a small step to deduce that this mechanism involves the exchange of flow control information between A and B that is of relevance *only* to the layer n functions in the two systems. This information is additional to any information exchanged between users and to any information exchanged within other layers. It is unique to layer n and is analogous to the gestures and expressions, and their conventional responses, used to control flow in a person-to-person conversation. The point was made earlier in this chapter that, in a personal conversation, flow control relies heavily on human experience, intelligence and adherence to generally accepted rules. Rules are even more necessary when the exchange of information is between two *machines*.

These rules for exchanging information for control purposes between instances of layer functions in different systems are called a *protocol*, because they resemble the rules of etiquette for human conversation. To return to our example, the layer n protocol defines the rules for exchanging flow control information between systems. Different layers have different roles but, in fulfilling these roles, each has a need to cooperate with the functions in its peer layer in some other system. Consequently, a protocol is required, in general, for each layer.

To return to the intuitive level of analysis, flow control is necessary only when information is actually flowing between users. It would seem sensible to include flow control information in the same transmission as, but separated from, the user data and separated from the control information needed by other layers for functions such as error detection or routeing. This is, indeed, the mechanism adopted by layered communications architectures where protocol control information is appended to the user data by successive layers of the stack in the sending system and used and removed by successive layers of the peer stack in the receiving system.

In this section the attempt has been made to establish, by a process of reasonable deduction, the technical case for layered architectures and some of their characteristics. The next section examines briefly the commercial case for layered architectures and some of the historical milestones in their development. The examples used here, and throughout the book, are the most widely implemented manufacturer-defined architecture, IBM's *Systems Network Architecture (SNA)*, and the most rigorously defined manufacturer-independent architecture, the *ISO Reference Model for Open Systems Interconnection (OSI)*.

## 4.3 The development of communications architectures

In the early 1970s, access to computers from remote terminals, for job entry or for interactive use, began to grow. A number of manufacturers had developed business applications for the batch processing of jobs submitted locally. These applications, and their supporting system software, needed to be redeveloped to incorporate functions to communicate with remote terminals. Initially this was done in an uncoordinated manner, resulting in many different implementations of terminal support functions, making it necessary for users to install a separate terminal and communications line for each application.

Manufacturers soon realized that a more structured and coordinated approach to the provision of communication between their systems was necessary. In other words they recognized the need for a communications architecture. Within a few years, in the mid 1970s, every major manufacturer had developed an architecture and products conforming to its rules. IBM announced SNA and the first SNA products in 1974.

All of these architectures incorporated the concepts of layers and their associated protocols. All of them were, and remain, different in detail. As detail is all important in a communications protocol, products from manufacturer X would not work with products from manufacturer Y. Indeed X or Y considered it commercially disadvantageous for this to happen and so did not encourage it.

Although enabling individual suppliers to present a uniform communications strategy to their customers, incompatible architectures presented those customers with problems if they wished to use products from different manufacturers. Communication between systems is essentially determined by the protocols at the various architectural layers. If these are incompatible, conversion of the protocol used by one system to that recognized by the other is required.

In 1977, the *International Standards Organization (ISO)* set out to define an architecture for the interconnection of data processing systems that would be open to all users. It came to be called the *Reference Model for Open Systems Interconnection*, or, the *OSI model*—a model to which designers of communications systems could refer. Any two systems implemented according to OSI rules would be able to communicate—they would be *open* to each other. The model was formally adopted as ISO standard 7498.

Since these early developments, data processing and telecommunications have continued to converge towards the common path of IT. The distribution of application processing, the availability of powerful microprocessors, the spread of LANs and the need to integrate them with WANs, the creation of new technologies, the provision of ever-increasing performance at ever-decreasing costs, all have combined to impose severe demands on communications systems and their underlying architectures. It is a tribute to the early workers in the field that the architectures, both proprietary and non-proprietary, have stood up well to these demands.

The situation at the time of writing is that both proprietary and non-proprietary architectures continue to develop. The idea of an architecture *developing* may seem dangerous in that if the rules change the architecture loses its value. By development, however, is meant the addition of new rules, to take into account the changes mentioned in the previous paragraph, rather than the changing of existing rules.

Proprietary architectures, particularly SNA, continue to dominate the field. The slow acceptance of non-proprietary standards, by both users and suppliers, is disappointing. This applies particularly to OSI (a major intellectual achievement), but this is understandable in that the spread of open networking needs commitment from manufacturers and a corresponding relaxation of their concentration on their own architectures. There are signs from many manufacturers that they are ready to relax—indeed, some would claim to be lending long-term practical support to OSI.

It is not implied here that the development of architectures by manufacturers and the development of general standards by standards organizations have been unrelated. The standards bodies rely on commercial suppliers for much of their technical resource. Proprietary architectures have influenced OSI standards and ISO and CCITT have influenced manufacturers to the point where a world of open, supplier-independent networking is not far away and where the full benefits of the convergence of data processing and telecommunications technologies can be realized.

## 4.4 Standards organizations

The communication of information between individuals, commercial organizations and governments is considered vital to the world's social, economic and political well-being. The need for communication transcends national boundaries and demands standardization at an international level. The relevant international standards organizations in the field of communication are the ISO and the CCITT. ISO covers many fields of human activity, while the CCITT is concerned with communication. They come together in defining the use of the world's telecommunication resources to support the exchange of information.

While there are significant structural differences between the CCITT and the ISO, they cooperate with each other to a surprising degree. The decision-making members of CCITT are the PTTs of the member countries, or their representatives in those countries (for example the UK and USA) where the telecommunications provider is separated from the government. Other organizations, including computer manufacturers, may influence the CCITT's recommendations, but executive power lies with national governments. This is reflected in the formal position of the CCITT as an arm of the United Nations. National governments have the power to impose the CCITT's standards, despite the fact that they are published as recommendations.

ISO has a different structure. It consists of a number of committees, subcommittees and working groups staffed by representatives of interested parties—governments, national standards bodies, suppliers and users. It defines standards whose adoption in a particular country depends on ratification by the standards body of that country (British Standards Institute, Deutsches Institut für Normung, Association Française de Normalisation and so on).

Despite the differences in structure and authority, the relationship between the ISO and CCITT is close and profitable. The CCITT's recommendations are adopted as ISO standards and vice versa. Both bodies are receptive to standards proposals from many sources—manufacturers (individually or collectively through manufacturers' associations), professional organizations (such as the Institute of Electrical and Electronics Engineers) or user groups.

## 4.5 The structure of a network

The term *network*, as we have seen, is frequently used not only in the communications world but in many other fields. The word is used in many familiar phrases—the rail, telephone and road networks, for example. The implication is that these things have something in common and it is not too difficult to deduce that the common factor is transportation—the movement of people or things or information from one place to another.

Continuing the intuitive approach adopted in this chapter, it becomes apparent that things do not generally travel directly through a network from their starting point to their destination. People change trains or the train changes tracks, telephone calls are routed through various exchanges, motorists encounter junctions and so on. Thus, the concept of a network as a set of interconnected points at which a routeing decision is taken begins to emerge.

Some further thought leads to the conclusion that networks have entry and exit points. Returning to our examples, railways have stations, the telephone network has handsets and roads have access points (such as private driveways). The processes that occur at these points seem to be different from the processes that occur at the routeing points. They are concerned with getting *into* the network rather than getting *through* it to the destination. This distinction will be developed in a general sense later in this chapter and more rigorously in later chapters.

The drawing of analogies between different types of network is useful in so far as it establishes a feel for the subject, which is the main purpose of this chapter. However, it loses value beyond this point—the 'private driveway' example given above is a rather artificial one.

In Chapter 3, a network was formally defined as being:

>a set of interconnected processes

This is sufficiently general to cover all our examples and has the merit of identifying two components—the processes and the interconnections. Railways have stations, junctions and tracks; telephone networks have subscriber equipment, exchanges and telephone lines.

A path from the intuitive approach to the analytical approach now begins to emerge. A network may be analysed in terms of the processes that occur at its various points. Formally, these points are termed *nodes*. There are entry and exit nodes and switching or intermediate nodes. The definition of the processes that occur at these nodes is very much part of a communications architecture. A network may also be analysed in terms of its topology—the placing of the nodes and the connections between them. This is not an architectural issue, but a design issue. This chapter, however, concerns architectural issues; the principles of network design are given in the previous chapter.

Having drawn some analogies between, at first sight, very different types of network, let us now return to the subject of communications networks—networks for transporting information. Do all nodes of a telephone or data network need to implement the same processes? The answer is fairly obviously 'no'. The processes in a telephone handset are different from those in an exchange. The former provide functions needed by subscribers while the latter provide functions needed to connect subscribers via a chain of exchanges. The processes in a data terminal provide functions needed by users while the processes in an intermediate switching node provide functions needed to connect users via a chain of switches.

User functions are not needed in switching nodes (you do not go to the telephone exchange to make a call). On the other hand, the ability to communicate with another node is needed in every node. A layered architecture distinguishes between functions that connect one node to another (the lower layers) and the functions that directly assist the user (the upper layers). It is tempting to deduce from this that all nodes need lower layer functions while only end nodes (the entry and exit points) need upper layer functions. A note of caution must, however, be sounded. Although nodes intermediate between entry and exit may not need upper layer functions in support of users, they may need those functions to support management of the network.

The concept of a communications architecture has so far been treated by reasonable deduction from common experience. It is now appropriate to introduce a more precise treatment of the subject.

## 4.6 The ISO's reference model for Open Systems Interconnection (OSI)

In Section 4.2 layered architectures were discussed in terms of two characteristics: the service provided by a particular layer to the layer above and the protocol governing the exchange of control information within a layer but between systems. The terminology is that of the OSI model, which adopts this distinction between service and protocol in a highly structured manner. The model was developed to provide rules for the design of communicating data processing systems with the intent that systems designed according to the rules would be open, that is able to communicate with any other system designed according to the rules.

The model is itself an ISO standard (ISO 7498) that embraces a large and growing number of standards that relate to specific parts of the communication process. It is a strictly layered model in which much thought was given to establishing the criteria for defining the layers. The result is a model with the seven layers shown in Figure 4.2. Each layer has a name and a number and may be referred to by either. The layers are introduced here in two groups and are discussed individually in more detail in the next chapter.

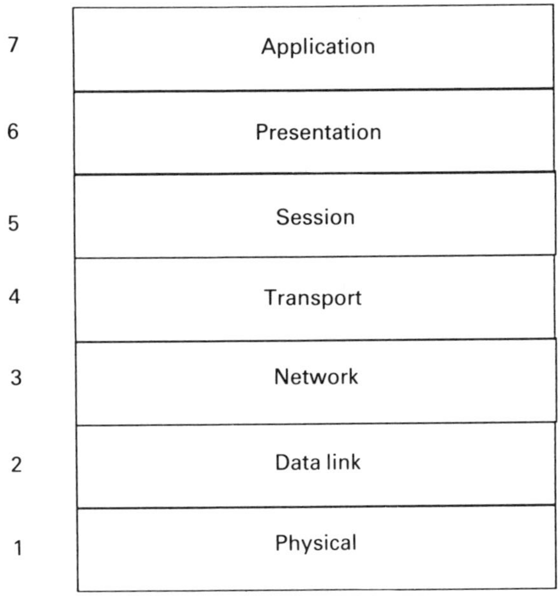

## Introduction to communications architectures

| | |
|---|---|
| 7 | Application |
| 6 | Presentation |
| 5 | Session |
| 4 | Transport |
| 3 | Network |
| 2 | Data link |
| 1 | Physical |

*Figure 4.2   The OSI model*

Each layer is defined by two primary standards, These specify, respectively, the service that the layer provides to the layer above and the type and format of the control messages exchanged within the layer between communicating systems, that is the layer protocol. Although adhering strictly to the principle of layering, the model is flexible in that it allows some functions within a layer to be optional while insisting on a mandatory subset.

A distinction was drawn in Section 4.5 between the lower layers of an architecture and the upper layers. It is convenient in this introductory treatment to apply this distinction to the OSI model by treating layers 1 to 3 (the lower layers) collectively but separately from layers 4 to 7 (the upper layers).

The purpose of an information network is to convey information from a source node to a destination node. In general, the information will travel via a number of intermediate nodes. A prudent network designer will provide a number of alternative routes between intermediate nodes to allow for failures of the links between them or to balance the traffic across the network. Each intermediate node may need to choose dynamically the next node in the route between source and destination. The role of the lower layers may be summarized as choosing the next node and a link to it (*network layer*), controlling the flow of messages on the chosen link (*data link layer*) and connecting to the physical medium that provides the link (*physical layer*).

The model specifies the functions that each layer must or may provide and embodies the specification in a service standard for each layer. Thus the data link service standard defines the service provided to the network layer in a node designed to conform to the lower layers of OSI. The model also specifies the set of control messages exchanged between the layer functions in adjacent nodes. For example, in the data link layer, a standard specifies the type, format and use of control fields that are appended as headers and trailers to messages generated by the network layer.

The composite role of the lower layers is to provide a means of sending a message from its source to any one of a number of destinations without loss or error. The network layer presents a service (the OSI network service) to its user. The user invokes the service, provides some necessary information along with the message, such as the identities of the source and destination, and we have a basic communication system. In many cases, this basic system is all that is required. In other cases, further functions may be needed but will be provided by the end systems without reference to the model. In the latter case, the users will need to agree on a private protocol to control these additional functions. The communication system is open but only to layer 3.

A user may require a type of service, such as an encrypted connection, that is not provided by the lower layers. Users may need to control the direction and rate of flow of information. They may require the syntax of a message to be changed. They may require a method of checkpointing and resynchronizing a conversation. These functions are essential in order to achieve reliable communication in many instances and particularly when communication is between application programs without human intervention. They must be provided either by the users themselves or by the communication system. The role of the upper layers of the OSI model is to define rules for the implementation of these more sophisticated functions.

The transport layer uses the network service and provides a service to the session layer by using the transport layer protocol. It therefore adds value to the network service by providing functions that raise the quality of that service to the level demanded, on behalf of the user, by the session layer. We have made a distinction between the lower three layers and the upper four layers. An equally valid distinction, although less common, is sometimes made between the lower four layers and the upper three layers on the grounds that the transport layer, with the cooperation of its lower layers, provides the service required by the user.

The session layer is responsible for controlling the user-to-user dialogue—its direction, if two-way simultaneous transmission is not available, and its synchronization. It provides the session layer service to the presentation layer and cooperates with its peer in the remote system through the session layer protocol.

The presentation layer, as its name suggests, is responsible for the presentation of information to a user in a format that the user can understand. In general, each user will generate information in a local syntax. The presentation layer will map the source information into a transfer syntax and, at the remote end, remap the information into local syntax. The situation is analogous to a conversation between two people one of whom speaks only language A, while the other speaks only language B. A employs an interpreter who speaks A and C, and B employs an interpreter who speaks B and C. The interpreters exchange information, in language C, translating to and from A or B for their respective users. A and B are the local syntaxes; C is the transfer syntax.

Finally, the application layer provides services directly to an application program. Application programs communicate for many reasons—for file transfer, remote entry of jobs to a computer, electronic mail, interactive enquiries and so on. This range of applications is reflected in the definition of a number of layer 7 services, each of which is specific to a particular use of the communication system. The layer also defines services that are likely to be required by all applications, such as a request to establish a temporary association with a remote application or the need to synchronize their processing.

The upper layers of the OSI model define standard services and control them through the use of standard protocols, to support reliable application-to-application communication. A system to provide such communication needs to provide the functions implied by the service definitions. If they are provided according to OSI rules, using OSI protocols, the system is open and will support communication with any system implemented according to the same rules. The application programmer can concentrate on the application, secure in the knowledge that it will communicate with any other application using an open system.

In addition to the primary service and protocol standards for each layer, there are a great many other documents associated with the OSI model. Some are approved international standards, some are draft standards, some are committee documents and some are still at the working paper level. The open systems movement slowly gathered momentum during the 1980s and is expected, during the 1990s, to take its place as a practical alternative to manufacturers' proprietary architectures. The provision of open systems is dependent on those manufacturers making a business case for the development of OSI products. Growing user and political pressure is increasing the momentum. In the unlikely event that open systems products never become widely available, the reference model will still be seen as a major achievement in the field of data communications.

## 4.7 Systems Network Architecture (SNA)

We now turn to the most widely used communications architecture—IBM's Systems Network Architecture (SNA)—as an example of an architecture developed to promote connectivity between a particular supplier's products and, of course, to promote their sales. SNA has been IBM's strategic networking vehicle since its announcement in 1974, several years before serious work began on the OSI model. Other manufacturers were developing communications strategies at the same time and, wisely, the founding fathers of OSI took note of, and were influenced by, these developments. Throughout the parallel, even converging, development of OSI and SNA, each has influenced the other while maintaining its individuality.

It has long been a popular pastime to compare OSI, layer by layer, with a proprietary architecture such as SNA. This temptation has been resisted here in favour of a discussion, in broad terms, of the similarities and differences between the two approaches.

The statement 'SNA is a network architecture while OSI provides for system interconnection' is often used. This merely repeats the words and leaves out the ones that are confusing, such as the word 'systems' in SNA. A network is a set of interconnected processes implemented in nodes of the network. These nodes may be end nodes or intermediate nodes. A network architecture defines rules that apply throughout the network in all node types. Hence, an SNA network is a set of interconnected SNA nodes. An OSI network is rather different. The upper layer protocols apply between end nodes (end systems). The lower layer protocols enable an end node to connect to an intermediate node. To anticipate our discussion of X.25 in a later chapter, X.25 defines a three-layer interface between *Data Terminal Equipment (DTE)* and *Data Circuit-terminating Equipment (DCE)*. In other words, it specifies how to connect a terminal (an end system) to a backbone network in order for it to communicate with another end system. In transit from one end system to the other, a message will generally pass through a number of intermediate nodes. Communication between intermediate nodes is not necessarily subject to the architecture in an OSI network. The protocol between the switches of an X.25 network is rarely, if ever, X.25.

SNA is a layered architecture, as is OSI. Indeed, with some ingenuity, it is possible to identify seven layers in SNA. Such an exercise tends, though, to conceal significant differences. In an OSI system, each layer provides a service to the layer above consisting of precisely defined functions and their associated parameters. The service definition is very close to being a programming interface. An OSI system may be built up to layer n (where n is between 3 and 7), for example up to and including the session layer. An application may then use the session service as a programming interface when it needs to communicate with a remote application. If the remote system is open to layer 5, the applications will agree a private protocol if they need the functions defined in layers 6 and 7. If the remote system has presentation and application functions that expect messages to be formatted according to the associated protocols, the local application will need to generate these protocols. In other words, the application itself implements layers 6 and 7.

This flexibility is not provided by SNA. The architecture does not define layer services and does not expose the layer boundaries for use by an application with the obvious, and important, exception of the uppermost layer. An SNA end node provides all layers but with subsets of the functions chosen to match the capabilities and purpose of the device in which the node is implemented. In only one case does an SNA node provide a programming interface, although this case has become increasingly important with the growth of application-to-application communication.

Earlier in the chapter, the distinction between layers 1 to 3 of OSI, considered as a whole, and layers 4 to 7 was made. This distinction is apparent, and a more obvious part of the architecture, in SNA. The lower layers of SNA (there are strictly only two, corresponding to layers 2 and 3 of OSI) constitute the *path control network*. The role of the path control network is to provide and control the path, or route, between end nodes. Path control functions are present in every node and communication between any pair of nodes is subject to the associated protocols.

The upper layers of SNA are collectively called *Network Addressable Units (NAUs)*. The name implies that they are units (of function) that are addressable by the (path control) network. The path control network provides a path between NAUs while the NAUs themselves supply the additional functions necessary to accept information from and deliver information to end users—people or programs or management functions within the NAU.

Three types of NAU are defined by SNA. *Logical Units (LUs)* are those sets of upper layer functions that enable users (people or programs) to communicate through the network. A coupling between users for the purpose of communication is called a *session* and is analogous to a telephone call. SNA nodes may be implemented in many different types of equipment—equipment that controls simple display terminals and printers, job entry terminals, personal microcomputers, minicomputers or mainframe installations. The architecture allows for this wide range of potential implementations by defining a number of session types. For example, LU-to-LU session type 2 (commonly called LU2) is defined to enable a person operating a keyboard/display terminal to use the network to access a remote application. Certain upper layer functions are required in the LUs to support the session, while others are not. The required functions are defined by SNA at each layer of the architecture. Each layer of each LU must provide these functions for a session to be possible. This has lead to the rather loose, but prevalent, use of the term LU2 in the above example to refer to the LU itself, or even to the terminal, rather than to the session type.

One of the strengths of SNA is its recognition of the need to manage the network—to detect problems, to bypass them pending resolution, to reconfigure the network temporarily or permanently, to measure the performance of the network and so on. A mechanism for managing the network is incorporated in the architecture in the form of the second type of NAU, the *Physical Unit (PU)*. Despite the necessarily abstract nature of an architecture and the use of terms like 'node', real networks consist of real hardware and software. The PU, although still a set of upper layer functions and, therefore, somewhat abstract, is closely associated with these real components. The PU is a set of functions implemented in every 'box' in the network that enable the box to be managed remotely by communication across the path control network. The PU functions enable the physical equipment in which they reside to be activated or deactivated to report problems and to gather and report performance and traffic statistics. The terminology is unfortunate in that LUs and PUs are both logical, in the sense of being abstract or conceptual.

The third type of NAU is the *System Services Control Point (SSCP)*. The SSCP is a repository and focal point for information necessary to operate and manage an SNA network. Each SSCP is responsible for a number of other NAUs (LUs and PUs) that constitute its domain of control. A large network may have several domains and several cooperating SSCPs, although many are single domain with one SSCP.

An SSCP exercises its control function by being in permanent session with every LU and PU in its domain. These sessions are established by the SSCP when the network is started and remain open, although often idle, until the network is closed, unless they are lost due to some failure. The SSCP sessions are used for the network management functions mentioned above. The SSCP-to-LU sessions are also used in establishing the LU-to-LU sessions that are necessary for user-to-user communication.

Consider a common example—a person wishing to log on to a remote application. A session between the LU representing the person (LUA) and the LU representing the application (LUB) is required. The process begins with a session initiation request from LUA to the SSCP controlling its domain. In most cases, the person will supply only a name for LUB. In particular this person will not supply the network address— this is provided by the SSCP using a directory function. This initiation request is sent on the permanent SSCP-to-LU session. The SSCP also holds information that essentially determines the functions required by each LU to support the session. The SSCP contacts LUB, via the SSCP-to-LU session, to indicate that a session has been requested and to pass information about the session. This information is largely derived from that held by the SSCP, but includes operator-entered data such as a user identification and password. It also includes the address of LUA so that LUB can communicate directly. The process is completed with a session establishment request from LUA to LUB and a response from LUB to LUA. The session is then established and communication can begin. The whole process is subject to upper-layer protocols defined by SNA. Sessions between LUs in different domains are established in a similar manner, transparent to the users but involving an extra stage using a session between the two SSCPs.

Although it takes far less time to happen than to describe, the process of session initiation highlights the hierarchical structure of an SNA domain. The use of a single focal point for session initiation is somewhat analogous to placing a telephone call through the operator. Many see this as a weakness in the architecture. It is certainly true that if the SSCP is unavailable, the network, too, is unavailable for new sessions. There are, however, advantages in the SSCP approach, particularly in having a single point from which the network can be monitored.

The SNA path control network consists of the data link control layer and the path control layer. The data link control layer is responsible for the transmission of messages across a link between two nodes without loss or error. It plays a similar role to the data link layer in OSI and the data link control protocol (the control information appended to messages) is virtually identical in the two architectures. The role of the path control layer is to choose the next node along the route and a link to it. This function is performed by the OSI network layer although the SNA and OSI protocols are here rather different. Consequently, a message formatted to pass through an SNA path control network cannot be handled by a network that provides the same functions in an OSI world and vice versa. An SNA network is not open, although we should note that SNA products are available that turn an SNA network into an X.25 network. This subject is returned to in Chapter 7.

As in OSI, the composite role of the SNA lower layers (the path control network) is to provide a means of sending a message from its source to one of a number of destinations without error or loss. In the OSI case, where this role is often fulfilled by a network offering an X.25 interface, the lower layers can be used directly by an application programmed to handle X.25 packets. This is not so in an SNA network. The path control network is used only to send messages to NAUs. A user must access the network through a LU.

The lowest of the upper SNA layers that constitute a NAU is the transmission control layer. This layer is responsible for session establishment, flow control and end-to-end error recovery. It also provides for the encryption of messages. The messages exchanged between NAUs in order to establish sessions are sent and received by a component of the transmission control layer. Flow control (called *pacing* in SNA) is provided by this layer, together with the matching of a request message to its response. In summary, the transmission control layer establishes sessions and controls the transmission of messages during the session.

Above the transmission control layer is the data flow control layer, which has nothing to do with flow control in a physical sense—this is provided by the layer below. Data flow control provides directional control. A session between two NAUs is, in principle, a full duplex channel, though it may be restricted, in a particular implementation, to half duplex operation. A telephone call is full duplex but is restricted to half duplex by the participants in the interests of efficient conversation. Data flow control provides half duplex operation if required by the session. SNA allows for a logical association between individual messages by chaining them together or by bracketing a set of messages that are associated in a transaction. Control of chains and brackets is also provided by data flow control.

The uppermost layer of a NAU has been subject to change in both structure and terminology as SNA has developed. The architecture originally allowed for simple implementations such as sessions between a VDU and an application. A structuring of the upper layer appropriate to such use was defined. It has subsequently been extended to more sophisticated implementations providing sessions for application-to-application communication. The most significant changes have occurred, as may be expected, in the layer closest to the user. We postpone a discussion of the purpose and structure of this layer until Chapter 7.

The essence of a communications architecture, and its success in promoting intersystem communication, lies mainly in its protocol definitions. It is the control information added to a message by each layer that allows that layer to play its part in the overall process of providing reliable transmission between users. OSI gives equal weight to the definition of layer services and protocols while SNA essentially defines only protocols. Of particular importance are the transmission header, added and used by the path control layer for routeing through the path control network, the request/response header added by transmission control and used by various components in the upper layers and the optional function management header added and used by the upper layer. The uniqueness of SNA is embodied in these headers and its development as an architecture is closely related to the development of their format and content.

In this and the previous section SNA and OSI have been introduced and the similarities and differences between them have been explored. In later chapters both architectures are described in more detail.

## 4.8 Local Area Networks (LANs)

Data networks, and their associated architectures, were originally developed to provide connections between data processing machines in separate geographical locations. A later development, encouraged by the availability of desk-top microprocessors, resulted in the appearance of a different type of network to provide connections between machines on the same site—in a building, between buildings, across a university campus and so on. These are Local Area Networks (LANs) as opposed to the more traditional Wide Area Networks (WANs). Further developments led to the need for connections from LAN to LAN and from WAN to LAN. It is now commonplace for a user to be able to send a message from a work station round the office or round the world. In the latter case, the message may travel across several LANs at each end and across several WANs in between.

A new networking subculture has emerged with new terminology and, apparently, needing new skills. LAN people are generally in a different part of the organization to WAN people. People write books on WANs with little reference to LANs and vice versa. This is an unfortunate trend as WANs and LANs are both networks that should have more similarities than differences.

It is not immediately obvious why there should be any differences and why wide area architectures, design and technology should not apply to LANs. In the general concept of layering, there is a mechanism for exploring questions of this kind. Let us apply it to a LAN.

The physical layer (to use OSI terminology) is responsible for connection to the physical medium that provides the links between nodes. The physical medium that connects stations on a LAN tends to be different from that which connects nodes on a WAN. It is shorter, allowing high-speed media to be used, which would be prohibitively expensive if used over a wide area. It is less likely to introduce errors as it runs in a more friendly physical and electrical environment. Some differences at the physical layer might be expected to exploit these advantages.

On moving up to the data link layer, a significant difference appears. It lies in the topology of the network. In wide area topology, it is usual for two nodes to be connected by a dedicated link. The link may consist of multiple physical circuits, but it is used only by those two nodes. (An exception, requiring special treatment, arises when a multipoint link is used). The resulting topology is some combination of mesh and tree structure. This topology could be used in a building to provide LAN connections, but a more economical use of cables is achieved by connecting all stations on the LAN to the same cable with a ring or bus topology.

What happens if two or more stations on the LAN attempt to send a message at the same time? The message is represented by electrical signals that are encoded to convey digital information. Interference between the signals, referred to as *collision*, will corrupt the information. The probability of a collision increases in proportion to the use of the network. Some means of handling the problem must be provided. The situation also arises on a telephone line shared by two extensions in a building or by two subscribers. A collision occurs if two people pick up a telephone at the same time. There are two aspects to the problem.

One is knowing that a collision has occurred or is about to occur; the other is recovering from it if it cannot be prevented. On a shared telephone line, user A picks up the telephone and listens. If A hears a dialling tone, A proceeds with the call. If A hears a conversation, A puts the telephone down and tries later. A potential collision has been avoided.

An architectural extension is required to deal with the problem on a LAN. The special case of multipoint links in a WAN was mentioned above. The problem was addressed there by a particular mode of data link control protocol that allowed one station to act as the primary station. Secondary stations may transmit only when invited (polled) by the primary station. The solution is not appropriate for a LAN of peer stations.

Two ways of dealing with collisions are used in LANs. One prevents them from occurring, while the other detects them when they have occurred and recovers afterwards. The first solution makes use of a *token*. This word is used in several places in network architectures to indicate the right to perform some operation. In the case of a LAN, the token is a specially formatted message that is generated when the network is started and passes continuously from station to station when the network is idle. When a station has a message to transmit, it captures the token and transmits the message. In the absence of the token, no other station can transmit and collisions never occur. When the transmitting station receives evidence that its message has been copied by the recipient, it restores the token to the network. The mechanism includes provision for priority messages and for restoring the token if it becomes lost or corrupted.

The second solution is more akin to the shared telephone line. A station with a message to transmit first 'listens' to the medium. If no message traffic can be detected, the station puts its message on the network. A collision may still occur, however, as the message takes time to travel through the network. A second station may listen, detect no traffic, as the first message has not arrived, and transmit. There are now two messages on the same medium and a collision will result. In order to detect a collision, a station continues to listen while transmitting and will eventually detect a garbled message. It will then back off and retransmit after a random delay. In order for the mechanism to work, a station must transmit for a minimum time to detect a collision occurring at the farthest reaches of the network. If it does not have enough information to fill this time, the message must be padded up to a minimum length. The technique is called *Carrier Sense Multiple Access/Collision Detection (CSMA/CD)*.

The data link layer has been described in some detail because it is the layer at which extensions are needed to incorporate LANs into a communications architecture. The data link layer is divided into two sublayers. The lower sublayer is the *Medium Access Control (MAC)* layer, which provides the additional functions needed for controlling access to the physical medium and for preventing or recovering from collision. There are separate standards at the MAC layer for token ring LANs and CSMA/CD LANs as well as other related standards. Each standard includes the definition of protocols that support the access control mechanism. The upper sublayer is the *Logical Link Control Layer (LLC)*, which includes those link control functions, such as flow control and error recovery, that are not related to media access.

Our purpose in this section is to position LANs in the wider context of layered architectures. Above the data link layer, no significant differences between LANs and WANs are apparent and the layer definitions, OSI or SNA or any other, are applicable to both LANs and WANs. The role of the network layer is reduced on simple LANs as every station receives every message and copies it to its own buffers only when it recognizes its own data link address. Different upper layer protocols may be used. For example, SNA LUs may be connected by a LAN rather than by the path control network.

## 4.9 TCP/IP

This introduction is completed by a brief summary of an architecture, or protocol suite, that is gaining popularity. For many years an important influence on the science of networking has been a network sponsored by the Defence Advanced Research Projects Agency of the United States Government Department of Defense (DoD). The network is known as *DARPAnet* and is used to connect academic and commercial research and development establishments in many countries. The protocol suite resulting from the development of this network is known, from the names of its most commonly implemented layers, as *TCP/IP—Transmission Control Protocol/Internet Protocol*.

DARPAnet connects many research institutions, each with its own approach to networking. The internet layer of a TCP/IP system provides for routeing between architecturally disparate networks to form a 'super network', or, internet. The internet protocol is unreliable. This is not a criticism but simply a consequence of a deliberate decision on the part of the protocol designers to provide a best efforts service and to put the onus of providing transmission without loss or error on the Transmission Control Protocol. TCP provides the error detection and recovery functions necessary to provide a reliable service across an internet. It is equivalent to the most powerful of the protocols defined for the transport layer of OSI. In fact, TCP has had a substantial impact on the development of the transport layer.

Many protocols are defined for upper layer communication in a TCP/IP system. The suite does not extend below the network layer and is content to make use of other standards at the data link and physical layers. TCP/IP is discussed more fully in Chapter 9.

## 4.10 Summary

In this chapter OSI, SNA, LANs and TCP/IP have been looked at briefly within the general framework of architectural layering and protocol suites. Each of these subjects has a later chapter devoted to it, which is intended to provide a foundation for detailed study of more specialized works. There are many other architectures, but, for the purpose of manageability only the main ones have been covered in this book.

*For many years, data processing was dominated by mainframe machines, particularly those from IBM. Networks were built mainly to enable remote users to enter information for mainframe processing and to receive the results. SNA is largely geared to this type of requirement. The WNB, in common with many other commercial organizations with large and scattered customer bases, traditionally installed IBM processors.*

*In the late 1970s and early 1980s, the financial services sector began to change. Banks extended the scope of their business into service areas such as house purchase loans, insurance and investment banking. In needing to sell these services, they began to reach out to their customers and compete with other financial services organizations. To support this expansion, IT departments needed to become more flexible and responsive to requirements from their own customers, the bank's business units. The WNB was no exception.*

*In considering the data requirements in the branch, the designers in the WNB realized that in order to provide any-to-any communication in an efficient way, it would be sensible to provide an open network. At the lower layers, this meant a packet-switched network designed according to the CCITT X.25 Recommendation. Throughout this period of planning and initial implementation, the WNB needed to maintain its core business, which was still largely supported by IBM central processors and SNA communication. The planners decided to provide the main branch accounting services, as an SNA service over an X.25 network. However, in order to satisfy the requirements of communicating with stockbrokers and the insurance and mortgage companies, a full OSI system was developed. The bank found itself in the not unusual position of operating a hybrid network of mixed architectures and using components from many suppliers. In some ways, this is not an ideal situation in that it introduces unnatural or inefficient combinations of components and a wide range of skills among the IT staff. It is, however, a necessary step in the migration of an existing business towards open communication.*

*Figures 3.3 and 3.4 in the last chapter indicate how data communication is provided to each branch. Noting that a large number of telephones and terminals would be required in the branches of the WNB, the planners in the WNB embarked on an extensive programme of rewiring the branches providing standard, unshielded twisted pair structured cabling for both voice and data. This cabling is used to connect telephones to the PABX and to provide a LAN. The LAN is controlled by means of a management device that allows stations to be disconnected or reconnected in order to facilitate diagnosis of LAN problems from the remote network management centre.*

*A variety of terminals are connected on the branch LAN and TCP/IP protocols are used to control data flow. Powerful UNIX processors are used to provide server functions for communication to the WAN, local application processing, local file handling and security. Work stations provide standard wordprocessing facilities. General management of the LAN is provided via the communications server. Work stations with a windowed graphical interface are used to provide access to a number of applications, both in the branch and elsewhere in the network.*

*In addition to the SNA and OSI transaction processing upper layer software, the communications server also provides an X.400 message handling system to allow standard documents to be sent to other offices on the private data network. The network itself is provided with a number of gateways to allow interconnection with other X.400 networks used by the customers of the bank and to allow conversion from X.400 to fax. Each branch is provided with its own fax machine to receive faxes directly from customers.*

*Open systems are seen, by the WNB's planners, as the ultimate strategic goal. It should be noted here that the word 'open', originally used in the context of OSI and with a precise meaning, has fallen into disrepute. Its meaning is no longer clear and it is often used to refer to anything that is popular at the moment. The WNB used the word in its more meaningful sense to indicate that its long-term IT strategy would be based on the OSI model, for both WANs and LANs.*

*It will be late in the 1990s when OSI products become readily available. In the meantime, the WNB needed to maintain its position in a rapidly changing and increasing competitive market. It decided to take the initial step of building an open backbone network, implementing the lower three layers of the OSI model and to integrate this data network with its private voice network in anticipation of eventually being able to provide integrated digital services. Its strategy for LANs would similarly be based on open standards at the lower layers. As an interim step to the higher layers, and interworking between networks, the use of TCP/IP would be encouraged. Full OSI stacks would be implemented where appropriate.*

*In the 1990s, open systems will become increasingly common, although unfortunately the term will continue, for some time, to mean different things to different people. Manufacturers are replacing their proprietary products with OSI products or are, at least, producing OSI products alongside products conforming to proprietary architectures. The WNB is well positioned to take advantage of this trend.*

# CHAPTER 5  X.25

## 5.1 Introduction

When a network is used to connect two data processing systems for the purpose of exchanging data, three distinct types of function may be regarded as essential:

- the physical connection of the systems to the network
- the reliable movement of messages through the network
- the ability to direct messages to the appropriate destination.

Without these functions, communication between the systems is not possible. They are provided in many public and private data networks by reference to *CCITT Recommendation X.25*.

Before examining X.25 in detail, it is useful to analyse a more familiar example from voice communication. The world-wide public telephone network is a remarkable achievement, providing communication between hundreds of millions of subscribers. It is made possible by adherence to the CCITT's recommendations and the same three types of function as those mentioned above may be discerned.

Telephone handsets are a familiar part of everyday life. Most people are also aware of telephone wires and telephone exchanges. The set of telephone exchanges, and their voice-circuit connections, constitute the telephone network. It is owned and operated by the telephone company. Its entry and exit points are the termination boxes provided on the premises of subscribers, who make use of the network by connecting their handsets to the termination boxes.

The physical characteristics of the connection are standardized locally by the telephone company while the electrical characteristics of the signals between the subscriber and the network are standardized internationally. Some of these signals are familiar, such as dialling and ringing tones, and have close analogies in data communication.

The functions that ensure acceptable quality of transmission are less apparent to the telephone user. These are the functions that provide for the electrical conditioning of the circuits to limit signal attenuation, noise, cross talk and echoes. They are less stringent than for data circuits as they are able to rely on the human correspondents to recover from errors and exercise flow control.

The routeing mechanism is embodied in the subscriber's telephone number, consisting of an international code, an area code (or its equivalent) and the subscriber's local number. This number identifies, uniquely, the subscriber's network entry/exit point or service access point. The full number is used by the exchange switches to set up a physical circuit between the subscribers for the duration of the call. Physical connection to the network, link control and provision of routeing information are all necessary to establish a voice circuit between any two access points of the international telephone service.

Telephone companies also provide public data networks on a national basis and collaborate to provide them internationally. Note that we are concerned here with a network dedicated to data transmission and not with the use of a voice network to carry data.

The functions of basic connection, link control and the provision of routeing information for public data networks are covered by a single CCITT Recommendation X.25. Since its introduction in 1976 (thus predating the OSI model), it has been enhanced during each four-year CCITT working cycle and a number of possible enhancements remain 'for further study'. In addition to its widespread provision by the world's PTTs it has been adopted by many commercial organizations for their private networks. It is also the most common means of providing the OSI network service discussed in the next chapter.

It is important to recognize what X.25 *is* and what it is *not*. It is a specification for the interface between a data processing system and a network. It specifies this interface in three layers corresponding to the physical, data link and network layers of the OSI model although, as it predates the model, the relationship between X.25 and OSI should not be overstated. The recommendation refers to other recommendations or standards for the lower two layers and itself defines the layer 3 protocol. There is, consequently, a misguided tendency to associate X.25 only with layer 3.

X.25 is not a network specification in that it does not necessarily apply to the internal protocols of the network. Manufacturers of switches for X.25 networks are free to adopt different proprietary means of transmitting messages between the switches. They must, however, provide an X.25 interface between the subscriber's equipment and the switch to which it is connected. If this interface is provided, the network is, by definition, an X.25 network. It must, of course, be matched by the interface provided by the equipment attached to the network.

In the following section the three layers of the X.25 interface are examined in more detail, from the top down.

## 5.2 The packet layer

The X.25 interface is designed to enable a computer to send data to and receive data from other computers across a network. The data may take a number of forms, ranging from a short message to a large file, and it would seem sensible, particularly in the latter case, not to send all the data as a single bit string. Errors may occur that necessitate retransmission and it would be inefficient to have to retransmit the entire file. In addition, intermediate nodes of the network may have limited capacity to store data before forwarding it to the next node. The X.25 interface therefore requires the user data to be sent in discrete units called *packets*. The default packet size allows for 128 octets of user data although network providers may accept packages containing as few as 64 octets or as many as 2048 octets.

The basic role of the network is to deliver packets to the destination specified by the user. The network provider does not guarantee to deliver packets but is obliged to ensure that packets which are delivered arrive in the order in which they were transmitted.

An analogy with sending a letter may be useful at this point. A letter is normally sent in an envelope. The letter contains information that is private to the correspondents. The envelope, however, carries control information that is needed by the postal service. This includes the delivery address and a stamp, the value of which determines (theoretically) the speed of transmission. The envelope may also contain an alternative delivery address and the sender's address.

This distinction between *user* information and *control* information applies also to an X.25 packet as the control data is attached to the message in the form of a *packet header*. The header and the user data together form a packet (the contents of the header will be examined later). The analogy should not be pushed too far however. For example, a request for acknowledgement would normally be included in a letter but is part of the header in an X.25 packet. The important point to remember is that a separation between the user data and the information required to deliver it with a specified quality of service is commonly adopted in communications protocols and X.25 is no exception.

The analogy between posting a letter and sending a packet breaks down when one considers the establishment of a connection between sender and receiver. It is not normal practice to ensure that the recipient is at home when a letter is posted. The service is connectionless. X.25, on the other hand, normally requires that a connection be established between sender and receiver *before* data can be sent. It is a connection-orientated service and, in this respect, is more analogous to a telephone call.

The connection between sender and receiver is called a *virtual circuit* in X.25 terminology. As far as sender and receiver are concerned, when a connection has been established, a circuit exists between them for the duration of the call. In the case of a telephone call this circuit is a physical connection. In the case of an X.25 call it is a virtual, or logical, connection in that packets entered at one end emerge at the other end but may travel by different routes in between.

Two types of virtual circuit are provided by X.25, although not necessarily by particular network providers. A *permanent virtual circuit (PVC)* may be established between two users. Data sent on a PVC is always delivered to the same user and so the processes of establishing and clearing a call are not required. A *switched virtual circuit (SVC)*, on the other hand, is established when required to a particular user and cleared when not required. The communication process then occurs in three phases:

- call establishment
- data transfer
- call clearing.

A virtual circuit is identified by a number, called the *logical channel identifier (LCI)*. The number is permanently assigned to a PVC and established dynamically for an SVC. Specifically it is chosen by calling the *Data Terminal Equipment (DTE)* at the sender's end at call establishment. At the receiver's end it is allocated by the *Data Circuit-terminating Equipment (DCE)* and supplied to the called DTE. In general, the identifiers by which each DTE refers to a virtual circuit will be different. Outgoing packets containing a particular LCI will all be delivered to the same destination, while incoming packets with a particular LCI will all have come from the same source.

Any DTE—from a small terminal to a large mainframe—may connect to an X.25 network. The DTEs connected to a network will thus often cover a wide range of data-handling capacities. However, the nodes of the network have a limited capacity for storing and processing messages. A mechanism is needed, therefore, to control the flow of messages between DTE and DCE and is incorporated in the X.25 protocol. Note that the flow control mechanism applies only to the interface between DTE and DCE as indeed does X.25 itself. Flow control may be exercised within the network itself, between intermediate nodes, but is outside the scope of X.25.

A common technique for flow control between two machines, say A and B, is to limit the number of messages that may be sent by A before waiting for an acknowledgement from B implying permission to send more. This number is generally called a *window*. The window is conceptually moved over the queue of messages that A has to send. At any one time, those messages that lie within the window may be sent. Movement of the window is activated by B, indicating that the previous 'windowfull' has been received. In some flow control schemes, the window size is fixed, while others allow for the window size to be adjusted dynamically to reflect the current utilization of the receiver.

Flow control by use of a window implies that messages need to be numbered and the numbers transmitted between DTE and DCE. Furthermore, as control needs to be exercised in both directions, numbers need to be maintained for both sent *and* received messages.

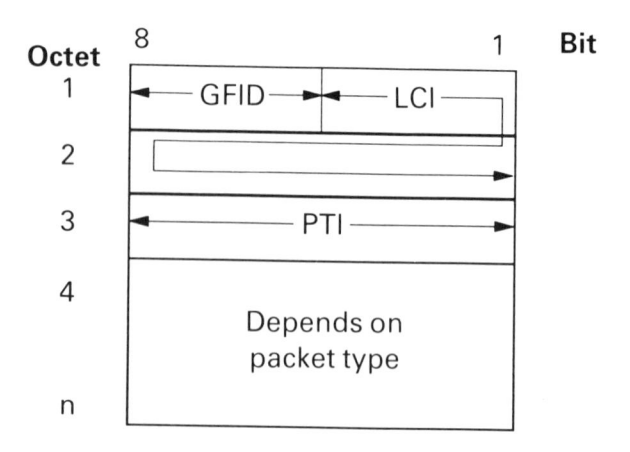

```
          8                    1  Bit
Octet  ┌────────────────────────┐
  1    │◄─GFID─►│◄──LCI──┐      │
       ├────────┴────────┴──────┤
  2    │                        │
       ├────────────────────────┤
  3    │◄────── PTI ──────►     │
       ├────────────────────────┤
  4    │                        │
       │      Depends on        │
       │      packet type       │
  n    │                        │
       └────────────────────────┘
```

*Figure 5.1   An X.25 packet*

Armed with this introductory information let us now examine the way in which these control functions are incorporated into the header of an X.25 packet.

**X.25 packet formats**

Every X.25 packet contains at least three octets. They are shown in Figure 5.1 and their contents discussed below.

**General Format Identifier (GFID)**

The GFID is a 4-bit field:

$$Q/A\ D\ x\ x$$

In Section 5.1 it was noted that, for flow control purposes, messages are counted and the counts transmitted with the message. The counting may be done modulo 8 (that is using numbers from 0 to 7 before recycling) or modulo 128. The former allows a maximum of 8 messages to be sent before acknowledgement, while the latter raises the maximum window size to 128. The xx bits indicate which type of counting is used:

$$xx = 01 \text{ for modulo 8 counting}$$
$$xx = 10 \text{ for modulo 128 counting.}$$

As counters are carried in some headers and they are of different sizes for the two types of counting, the xx bits determine the format of the header—hence the name Format Identifier (the use of the Q/A and D bits will be explained later).

**Logical Channel Identifier (LCI)**

The 16-bit LCI contains a number that identifies the virtual circuit for which the packet is destined and, hence, effectively, the destination. An LCI of all zeros is reserved for packets that are destined for the network itself rather than for another user. The remaining 4095 numbers are

# X.25

available for virtual circuits so that, in principle, a DTE may have simultaneous calls to 4095 destinations.

**Packet Type Identifier (PTI)**

The third octet in the header identifies the type of packet. For a data packet, bit 1 is set to 0. For all control packets, bit 1 is set to 1 and the type determined by the rest of the field.[1]

These first three header octets contain information needed in every packet:

- the format of the rest of the header
- the virtual circuit for which it is intended
- the packet type.

Most packet headers contain other information specific to the packet type.

**Call establishment and clearing**

Four packet formats are defined to enable SVCs to be established and cleared. They have different names depending on whether they are sent from DTE to DCE or vice versa, as follows:

| *Call processes* | *Packet type* | |
| --- | --- | --- |
| | *From DTE to DCE* | *From DCE to DTE* |
| Call establishment | Call request<br>Call accepted | Incoming call<br>Call connected |
| Call clearing | Clear request<br>DTE clear confirmation | Clear indication<br>DCE clear confirmation |

The format of a call setup packet is shown in Figure 5.2.

To establish a call, a DTE sends a call request packet to its local DCE and the local DCE at the destination sends an incoming call packet to the destination DTE. If it is willing and able to accept the call, the destination DTE sends a call accepted packet to the network and the network sends a call connected packet to the caller. If the called DTE refuses the call, it sends a clear request packet and the caller receives a clear indication packet that indicates the reason for rejecting the call.

To clear the call, the local DTE sends a clear request packet to its local DCE. The remote DCE informs the remote DTE with a clear indication packet. The remote DTE accepts the clearing with a DTE clear confirmation, and finally the local DCE confirms the request to the local DTE with a DCE clear confirmation.

---

[1] The least significant bit in an octet is numbered 1 and is transmitted first. The reader is warned that in some diagrams in the literature bit 1 is on the right and in others on the left.

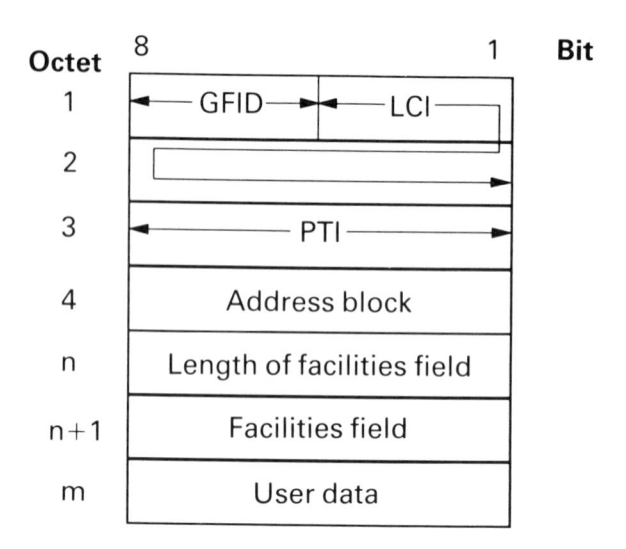

|  | 8 | 1 |
|---|---|---|
| Octet | | Bit |
| 1 | ←—GFID—→ ←—LCI—→ | |
| 2 | | |
| 3 | ←——— PTI ———→ | |
| 4 | Address block | |
| n | Length of facilities field | |
| n+1 | Facilities field | |
| m | User data | |

*Figure 5.2  X.25 call request/incoming call packet format*

The headers of the above set of packets provide for two addresses, those of the *calling* DTE and the *called* DTE. As the lengths of the addresses may be different for different networks, the headers also indicate the lengths of the addresses in half octets. Addresses are expressed as binary-coded decimal digits, two per octet.

The most significant bit of the GFID, called here the A bit, indicates the type of addressing used. If the A bit is 0, the length fields are each 4 bits long and the address fields contain only address digits. If the A bit is 1, the length fields are 8 bits long and the address fields consist of 3 subfields. The first subfield (4 bits) indicates the *Type of Address (TOA*—e.g., international number, national number), the second subfield (4 bits) indicates the *Numbering Plan Identification (NPI*—e.g., X.121, network dependent) and the third subfield contains the address digits. The use of TOA/NPI is an additional optional user facility included in the 1988 revision of the recommendation.

A DTE requesting a call obviously needs to specify to its local DCE the address of the destination DTE. Not quite so obviously, the local DCE at the destination needs to specify the address of the caller. This enables the called DTE to reject the call if it so desires. The called address is required in call request packets and the calling address is required in incoming call packets. These packets may optionally include both calling and called addresses. Addresses are not required in call accepted and call connected packets, although the fields may be used in special cases.

It is common to be able to specify special conditions when requesting a communications channel. Familiar examples from the telephone system are transferring the cost of the call to the recipient or receiving notification of the cost at the end of the call. In a telephone system, most of these special facilities require operator intervention, but special (optional) facilities are provided automatically by the X.25 protocol. They are requested in the facilities field of the call request packet and the destination DTE is informed via the corresponding field in the incoming call packet. As the number and type of facilities may vary, a length field precedes the facilities field itself.

In the original implementations of X.25 networks, the use of a particular facility needed to be agreed with the network provider when an application for service was submitted. The 1984 revision of the recommendation, however, allows a user to request registration of a facility on-line by sending a facility registration packet to the network. This packet is an example of the use of a LCI of all zeros to convey information to the network provider.

Some of the facilities that may be requested are described briefly below.

**Reverse charging** — The caller normally pays for an X.25 call but may request the *reverse charging* facility. If the called DTE accepts the call, it bears the cost. It may accept reverse charged calls from some DTEs and not from others. It needs to know the source of the call, hence the calling address in the incoming call packet. The called DTE may not wish to receive any reverse charged calls, in which case, it requests the facility to reject all incoming reverse charged calls. Such calls are then rejected at the DCE local to the called DTE.

**Incoming calls barred** — If this facility is requested, all incoming calls are rejected by the destination DCE.

**Call redirection** — A DTE may request that, in the event of its not being available, incoming calls are sent to an alternative DTE.

**Called Line Address Modification Notification (CLAMN)** — If a call is redirected, the caller is informed by the appearance of a *CLAMN* in the facilities field and a modified address in the called address field of the call connected packet. This is one of the special cases of the use of these fields referred to above.

**Closed User Group (CUG)** — A *CUG* enables a group of DTEs to communicate with each other but not with other DTEs outside the group. The CUG may be made less restrictive by additionally allowing calls to be received from all users or made to all users. A CUG effectively enables a private network to be implemented using public facilities.

**Extended sequence numbering** — The change from modulo 8 sequence numbering to modulo 128 is effected by means of this facility.

**Fast select** — A normal call request packet may have up to 16 octets of call user data appended to it, following the facilities. These are intended to contain information such as a user identifier and password. No user data is allowed in a normal call accepted packet. The DTEs cannot normally exchange information without establishing a call, sending data packets and then clearing the call.

The *fast select* facility provides a means of exchanging limited amounts of data without going through the full three-phase process. The call user data in the call request packet is increased to a maximum of 128 octets. Extended format call accepted, call connected, clear request and clear indication packets enable up to 128 octets to be returned to the caller in these packets.

The calling DTE may restrict the response to a fast select call to be clear only, in which case the called DTE may only respond with a clear request. As a result, up to 128 octets of user data have been sent in each direction without the full call setup and clear procedures and without data packets. If the response is not restricted by the caller, it is treated as a normal call that the called DTE may accept, with a call accepted packet, or reject, with a clear request.

All of the above facilities, and others not described here, are optional. Some rely for their provision on the capabilities of the DTEs, while others rely on the network provider. Different networks provide different options. Each CCITT revision of the recommendation adds to the list to cater for growing user needs.

## Facilities registration

The 1984 revision of the X.25 Recommendation provided for on-line facility registration and defined registration request and registration confirmation packets. These packets enable a DTE to initiate or terminate use of one or more of the optional user facilities. The packets are exchanged between DTE and DCE on logical channel 0.

The coding of the information describing a particular facility in both the facilities field of call setup packets and the registration field of registration packets is identical. Facilities are divided into four classes—A, B, C and D—that have, respectively one, two, three and a variable number of parameter octets.

## Data transfer

Once a call has been established, data packets may be exchanged between DTE and DCE. The packet format is shown in Figure 5.3. The header consists only of the GFID, LCI and packet type fields. Bit 1 of the packet type field is set to 0, which uniquely identifies a data packet. The remaining bits are used rather differently to the way they are used in other packets. They contain the send and receive sequence counters used to support the windowed flow control mechanism. The use of two counting systems, modulo 8 and modulo 128, has already been mentioned and these require, respectively, the counters to be 3 bits wide and 7 bits wide. Consequently, the type field is 1 octet in modulo 8 numbering and 2 octets in modulo 128.

The user data follows the header. Although the X.25 Recommendation does not specifically require the user data to be an integral number of

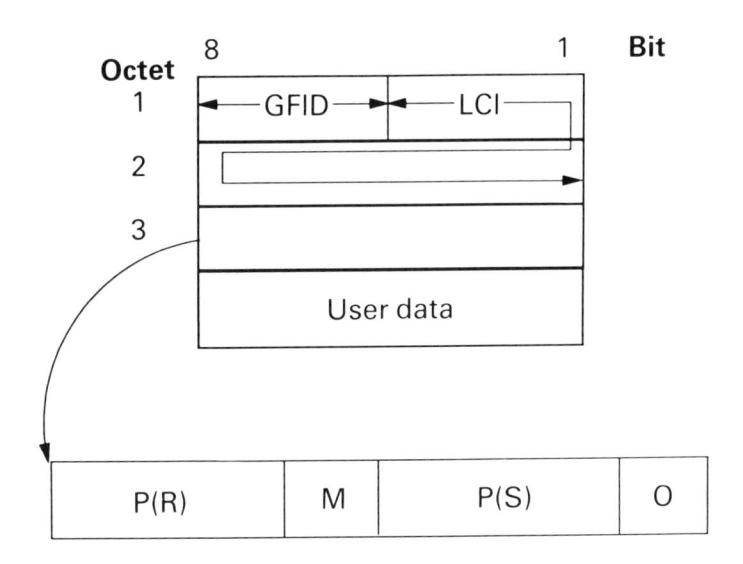

*Figure 5.3  X.25 data packet*

octets, most networks impose this restriction. The maximum number of octets is also dependent on the network provider. It has a default value that is normally 128. An optional facility (non-standard default packet size) enables the default to be changed. A further facility (flow control parameter negotiation) enables the packet size to be negotiated between DTEs on a per call basis.

Data packets are sent in sequence and are subject to flow control. Only those packets within the window may be sent and then in strict order. Occasions may arise in which a user wishes to send a packet without waiting for authorization from the receiver. An interrupt procedure is provided for this purpose with associated *interrupt* and *interrupt confirmation packets*.

An *interrupt* packet is similar to a data packet except that the type field in the header does not contain counters as the packet is not subject to flow control. It may contain a maximum of 32 octets of user data. Interrupt packets, unlike data packets, must be acknowledged by the receiver with an *interrupt confirmation* packet. Each interrupt must be individually confirmed and hence the interrupt procedure is not suitable for general data transfer.

The observant reader may have noted that one bit in the packet type field of a data packet has not been mentioned. It is the *M bit* (more data bit) and is bit 5 of octet 3 or bit 1 of octet 4 (extended counting). When set by the sender, it indicates to the receiver that the packet is part of a sequence that, when linked together, forms a single message. Such segmenting of a message may be forced by the maximum permitted packet size.

The most significant bit of the GFID also plays a part in the protocol for data packets. It is now called the *qualifier bit* and is available to the user to distinguish between two types of information, such as real user data and control data for a higher level protocol but carried as user data. The use of the D bit (the delivery confirmation bit) is described in the next section.

## Flow control

X.25 specifies an interface between a DTE and a DCE, that is between a host and a network. It incorporates a mechanism for flow control at the packet layer between the DTE and the DCE at the entry points to the network. The mechanism operates in both directions at these interfaces and applies to individual virtual circuits. It does not apply to the flow of packets through the network, although some means of controlling this flow is likely to be implemented.

The flow of packets across an X.25 interface is controlled by the receiver using a window technique. The window is a number between 1 and 8 for modulo 8 sequence numbering and between 1 and 128 for modulo 128 numbering. It defines the number of data packets that the sender may transmit before waiting for permission from the receiver to resume the flow.

The sender and receiver each maintain two state variables. The *send state variable V(S)* is the number of the next data packet to be sent. When a packet is sent, the send counter in its header is set to V(S) and V(S) is incremented by one. The *receive state variable V(R)* is the number of the next data packet that it expects to receive. These variables are initialized to 0 at the start of an exchange of data packets. The lower limit of the window, $W_{min}$, is also set to 0.

Let us assume a window size of W. The X.25 flow control procedure allows packets to be sent provided the sequence number is less than $W_{min} + W$. Hence, if W is 2, packets numbered 0 and 1 may be sent before an acknowledgement is received. At the sender, V(S) will now have been updated to 2 and V(R) will still be set to 0. At the receiver, V(R) is updated to 2 and V(S) remains at 0.

There are two ways in which the receiver may acknowledge receipt of a packet, both of which involve sending the receiver's V(R) value to the sender. If the receiver has data to send, it may do so and include its V(R) in the header. If not, it may send a *Receive Ready (RR)* packet with V(R) in the header. This packet, as its name suggests, indicates that the receiver is ready to receive more packets. When the sender receives either of these packets, it resets $W_{min}$ to the value of the receive count in the incoming packet (which is 2 in this example). The flow control procedure now allows packets numbered 2 and 3 to be sent.

The detailed working of the flow control procedure sometimes causes confusion. The important things to remember are that the send sequence count (which only appears in a data packet) contains the number of the packet in which it appears, the receive sequence number (which appears in several packet types used for acknowledgement) contains the number of the packet that is expected next. The latter number resets the lower boundary of the flow control window allowing W more packets to be transmitted.

The receiver uses the RR packet to authorize more packets to be sent. If it is temporarily unable to accept more packets, the *Receive Not Ready (RNR)* packet is transmitted to the sender. An RNR packet also contains the receive sequence number. The packet indicates to the sender that a packet with this number may be sent next but not yet. Flow is resumed on receipt of an RR packet from the receiver.

Flow control operates between the DTE and its local DCE, that is across the X.25 interface. Acknowledgement of a particular packet by the local DCE does not imply that it has been received by the destination DTE. A 1980 revision of the recommendation provided a mechanism for end-to-end acknowledgement through the use of the D bit (bit 7 of the GFID). If a data packet numbered, say, n is sent by a DTE to its local DCE with the D bit set, and is subsequently acknowledged (by receipt of a packet with a receive count of $n + 1$), the DTE knows that the packet has been delivered to, and has been acknowledged by, the destination. This mechanism obviously requires cooperation between the two local DCEs. Note that the use of the D bit does not demand acknowledgement by the remote *user*. It is essentially an instruction to the network provider.

## Error situations

The packet layer protocol of X.25 defines a number of packets used when problems arise. These are the *reject, reset, restart* and *diagnostic* packets. *Reject* is used by a receiver to indicate to the sender that it has been forced to discard packets. It contains the receive sequence number to indicate to the sender the point in the sequence from which to retransmit. *Reset* returns the virtual circuit to its initial state. The send and receive state variables, and the lower edge of the window, are reset to 0 and all data and interrupt packets in transit are discarded. Retransmission of lost data is the responsibility of a higher level protocol.

*Restart* is a more drastic procedure in that the packet layer as a whole is reinitialized, thus affecting all virtual circuits. Both reset and restart need to be confirmed by the recipient.

Finally, a *diagnostic* packet may be sent by the DCE to the DTE to indicate errors, such as receipt of an erroneous packet or expiry of a timer.

The packet layer of the X.25 Recommendation, in addition to defining the packets and their contents, describes the states in which the interface may be found and the cause and effect of transitions between them. Procedures are described for reacting to particular events in particular states. These procedures make much use of time-outs to ensure that the interface does not 'hang'.

The user of the communication facilities offered by X.25 is any process able to generate and respond to X.25 packets. The nature of that process and its relationship to the X.25 packet layer is an implementation decision. It may be an application program, an application-enabling process providing a programming interface or a higher layer of a communications architecture.

Of particular interest is the use of X.25 to provide the network service defined by the OSI Reference Model. The X.25 Recommendation was well established, although not widely implemented, when work began on the OSI model. Some relatively minor enhancements were made to X.25 by CCITT, in its 1984 revision, to enable compatibility with the OSI network service. Discussion of these facilities is postponed until Chapter 6 where the network service is described.

## 5.3 Layer 2

You will recall that the X.25 Recommendation is a three-layer interface. The packets discussed in the previous section are not transmitted directly between the layer 3 functions. They are passed to the next layer—layer 2—which has its own part to play in controlling communication between the terminal and the network.

The connection between a DTE and its local DCE is made via a physical medium, the data link. The link may be permanently established on a leased circuit or may be established by dialling via a telephone network. In either case there is one physical connection, in contrast to the multiple logical connections that may exist at the packet layer. The role of layer 2 is to ensure reliable communication across this physical connection. The X.25 layer 2 protocol is designed to achieve this.

In the early 1970s much attention was devoted by computer manufacturers and standards organizations to the definition of an efficient and effective protocol for synchronous data transmission. One result of this effort was the definition, by ISO, of the *High Level Data Link Control (HDLC)* protocol. When the X.25 Recommendation was first made in 1976, a variant of HDLC was proposed as the layer 2 protocol. First the HDLC will be discussed, while the variant will be covered later.

The function of a data link protocol is to ensure that units of information are conveyed from sender to receiver without error, without loss and without duplication. This basic statement contains the essence of the protocol. It is easier to provide for reliable transfer of information and, in particular, recovery from error if the information is broken down into standard units. Transmission without error implies a means of detecting errors. Transmission without loss or duplication implies a means of recognizing each unit.

The user of the facilities provided by layer 2 is the packet layer, layer 3. The packet layer protocol provides, by the use of headers, control information at the virtual circuit level. It does not provide any information that enables transmission across the DTE-DCE link as a whole to be controlled. This is provided by the layer 2 protocol. The layer 3 packets, including their control information, are the units that layer 2 must transmit reliably.

The devices attached to an HDLC link are referred to as stations. The protocol provides for three modes of operation of the link depending on its configuration and the capabilities of the attached stations. These are as follows.

- *Asynchronous Balanced Mode (ABM)* is used on point-to-point links. Balanced mode indicates that no distinction is made between the two stations on the link—each may request or terminate a connection. Activity on the link is asynchronous in the sense that a call may be established by either station at any time.
- *Asynchronous Response Mode (ARM)* is an unbalanced mode of operation for point-to-point links. It is unbalanced in the sense that one station (the primary station) is assumed to have greater functional capability, enabling it to exercise control over the other station (the secondary station). Despite this distinction, either station may initiate a call at any time when the link is idle.
- *Normal Response Mode (NRM)* is also unbalanced but in this mode the primary station is in control of the link. Secondary stations may send data only when invited to do so by the primary station. NRM is intended for use on multipoint links.

The unit of information handled by the HDLC protocol is called a *frame*. If it is sent from a primary station to a secondary station it is called a *command*. If sent from a secondary to a primary it is called a *response*. Several frames are defined, some for carrying information and some for control purposes. The general format of an HDLC frame is shown in Figure 5.4.

The flags, each consisting of one octet containing the bit pattern 01111110, delimit the frame. To prevent a sequence of six 1 bits elsewhere within the frame being mistaken for a flag, the sender inserts a 0 bit after five successive 1 bits. This inserted bit is removed by the receiver. The technique is known as *zero bit insertion* or *bit stuffing*.

The address octet identifies the sending or receiving station. The address field is significant only on a multipoint link where it allows up to 255 secondary stations to be addressed. If the frame is a command, the address field contains the address of the secondary station for which it is destined. If the frame is a response, it too contains the secondary

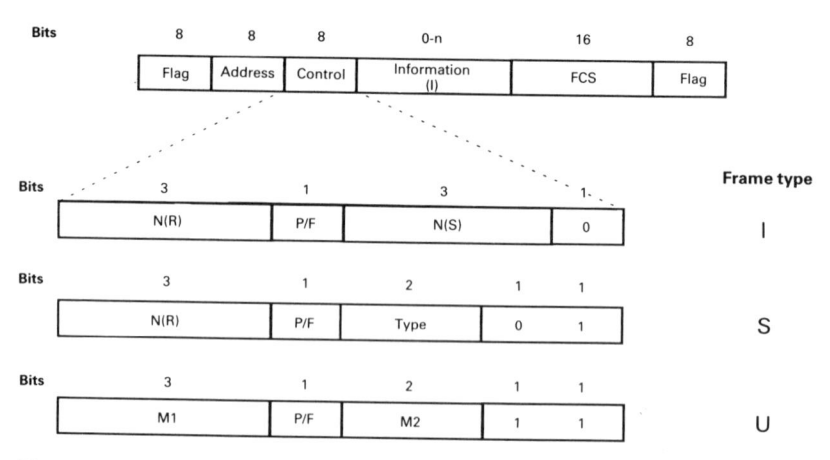

*Figure 5.4   HDLC frame (basic format)*

address so that the source can be identified. On point-to-point links, although the address is not required, it is filled in with a fixed value.

Three types of frame are defined by the protocol and are distinguished by the contents of the control field. The frames and the details of the control field are shown in Figure 5.4.

## HDLC frame types

**Information frames (I-frames)**

The 0 in bit 1 identifies the frame as an *I-frame*. The send counter, N(S), is the sequence number of the frame and the receive counter, N(R), is the number of the next frame expected. These counters are used for flow control and error recovery (their use is described below). The *Poll/Final bit (P/F)* has different uses in normal and aynchronous modes (and is also described below).

The information field of an I-frame contains user data, if any. Its length is not defined by the HDLC standard, but, in practice, an implementation will define a maximum length and most implementations require it to be an integral number of octets.

**Supervisory frames (S-frames)**

*S-frames* are used to control the flow of data on the link. The frame is identified as a supervisory frame by 01 in bits 2 and 1. The type field allows for four types of supervisory frame:

- Receive Ready (RR)
- Receive Not Ready (RNR)
- Reject (REJ)[2]
- Selective Reject (SREJ)[2]

All supervisory frames can be commands or responses. The use of these frames is described below.

---

[2] Optional.

**Un-numbered frames (U-frames)**

*U-frames* are used for link control. They are un-numbered in the sense that they do not have sequence numbers, although neither do supervisory frames. They were known originally by the rather better name 'non-sequenced'. The frame is identified as an un-numbered frame by 11 in bits 2 and 1. The *modifier bits*, *M1* and *M2*, identify the frame type. Not all 32 possibilities are defined by HDLC, but there is a substantial number of un-numbered frames, some of which are optional. A few of them may include an information field containing control information and one of them (the *Un-numbered Information frame*, *UI-frame*) may be used to carry user data outside the normal flow control procedure. Listed here are only those un-numbered frames that are mandatory and which constitute the basic HDLC repertoire. These are:

c  Set Asynchronous Balanced Mode (SABM)
c  Set Normal Response Mode (SNRM)
c  Set Asynchronous Response Mode (SARM)
c  Disconnect (DISC)
r  Un-numbered Acknowledgement (UA)
r  Disconnected Mode (DM)
r  Frame Reject (FRMR)

c = command
r = response

**The link access procedure in X.25**

The link access procedure recommended for the X.25 interface is a variant of HDLC called *LAPB*—the 'B' indicating the use of *balanced mode*. X.25 originally recommended asynchronous response mode, but this has now been superseded by LAPB. Point-to-point links are thus assumed.

LAPB includes I-frames, the RR, RNR and REJ supervisory frames and the basic repertoire of un-numbered frames for balanced operation (SABM, DISC, UA, DM and FRMR). It optionally allows the use of extended sequence numbers (modulo 128) in which case the mode setting command is SABME.

The following sections describe the use of these frames to set up the link, to transmit information and to disconnect the link.

**Link setup**

An X.25 link may be set up either by the DTE or by the DCE. The procedure requires the initiator to send SABM and the responder to return UA. If the responder is unable to set up the link, the appropriate response is DM. SABME is used to set up a link on which extended sequence numbers will be used.

**Information transfer and flow control**

Once the link is established, it enters the data transfer phase and I-frames may be exchanged. Each station maintains $V(S)$ and $V(R)$ that hold the sequence numbers of the next frame to be sent and the next frame expected to be received respectively. They are set to 0 when the link is set up. When an I-frame is sent, the values of these variables are copied into the control octet and the sender's $V(S)$ incremented using modulo 8. When an I-frame is received the recipient's V(R) is incremented.

A window mechanism similar to that used at the packet layer is used to control the flow. For a window size of W, the sender may send frames provided its V(S) satisfies the condition:

$$V(S) < N(R) + W$$

where N(R) is the last sequence number received. Frames may be acknowledged by receipt of an I-frame, RR, RNR or REJ, each of which carries an N(R) value.

A situation may arise in which the sender is allowed to send frames but the receiver is temporarily unable to accept them. The RNR frame is used to signal this condition to the sender, which then suspends transmission. The usual way to resume transmission is for the receiver to send an RR frame.

If a gap appears in the expected sequence of received I-frames, indicating loss of one or more frames, or a frame is received but fails the error check, information must be retransmitted. The REJ frame is used to inform the sender and its N(R) value indicates the first frame that must be retransmitted.

HDLC allows for both modulo 8 and modulo 128 frame sequencing. The basic format has modulo 8 counters and an 8-bit control field, as shown in Figure 5.4. The extended control format has 7-bit counters and a 16-bit control field. An extended mode command—SABME—is used to establish the use of extended format frames.

**The P/F bit**

The most obvious use of this bit is in normal response mode where the link is fully controlled by the primary station. Information may be sent by a secondary station *only* when it is polled by the primary, that is when it receives a command with the poll bit set. The secondary may then send response frames including I-frames. It must set the final bit (same bit, different name) in the last frame that it sends and must then wait to be polled again. The bit is used in asynchronous mode to match responses to commands.

**Error detection and the Frame Check Sequence (FCS) field**

Each HDLC frame carries with it a number enabling the receiver to detect errors in transmission. The number is carried in the *FCS* field in the link trailer. The error detection technique is an example of the use of a *cyclic redundancy check*.

The details of the technique are beyond the scope of this book and the approach is merely outlined here. If a number x is divided by a number y there is generally a remainder r. If r is subtracted from x, the result is divisible by y. If this simple arithmetic is performed on binary numbers modulo 2, then addition and subtraction are equivalent and x + r is also divisible by y.

A message coded as a bit string is a binary number. It is common in describing error detection techniques to represent a bit string as a polynomial with coefficients that are either 0 or 1 depending on the setting of the bits in the string. For example the binary number

$$101100101$$

is represented as

$$1 + x^2 + x^3 + x^6 + x^8$$

When an HDLC frame is to be transmitted, it is first divided by the 17-bit number

$$G = 1 + x^5 + x^{12} + x^{16}$$

This number is an example of a generating polynomial. It must be carefully chosen if the technique is to detect a high proportion of bit errors. The particular generating polynomial shown above is included in CCITT Recommendation V.41.

The remainder resulting from this division is a number with no more than 16 bits. The remainder is added to the number representing the message after the latter has been shifted left by 16 places to accommodate the addition. This forms a new number that is divisible by G. Division by G is checked at the destination and if it yields a 0 remainder, the frame is assumed to be uncorrupted.

The whole process of generating and checking the frame check sequence is easily accomplished by hardware in the two stations.

**Disconnecting the link**

Either station may disconnect the link by sending a *DISC* command, to which the response is *DM*. The P bit in the DISC should be set and the F bit in the DM response. This enables the response to be distinguished from a DM response sent by a station to indicate that it has entered the disconnect phase and requires a mode setting command to re-establish the link.

## Relationship between layer 2 and layer 3

Layer 3 of X.25 generates packets and passes them to layer 2 for transmission across the link between DTE and DCE. Layer 3 operates at the logical channel level and a number of logical channels may exist between DTE and DCE at a particular time. Packets for all logical channels are of course carried on the one physical link. The type and content of these packets is of no significance to layer 2—they are just information to be carried in an I-frame. The link layer protocol ensures that none of them is corrupted, lost or repeated.

When the X.25 interface is initialized, the link is established and its state variables are set to 0. Layer 2 enters the information transfer phase and waits for packets to send. On receipt of a packet from layer 3, it puts it in an envelope (an I-frame) and passes the frame to layer 1 for physical transmission to its destination.

The following section describes the operation of the third and lowest layer of the X.25 interface.

## 5.4 The X.25 physical layer

The X.25 Recommendation enables network providers to offer one or both of two physical interfaces. These are X.21 and X.21 bis and both are covered in detail by the corresponding CCITT Recommendations. The X.25 Recommendation merely clarifies the use of certain features of these interfaces. X.21 describes the physical interface to networks that provide digital data circuits while X.21 bis allows for connections via modems to analog circuits. Only the former is described here, as it is the interface likely to be more widely used as digital circuits become more common.

The mechanical shape, size and pin positioning of the plug that connects a DTE to a network are themselves standardized. The concern here is with the electrical characteristics of the interface, such as the meaning of particular voltage levels on particular circuits.

X.21 refers to a number of individual electrical circuits that together make up the interface. In describing the protocol at this layer, four of these are covered here. The *Transmit (T)* and *Receive (R)* circuits, as their names suggest, respectively transmit data to the DCE and receive data from the DCE. The *Control (C)* and *Indication (I)* circuits indicate the state of the DTE to DCE connection. The T and R circuits transmit bits; the C and I circuits are either on or off, these states being distinguished by differing voltage levels. Figure 5.5 shows how these

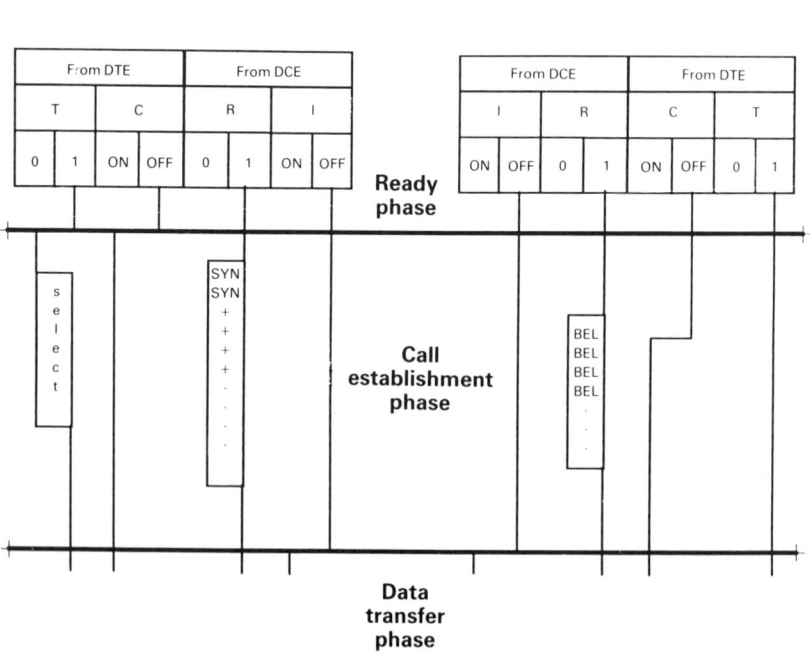

*Figure 5.5   X.21 call establishment*

circuits are used to establish a call between two DTEs. In describing the process, it is helpful to return to the telephone call analogy.

Under normal circumstances, both the DTE and the DCE are in the ready state—the telephone is on the hook. The state is indicated by $t = 1$, $c = $ OFF, $r = 1$ and $i = $ OFF. T and R are transmitting continuous 1 bits and C and I are OFF.

When the DTE wishes to make a call, it changes state to $t = 0$, $c = $ ON—the caller picks up the telephone. The DCE responds by transmitting continuous ' + ' characters preceded by two or more 'SYN' characters—this is the equivalent of a dialling tone. The I circuit remains OFF. The next stage is to select the destination DTE.

The selection signal is preceded by 'SYN' characters and contains the destination network number. It also enables the caller to select optional facilities, such as reverse charging and closed user groups. These facilities are not normally provided by a public telephone service. The DTE is now waiting for something to happen, as is the telephone caller. In the case of an X.21 call, the DCE informs the caller of progress using a sequence of call progress signals.

Throughout this process, the destination DTE and DCE remain in the ready state. The first indication that something is about to happen is the appearance of an incoming call signal on the R circuit at the destination —the telephone rings. The incoming call signal consists of continuous 'BEL' characters. The destination DTE should accept the call within a specified period of time by changing to $c = $ ON—the telephone is picked up. The DCE will then provide information about the incoming call, such as the caller's number and the optional facilities selected.

When call progress and DCE-provided information is completed, each DCE will indicate the 'ready for data state' by switching the I circuit from OFF to ON. The circuit is now in the state $t = 1$, $c = $ ON, $r = 1$ and $i = $ ON, which defines the data transfer phase. Subsequent signals on the T and R circuits are treated as data. In the case of an X.25 interface, the data are LAPB frames generally containing X.25 packets that themselves generally contain user data.

A DTE indicates its wish to clear a call by signalling $t = 0$, $c = $ OFF— the telephone is put down. The DCE responds with the clear confirmation signal $r = 0$, $i = $ OFF and then reverts to the ready state once more—$r = 1$, $i = $ OFF. The DTE, following receipt of the clear confirmation signal, also reverts to the ready state.

The other DCE will inform its DTE by means of the clear indication signal of $r = 0$, $i = $ OFF—this is the resumption of the dialling tone. The DTE responds with the clear confirmation signal of $t = 0$, $c = $ OFF and finally both DTE and DCE enter the ready state.

The protocol at the physical layer is designed to enable calls to be set up and cleared down. It is implemented by the electrical states of the four circuits involved. Signals on the T and R circuits are treated as data only when C and I are both ON. During the data transfer phase, the T and R circuits act as a duplex 'pipe' between the DTE and DCE layer 2 implementations. The layer 2 protocol ensures the controlled and error-free movement of frames through the pipe. From a layer 3 perspective, the pipe carries a number of logical channels. The layer 3 protocol controls the flows through each of these channels independently. This summary of the X.25 interface is illustrated in Figure 5.6.

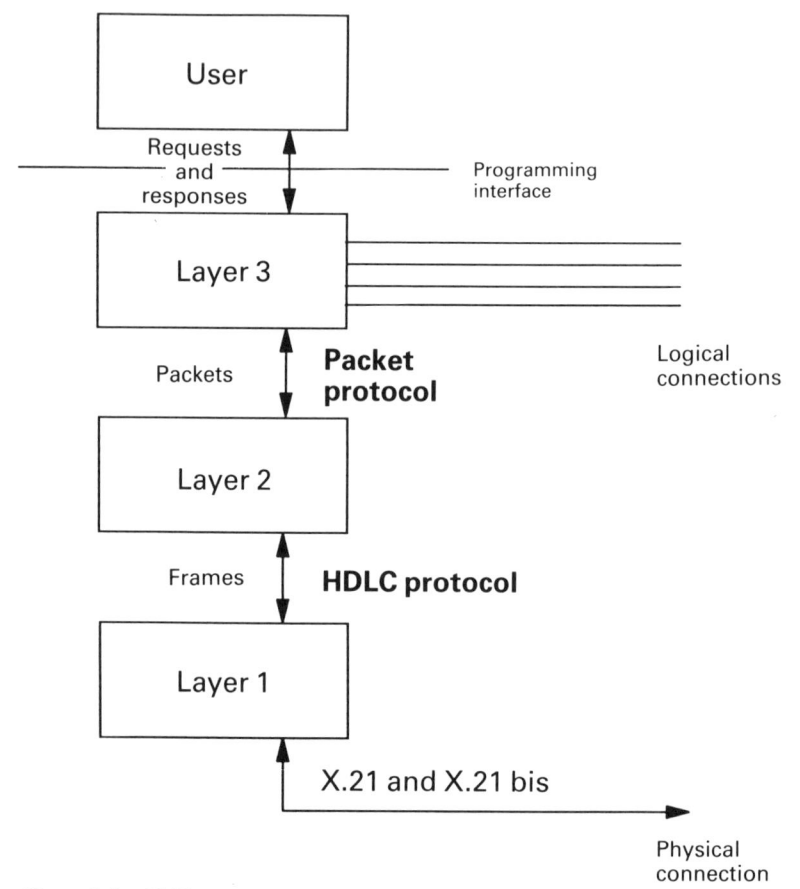

*Figure 5.6   X.25 summary*

The description in Figure 5.5 of the X.21 interface excludes many details of the recommendation that allow for unusual situations and define time periods during which certain things should, or should not, happen. The same caveat applies equally to the descriptions of the other layers.

## 5.5 Packet Assembler/Disassembler (PAD)

In order to connect to a network across an X.25 interface, a terminal (a DTE) needs to be capable of handling packets. Such DTEs are called *packet-mode* or *packet-oriented terminals*. Not all terminals have this capability but need to be connected to public data networks. So-called *dumb terminals*—terminals with fixed communications functions that cannot be programmed—are widely used to access remote applications. The revolutionary growth in the use of personal computers with simple asynchronous communications capability has added to the need. The solution lies in the provision of a *PAD*.

Simple terminals send and receive data as a stream of individual characters rather than in packets. In order to attach them to an X.25 network, a mechanism is needed that asssembles the character stream into packets for transmission into the network and accepts packets from the network, producing a stream of output characters to the terminal. This device is called a PAD. It may be supplied by the network provider and accessed by means of a dialled connection via the telephone network or it may be provided by the user in the form of an intelligent controller serving a cluster of dumb terminals.

Dumb terminals come in various guises—VDUs with a range of screen sizes, printers, teletypes or not-so-dumb personal computers. A packet that can be satisfactorily sent to a printer may overflow the screen if sent to a VDU. The interface mechanism needs to take into account the different capabilities of its potential users.

A set of three CCITT Recommendations is associated with the definition and use of PADS: X.3, X.28 and X.29. They are often referred to collectively as 'triple X' and are currently defined only for start/stop DTEs.

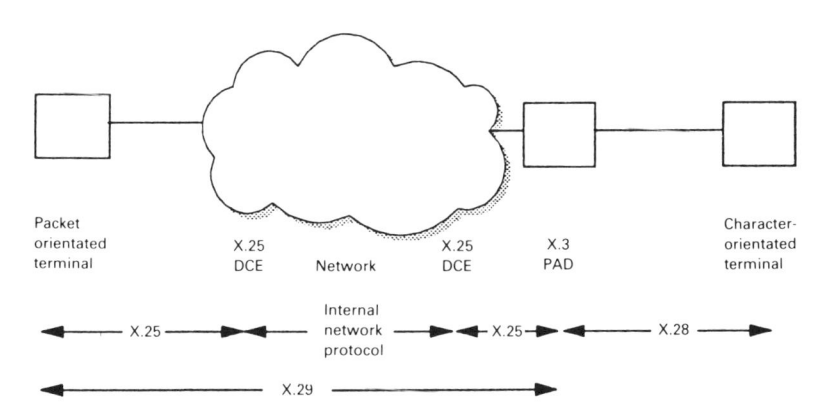

*Figure 5.7   PADs and the 'triple X' recommendations*

The use of a PAD is illustrated in Figure 5.7. The character mode DTE is connected to the PAD, often by means of a dialled telephone connection. The PAD receives asynchronous characters from, and delivers them to, the dumb terminal. It communicates with a data network across an X.25 interface and thence with a packet mode DTE, which may itself be another PAD acting on behalf of another asynchronous device. Conceptually, data flows in the way shown in the lower part of Figure 5.7.

The PAD acts as a protocol converter between the asynchronous world and the X.25 world. It should be capable of supporting a number of asynchronous devices with different presentation spaces (screen sizes, paper sizes and so on). It should be able to recognize, and act upon, control characters from the devices attached to it. The requirements imply that the functions of a PAD need to be dynamically configurable to suit different calls.

The obvious way to set up the PAD for a particular call is for the participants in the call—the packet DTE and the character DTE—to configure it. A protocol for communication between the PAD and each DTE is consequently required. These protocols are defined by X.28 and X.29 respectively. Finally, rules and parameters for the configuration and operation of the PAD are required. These are provided by X.3. In the following section the main features of the protocols that make up the triple X Recommendations are described.

## X.3

The 1988 version of X.3 defines 22 parameters for configuring a PAD together with their possible values. Numbers 1 to 12 are considered essential, to be provided internationally, and the remainder may or may not be provided by a particular network. The essential parameters, with their identifying numbers, include the following.

**PAD recall (1)** — This enables the DTE to escape from the data transfer phase in order to send commands to the PAD. A setting of 1 indicates that the DLE character will be used for this purpose.

**Echo control (2)** — This parameter determines whether or not the PAD will echo characters to the start/stop DTE.

**Data forwarding character (3)** — This determines the character (usually the carriage return character) the receipt of which from the DTE will cause a data packet to be sent to the network.

**Idle timer delay(4)** — The PAD will also forward a packet if it has not received a character from the DTE for n twentieths of a second where n is the value of the idle timer delay.

**Service signal control (6)** — Service signals are analogous to the call progress signals transmitted by an X.25 DCE to the DTE. This parameter enables them to be suppressed or transmitted in different natural languages.

**Receipt of break signal (7)** — This determines the reaction of the PAD to receipt of a break signal from the DTE. The options include sending an interrupt packet to the packet DTE and resetting the call.

**Line folding (10)** — This indicates the length of a line at the DTE. When set to n ($>0$) the PAD will insert a line feed after n characters.

**DTE speed (11)**  The PAD is able to determine the speed of the DTE in bits per second. The value is held in this parameter and can be read by the packet DTE.

**Flow control (12)**  Flow control using the DC1 (X-On) and DC3 (X-Off) characters may be exercised between PAD and DTE. It is selected according to this parameter.

The X.3 Recommendation also defines the basic functions of a PAD including:

- assembling packets
- disassembling the user data field of incoming packets and sending the individual characters to a DTE
- implementation of the X.25 procedures and packets for call setup and clearing, reset and interrupts
- sending service signals to attached DTEs (these are analogous to the call progress signals provided by an X.25 network)
- a mechanism to control the forwarding of packets to the X.25 network
- handling break signals from the DTE
- editing of PAD command signals (these are the means by which the DTE controls the PAD)
- a mechanism for reading and setting the PAD parameters that determine the mode of operation of the PAD.

Some optional functions are also listed in X.3, including:

- selection of a predefined set of parameters
- allowing the packet DTE to request a call to the start/stop DTE.

These functions, controlled by the configuration parameters, determine the behaviour of the PAD for a particular call. Configuration of the PAD is determined by the users—the start/stop DTE and the packet DTE. Interfaces are defined for this purpose. In the case of the start/stop DTE, the interface is defined by the X.28 Recommendation.

## X.28

The DTE may access the PAD by a variety of means, including the public telephone network, a public data network such as a telex network or by leased analog or digital circuits. X.28 refers to the appropriate V or X series Recommendation for establishing a physical level connection.

To establish a call, via the PAD, to a remote DTE, the start-stop DTE sends a service request signal, followed by a selection command. The selection command consists of a facility request block, to select one or more of the optional facilities provided by X.25, an address block, to indicate the address of the remote DTE and, optionally, a limited amount of user data. At this stage, the DTE may transmit other PAD commands, for example to set the PAD parameters. To set echo control (parameter 2) off and to set flow control (parameter 12) on, the DTE will send the characters 'SET 2:0, 12:1'. A complete predefined set of the 12 essential parameters may be selected by the 'PROF' command.

The format and timing of all control commands to the PAD and service signals from the PAD are defined in X.28.

After call setup, the connection enters the data transfer phase. During this phase, data characters are sent to the PAD and assembled into a packet, which is released when it is full or on receipt of a data forwarding character or on expiry of the idle timer. PAD commands may also be sent during the data transfer by sending the DLE character (or a user-defined character). The PAD will now interpret characters as commands until another recall character or a command delimiter (CR or + ) is sent. The call is cleared by the DTE by sending the clear request PAD command.

## X.29

The third recommendation in the triple X set provides procedures for exchanging control information between a PAD and a packet-mode DTE or another PAD. As these devices are connected to an X.25 network, a ready-made mechanism, the user data field of an X.25 packet exists for the exchange of information. The same mechanism is, of course, used to transfer user data between the communicating DTEs. The Q bit in the packet is used to distinguish packets containing PAD control messages from those containing user data.

X.29 defines the format and use of PAD control messages. It essentially defines a protocol over and above X.25. The messages enable the parameters of a PAD to be controlled by the packet-mode DTE or by another PAD. Parameters may be set, read or set and read individually or collectively. Other messages enable the PAD:

- to inform the start/stop DTE that a break has been indicated
- to clear the call
- to clear the call and re-establish a call to the same or another DTE
- to transmit an error message.

In addition to sending PAD control messages in qualified data packets, the X.29 protocol makes use of the call user data field in call request and incoming call packets. The field is used to identify the protocol that is being handled by the PAD. The use of a PAD to support start-stop mode DTEs is the only protocol currently defined in X.29, but there is ample scope for the use of this field in future CCITT Recommendations.

## 5.6 Summary

X.25 networks are to data communication what the PSTN is to voice communication. Most of the world's national public data networks are based on this recommendation. Interworking between X.25 networks is achieved by means of the companion recommendation, X.75, enabling a world-wide public data service to be provided. X.25 networks are also widely implemented by private organizations. Packet switches have been developed with increasing capacity and function and are available from many manufacturers. The recommendation has been enhanced to enable an X.25 network to provide the OSI network service. OSI is the subject of the next chapter.

*The WNB's strategy is to move towards open systems and distribute its data processing to those network end nodes where it is most beneficial to staff and customers. The strategy is being implemented on a number of fronts. The first of these was the provision of an open backbone network conforming to the X.25 Recommendation. This is the network shown in Figure 3.3. It presents the X.25 interface at its entry points and provides any-to-any connectivity between the WNB's offices. Connections to foreign locations are provided through the international public X.25/X.75 service.*

*Switches in the lower tier (L) of the topology provide a low-speed DCE appearance to branches and other offices in the peripheral network (P), and switches in the upper tier (U) provide a high-speed DCE appearance to the data centres (D). Protocol conversion is required for those data centre machines that do not present an X.25 DTE appearance. Communication between switches is not subject to X.25 protocol. The use of the CUG facility restricts connectivity to those locations authorized by the bank.*

*X.25 was chosen for many reasons. It has the blessing of the CCITT and is regularly updated to take into account new technology and user needs. Its widespread use in public data networks encourages manufacturers to develop switches that keep pace with the development of the recommendation. It is the foundation for open networking. X.25 is fast enough, in its call setup and packet delivery functions, for most applications, although the need for communication across a WAN between high-speed LANs has called into question the complexity and layering of the protocol. X.25 also lends itself readily to accounting for use of the network.*

# CHAPTER 6  The OSI reference model

## 6.1 Introduction

The fact that it is possible to pick up a telephone and establish a connection with virtually any other telephone in the world deserves greater recognition and praise than it usually gets. It results from the definition and agreement of standards for electrical connection and signalling between the world's telecommunication authorities. Equally remarkable, and for the same reasons, is the ability to send a telex or a fax to any machine in the world.

In terms of the architectural layering discussed in Chapter 4, such communication makes use of the lower layer functions—those that establish physical connections and provide routing. Although it is possible to connect two telephones or two fax machines together, it may be less easy to establish an exchange of information due to lack of a mutual language. A translator may be needed, represented in a communications architecture by one of the upper layers.

More and more information is being generated and processed by computers and needs to be exchanged between them. Here the situation is far less impressive. The difficulties of exchanging information between an application program in a machine from manufacturer A and one in a machine from manufacturer B are notorious. These difficulties may well have contributed to the inability of businesses to take full advantage of the convergence of data processing and telecommunications technologies.

The problem is less apparent in the lower layers. The CCITT Recommendation X.25 defines a three-level interface to a data network and many of the world's public and private networks provide this interface. Computers that match this interface may connect to their local X.25 network and, hence, to each other via the world's interconnected public networks operated by the PTTs. Packets of data may be sent from an application in one computer to an application in the other.

However, in order for an exchange of data packets to represent an exchange of information, the applications need to establish bilateral agreement on the syntax and semantics of the data. Such agreement is impractical for the exchange of information between machines from different manufacturers operated by enterprises that may not even be aware of each other's existence.

What is required for full application-to-application communication is the same level of standardization in the upper layers as X.25 provides at the lower layers. Individual manufacturers achieve application-to-application communication by defining upper layer functions in their proprietary architectures and implementing these functions in their products. Two IBM computers each implementing the functions of a particular type of SNA logical unit will happily communicate with each other. Two machines from the Digital Equipment Corporation (DEC), each implementing a compatible subset of Decnet upper layer functions, will also happily communicate with each other. One of the IBM machines can send packets of data to one of the DEC machines across an X.25 network or vice versa—even this requires some enhancements to the respective products. The data will mean nothing to the receiver.

The development of computer networking began in the late 1960s and had become well established by the 1970s. Each major computer manufacturer recognized at that time the need to provide connectivity between its products to take advantage of the convergence of data processing and telecommunications and to provide a platform for distributed processing. Each manufacturer defined a communications architecture and began to develop products conforming to that architecture. It was not seen to be in the commercial interests of a particular manufacturer to facilitate connectivity to its competitors' products. Consequently, many different architectures and incompatible product lines were developed.

The ISO recognized the need for a non-proprietary architecture to encourage the development of vendor-independent networking and to facilitate the connectivity of multivendor equipment. The ISO began, in 1977, to develop a general architectural model for the interconnection of data processing systems. This model—the OSI reference model—is the subject of this chapter.

## 6.2 Fundamentals of the reference model

A reference model is something to which people refer for guidance. The OSI model provides guidance in the development of communication systems between computers. In fact, it provides more than guidance. It provides precisely defined rules for the implementation of such systems.

Chapter 4 introduced, in an intuitive manner, the concept of layered communications architectures. This concept is based on the observation that the many and diverse functions involved in communication may be divided into groups, or layers, such that the functions in a particular layer are manifestly similar to each other and manifestly different from those in other layers. The OSI model is the most rigorously layered of all communications architectures.

The model treats the communication functions in a data processing system as a layered stack—the OSI stack. The purpose of the stack is to provide all the functions necessary for an application in one system to communicate with an application in another. The functions uppermost in the stack provide a communications service directly to an application. Those lowest in the stack interface directly to the physical medium that connects machines. Each layer adds value to the functions provided by the layers below. The model defines seven layers from layer 1 (the physical layer) to layer 7 (the application layer). Layers cannot be omitted but a partial stack may be implemented by truncation from the top. Thus, a stack consisting of layers 1, 2, 3, 4 and 6 is *not* permitted, while one consisting of layers 1, 2, 3, 4 and 5 *is* valid. In the latter case, the functions of the missing upper layers, if required, need to be provided by the application.

Each layer is formally defined in terms of two standards. The first standard defines the *service* that, say, layer n provides to layer $n + 1$. In providing this service, layer n takes the service provided by layer $n - 1$, adds value through its own functions and presents the enhanced service to layer $n + 1$. In this way, an increasingly powerful service is built up before being made available to the application.

The stacks in two interconnected systems—A and B—collaborate to provide communication between applications. Collaboration is achieved by the exchange of control information between corresponding layers in the two stacks. Layer n in stack A adds its control information to the data passed to it by layer $n + 1$ and passes the composite message to layer $n - 1$. This n-layer control information essentially describes the functions performed by layer n in stack A and the functions that need to be performed by layer n in stack B.

The format and content of the control information are governed by the second of the pair of standards associated with each layer. It is called the *protocol standard*. Each layer is defined by one or more service standards, each with an associated protocol standard.

Layer n in an OSI stack provides a service to layer $n + 1$. Layer $n + 1$ is the user and layer n is the provider. Thus, the network layer provides a service (the network service) to the transport layer, the session layer provides a service (the session service) to the presentation layer and so on. Each service consists of a set of functions that the user may request the provider to perform as part of the overall communications process. The functions that constitute the service are called the *service primitives*. A service standard defines the primitives, the information that is given by the user to the provider and the information that is given by the provider to the user.

Consider a simple example. A user (layer $n + 1$ in system A) needs to send a message to layer $n + 1$ in system B. Layer n provides the 'guaranteed delivery' service despite the fact that layer $n - 1$ only provides a 'best efforts delivery' service. The value added by layer n is to guarantee delivery given an unreliable service. *How* it does this is an implementation decision.

Layer n in system A provides its service by collaboration with layer n in system B. The mechanism for ensuring delivery is embodied in the layer n protocol—the control messages exchanged by the layer n entities. It may, for example, be a system based on send and receive counts maintained at each end and transmitted with the messages.

Layer n + 1 in A requests guaranteed delivery of data to layer n + 1 in B by issuing a guaranteed delivery request to layer n. Layer n adds control information to the message and issues a data delivery request to layer n − 1. The process continues in system A, with each layer adding its own control information until the physical layer is reached that is responsible for putting data onto the physical medium that connects system A to the network. The network is responsible for delivery of the data to system B.

System B receives the data in its physical layer and it is passed upwards through the stack, with each layer using control information to perform its part in the communication process. When the data is passed to layer n, it informs layer n + 1 that a message has arrived by issuing a guaranteed data indication.

This combination of a primitive in its request form (to solicit a service) and in its indication form (to alert the user that a service has been requested) is the means by which an OSI stack provides application-to-application communication. Each layer in the stack accepts requests and provides indications and exchanges control information with its peer according to the standard layer protocol.

Many primitives have two other forms to allow for confirmation that a request has been performed. The *response* form allows a user to respond to an incoming message and the *confirmation* form allows a provider to confirm to a user that a request has been fulfilled. A service having all four forms is a *confirmed service*, while a service having only request and indication forms is an unconfirmed service.

An OSI service standard will typically define the primitives of the service, the forms in which they must be provided and the parameters associated with each form. An implementation claiming to provide the service must provide these primitives or a defined subset. Two systems that implement a compatible subset at each layer will provide application-to-application communication.

The formal terminology associated with the layers of an OSI stack is shown in Figure 6.1. The information passed to a layer when a service request is made is called a *Service Data Unit (SDU)*. When describing a non-specific layer n, the term *(n)-SDU* is used to indicate the SDU passed to layer n. When describing a specific layer, such as the session layer, the initial letter of the layer name is used, thus becoming SSDU.

As described above, the functions of a particular layer are controlled by information attached (as a header or sometimes a header and a trailer)

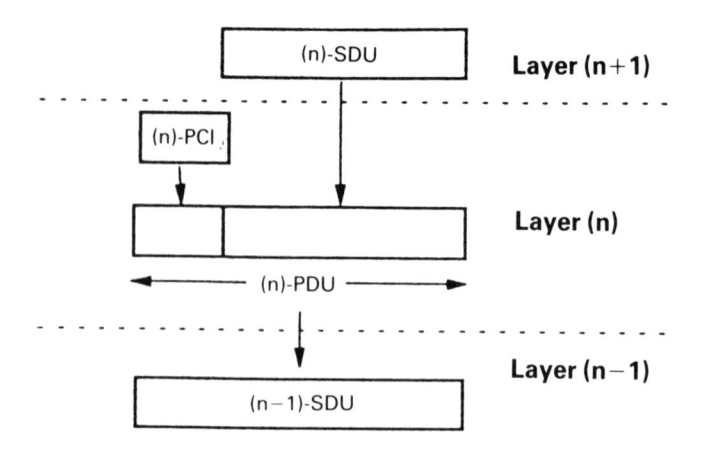

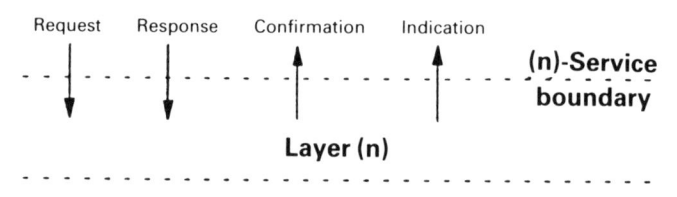

*Figure 6.1  OSI terminology*

to the data with which the layer is presented. This control information is called *Protocol Control Information (PCI)* and the combination of the SDU and the PCI forms a *Protocol Data Unit (PDU)*. This results in expressions such as n-PDU and SPDU. The PDU produced by layer n becomes the SDU for layer n − 1, that is the (n − 1)-SDU. The OSI protocol standards for each layer essentially describe the number, format and content of the PDUs for that layer.

## 6.3 The layers of the reference model

The functions of a communication system consisting of a full OSI stack are divided into the seven layers shown in Figure 6.2.

In this chapter, the lower three layers are considered first as a composite group and then the upper layers are examined individually.

The lower three layers are concerned with accepting a message from a data processing system and delivering it to some other system. There is a strong case for reserving the word 'network' for the layers that provide this delivery service, but the word is used so often that any attempt to

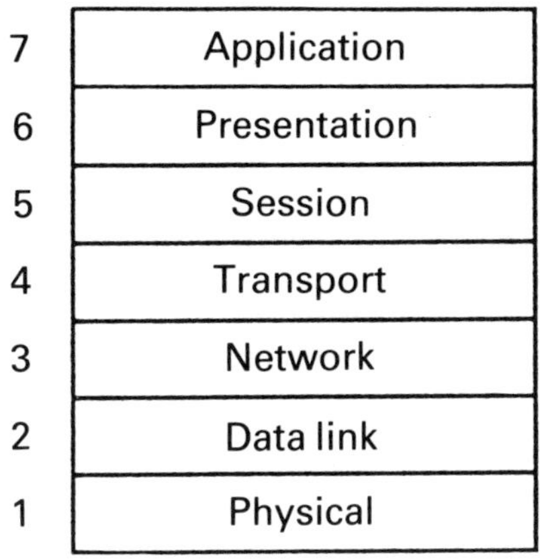

| | |
|---|---|
| 7 | Application |
| 6 | Presentation |
| 5 | Session |
| 4 | Transport |
| 3 | Network |
| 2 | Data link |
| 1 | Physical |

*Figure 6.2  The layers of the OSI reference model*

restrict its use would be pedantic. It is used in the restricted sense in phrases such as 'an X.25 network' or 'the telephone network', but has a wider and looser meaning in 'an SNA network' or 'an OSI network'. For the moment, then, 'network' is used here in the more restricted sense.

A network may be thought of as a rather complicated multiway switch. End systems are connected to the switch and, hence, may be connected to each other. The internal structure of the switch is of little concern to the end systems, which probably explains why there is a universal convention of representing a network pictorially as a cloud. End systems are concerned with having a means of connection to the switch and a means of addressing other end systems.

Networks generally consist of a set of interconnected machines (network nodes) the role of which is to send a message to the next node and, ultimately, to the destination end system. Some nodes connect directly to end systems, containing end nodes, and are sometimes called *boundary nodes*; others connect only to intermediate nodes. Local telephone exchanges and PTT switching centres are, respectively, examples of the two categories.

Nodes (end, boundary or intermediate) are connected to each other by physical media, variously called links, circuits, channels, wires or cables. All types of node need functions that enable them to decide where to send a message, to transmit data to another node and to connect to a physical medium. These are the functions defined by the network, data link and physical layers of the OSI model.

There are a number of reasons for considering these three layers and the functions they provide as a group. They are required in every type of node and together constitute the networking functions. They are the only functions generally provided in public telecommunications networks. They are essential for end node-to-end node communication, other than for the trivial cases of permanently connected end systems. Together they provide an important networking keystone—the OSI network service.

## 6.4 The OSI network service

This service is defined (by ISO standard 8348) as a number of primitives providing the user with the following facilities:

- *N-Connect*: to establish a connection to another user
- *N-Data*: to send data to another user
- *N-Data-Ack*: to acknowledge the receipt of data
- *N-Expedited-Data*: to send data bypassing queues in nodes
- *N-Reset*: to reset a connection to a predefined state
- *N-Disconnect*: to terminate the connection.

The forms in which the primitives are implemented (for example request, confirmation) and the associated parameters are also defined by the standard. The service outlined above is the OSI *Connection-orientated Network Service (CONS)*. In connection-orientated mode, a connection must be established before data transfer can occur. An alternative form of network service, the connectionless mode, does not require a connection to be established before data transfer.

The ability of a network to provide the OSI CONS is dependent on the control protocol used by the network layer. The PCI added by the network layer must be capable of conveying the required control information between users to support the above primitives and their parameters. The service is now examined in more detail.

**Connection establishment**

The CONS requires a connection to be established between its users before data transfer. OSI provides the network connection establishment service with four primitives. Some of the parameters of these primitives are fairly obvious—the user must give the provider (the network) the address of the destination user and the provider must tell the destination user the address of the source user. Other parameters are less obvious and are associated with the nature of the subsequent data flow and the quality of the connection.

The service defines two options: confirmation of receipt of data and provision of expedited flow. They are options in the sense that the network is not obliged to provide them. Even if they are provided, the destination is not obliged to accept use of them. If the source wishes to use these options, it indicates its wish when requesting a connection.

The type of connection required by the user is indicated by a number of *Quality of Service (QOS)* parameters that include throughput, transit delay and the security of the connection against active or passive attack on data in transit.

The purpose of connection establishment is to establish the type of connection required by the calling user, although this may not always be possible—the network may be unable to provide such a connection or the called user may be unable to handle the connection.

Finally, a limited amount of data (such as a password) can be included in a connection establishment message.

The primitives of the connection establishment service and their parameters are as follows.

N-Connect request with parameters:
- called address
- calling address
- receipt confirmation selection
- expedited data selection
- QOS parameters
- user data

N-Connect indication has the same parameters as those for request above. The same information is passed to the called user as is provided by the calling user. However, the values of some parameters (QOS, receipt confirmation and expedited data) may change. For example, if the calling user requests expedited data, but the network cannot provide it, the parameter is set to 'Off' in the indication. The parameter would also be set to 'Off' in the *response* and *confirm* primitives so that the calling user knows that the request for expedited data has not been accepted.

N-Connect response with parameters:
- receipt confirmation selection
- expedited data selection
- QOS parameters
- user data
- responding address

N-Connect confirm has the same parameters as those for response above. The address parameter in the response and confirm (the responding address) allows for a response from an address that is different to that of the original called address. This may result, for example, from redirection of messages.

## Data transfer

When a connection with which both users are satisfied is established, *data transfer* can take place. The standard primitives for data transfer are as follows.

N-Data request with parameters:
- user data
- confirmation request

N-Data indication has the same parameters as those for request above.

This is an unconfirmed service in the sense that there are no corresponding response and confirm primitives. Confirmation of receipt is provided by two further primitives that may optionally be implemented by the network. They are shown below. Neither primitive has parameters.

- N-Data acknowledge request
- N-Data acknowledge indication

*Expedited data* is also a network option. If provided, it is requested by the following. In both cases, the parameter is the user data.

- N-Expedited data request

is indicated to the called user by the following:
- N-Expedited data indication.

Things may go wrong during data transfer. A temporary network failure may occur that, although recoverable, may result in loss of data or uncertainty over its delivery. A recoverable problem on the part of one of the users may arise, such as inability to handle the volume of incoming data. The CONS allows for this by defining a reset service that results in data being flushed from the network and the data transfer process being restored to a previous state from which it can be picked up.

*Reset* is an example of a service that may be initiated either by the user or by the provider in that the network itself may reset the connection. In this case, both users are informed and it is their responsibility to resynchronize the data flow. The reset service has the following primitives:

- N-Reset request where the parameter is the reason for the reset
- N-Reset indication where the parameters are the reason for the reset and originator
- N-Reset response where there are no parameters
- N-Reset confirm where there are no parameters.

## Connection release

The *connection release* service is provided to users to enable them to disconnect from the remote user. It can also be initiated by the network if it cannot continue to support the connection. A Quality of Service parameter enables the user to specify a priority, when requesting the connection, in the hope that the network will maintain high priority connections as long as possible. The primitives and parameters of the connection release service are shown below.

N-Disconnect request with parameters:
- reason
- user data
- responding address.

N-Disconnect indication with parameters:
- originator

- reason
- user data
- responding address.

## Provision of the OSI Connection-orientated Network Service (CONS)

The OSI CONS has been discussed in some detail because of its importance to open networking. The transport layer in an OSI stack expects to find an OSI network service at the service boundary of layers 3 and 4. If two end systems can rely on the provision by a network of the services described above they are able to exchange data. The network service standard describes to implementers precisely what to do to establish connections and to exchange messages and what the reaction of the network will be.

The most common means of providing end systems with the OSI CONS is based on the X.25 Recommendation discussed in Chapter 10. X.25 and the OSI CONS have grown up together and have always been close. The protocol at the X.25 packet level enables all mandatory and optional primitives of the network service to be provided by an X.25 network.

It is worth re-emphasizing here the interface nature of X.25. The recommendation defines the physical-, link- and network-level interfaces between a DTE and a DCE—between the end system and the network. Any network that provides this interface is an X.25 network. An SNA path control network, suitably enhanced, provides the interface and, by definition, is an X.25 network. (The relationship between SNA and X.25 is examined in Chapter 7).

It is also possible to provide the OSI CONS without using X.25. For example, a packet protocol may be superimposed on the link and physical layers of a LAN to provide the OSI network service.

The common element in all implementations of the OSI network service is the provision to the user of the set of primitives described above. This imposes a requirement on the control protocol to support the functions expressed by the primitives.

## 6.5 The upper layers of the OSI model

In the discussion of X.25 in Chapter 5, each of the lower layers was examined individually and in Chapter 7, the lower layers of SNA are considered. In this chapter, the lower layers of the OSI model are treated as a group, the purpose of which is to provide the network service to the transport layer.

This separation of the lower three layers from the upper layers is common practice for the reasons mentioned in Section 6.2. There is also a case for including the *transport layer* in the lower group. A user of a network should be able to assume that the network provides a reliable connection to another user with a quality of service acceptable to both users. The network service is not always able to justify this assumption. For example, a requested QOS parameter may be rejected by the network, the network may recover from a failure, it may or may not notify the users that an error has occurred and it probably will not be able to indicate to the users the impact on their data. In short, networks have varying degrees of reliability.

The main purpose of the OSI transport layer is to enhance the network service so that it is acceptable to users and to provide this enhanced service in the form of the primitives of the OSI transport service. It is the transport service that justifies the users' assumption of a transparent data transfer mechanism.

So far, the concern has been to ensure that connections between users are provided with an acceptable quality (transit delay, throughput, protection and so on) and that messages are exchanged between users without error, loss or repetition. When we come to the *session layer*, we move from the world of raw data to the world of useful information.

Both participants in a human conversation may speak at the same time. This is neither a polite nor an efficient way to exchange information. Alternatively, a conversation may be interrupted and will need to resume from a point at which the participants had reached a common level of understanding. In order for an exchange of data to convey information between users, therefore, it is clear that certain disciplines are necessary to control the direction and synchronization of data transfer. The role of the session layer is to provide this discipline for machine-to-machine communication.

A controlled exchange of data may still not result in an exchange of information. For example, a controlled conversation between a person speaking and understanding only French and a person speaking and understanding only English leads to frustration rather than information. Translation—a syntax transformation process—is required to achieve understanding. In an OSI stack it is provided by the *presentation layer*.

The need for application-to-application communication arises in many areas of data processing. Computers exchange large data files. Computers provide systems for people to exchange messages. Information provided to one computer may be used as input to a process in a remote computer. Execution of a data processing task may be distributed between many computers. All these requirements should be met by a general-purpose communications vehicle. OSI seeks to provide such a vehicle.

The variety of ways in which computers are used to process data is reflected in the variety of services provided in the uppermost layer of an OSI stack—the *application layer*. Some of these services are common to all applications, such as the need to request a connection to another application or the need to synchronize processing across a distributed system. Others are specific to particular needs, such as transaction processing, file transfer or message handling. They are all the concern of the application layer.

Before each of the upper layers is examined in more detail, it should be emphasized that the purpose of a full OSI stack is to provide application layer services to applications. In fulfilling these service requests, the network layer provides a service to the transport layer, the transport layer to the session layer and so on. These service requests are triggered by a request from an application and it is the application that must supply all the information required as parameters at each service boundary in the stack. If information is *not* used by a particular layer, it is passed down the stack until it reaches the relevant layer. For example, quality of service parameters are supplied by the application (as it is only the application that knows the QOS requirements), but they are not used until the session or transport layers.

## The transport layer

In an OSI stack, the transport layer is the user of the network service and itself provides the transport service to the session layer. Earlier in the chapter it was intimated that although a network may provide the network service, it may not provide it very reliably. It may also not meet the quality of service required by the user (ultimately the application). The role of the transport layer is to bridge the gap between what is *needed* by the *application* and what is *provided* by the *network*.

The case for including the transport layer functions with the networking functions rests on this role. The enhancement of the network service by the transport layer enables the upper layers of the stack and the application to concentrate on a controlled exchange of information secure in the knowledge that they have a reliable data transport service.

The transport layer functions necessary to achieve this service depend on the quality of the underlying network. The lower the quality of the network, the more the transport layer has to do to provide a reliable transport service. The provision of a service by a particular layer is a cooperative effort between the functions of that layer in one end system and those in the same layer in another end system. This cooperation is achieved through the layer protocol. Consequently, additional work in the transport layer is reflected in an increase in the complexity of the transport protocol. OSI defines different classes of transport protocol to allow for different network qualities (these transport classes are discussed more fully later).

It may be that a particular implementation of the transport layer on a particular quality of network is unable to meet the quality of service specified by the user when requesting a transport connection. In such cases, the transport layer will reject the connection request.

**Elements of the transport service**

The *connection establishment* element of the transport service consists of the following primitives:

- T-Connect request

- T-Connect indication
- T-Connect response
- T-Connect confirm.

Parameters are similar to those for the establishment of a network connection. Connection establishment is a confirmed service. The responding address will normally be the called address, but the service does allow them to differ. The inclusion of user data at connect time is optional and its length is limited. The data transfer services are unconfirmed and consist of the *T-Data/expedited data request* and *T-Data/expedited data indication* primitives.

*Connection release* is unconfirmed (request and indication primitives only). It may also be provider-initiated (by the transport layer itself) and signalled to the users of the connection via the T-Disconnect indication, with a code indicating the reason for the disconnection.

**The transport protocol**

The provision of the transport service relies on the exchange of control information by peer elements of the transport layer in the form of *Transport Protocol Data Units (TPDUs)*, which carry parameters and other information from one end system to another.

The TPDUs supporting the connection-orientated transport service, with their short names, are:

- Connect Request (CR TPDU)
- Connect Confirm (CC TPDU)
- Disconnect Request (DR TPDU)
- Disconnect Confirm (DC TPDU)
- Data (DT TPDU)
- Acknowledge (AK TPDU)
- Expedited Data (ED TPDU)
- Expedited Data Acknowledge (EA TPDU)
- Error (ER TPDU)
- Reject (RJ TPDU).

The content and format of these TPDUs, together with the circumstances in which they are used, are defined by the transport layer protocol standard. They are, of course, carried as user data by the corresponding network service primitives.

**Protocol classes**

It has been mentioned previously that different networks provide different qualities of service and that the role of the transport layer is to enhance the network quality to a level acceptable to the user. The quality of a network connection may be considered from two points of view.

The first is related to the probability that user data may be corrupted, lost, duplicated or delivered out of sequence, with the user being left to determine that an error has occurred. Such errors are known as *residual errors*. The second is related to the probability that the connection may be lost or reset, but with the user being informed of this such errors are known as *signalled errors*. Networks are classified according to the likely rate of these two categories of errors:

- *Type A*: low number of residual errors and low number of signalled errors
- *Type B*: low number of residual errors but unacceptably high rate of signalled errors
- *Type C*: unacceptably high level of residual errors.

The functions that the transport layer needs to provide in order to offer an acceptable service to its user, and the complexity of the supporting transport protocol, are determined by the class of the underlying network. Several transport protocol classes are defined to enable implementers of the transport layer to determine what functions need to be provided. The details of these classes are beyond the scope of this book, but the salient features of each class are indicated below:

- *Transport class 0 (simple class)*: class 0 protocol is used with Type A networks; it provides the basic facilities of connection establishment, data transfer and connection release using the CR, CC, DR, DT and ER TPDUs
- *Transport class 1 (basic error recovery class)*: class 1 is used with Type B networks, which are likely to release or reset the network connection, and such an implementation needs to supplement class 0 with functions such as recovery from loss of the network connection, recovery from a reset of the network connections, storage of TPDUs until acknowledged and TPDU numbering and resynchronization
- *Transport class 2 (multiplexing class)*: class 2 protocol augments class 0 by enabling multiplexing of several transport connections onto a single network connection and consequently requires TPDU numbering and acknowledgement and also the use of flow control (it is used only on a Type A network)
- *Transport class 3 (error recovery and multiplexing class)*: this class essentially combines the functions of classes 1 and 2 and is used for Type B networks
- *Transport class 4 (error detection and recovery class)*: the most complex protocol class, it enables residual errors to be detected and recovered and is intended for use on Type C networks; class 4 provides all the functions of Class 3 and, additionally, is required to implement mechanisms for error detection by checksum, retransmission of TPDUs, resequencing and detection of inactivity on the connection.

Products that implement the OSI Transport Layer are described in terms of the protocol classes that they support. A common offering is classes 0, 2 and 4, enabling the product to be used on any type of network.

The OSI transport layer functions are concerned with exchanging data between session-layer entities in communicating end systems. In contrast, the lower three layers are concerned with attachment to and routeing through a network. Consequently these lower layer functions are required in end nodes, boundary nodes and intermediate nodes, whereas transport layer (and above) functions are implemented only in end nodes. Note, however, that different implementations of lower layer functions may exist in different parts of the network. The significant factor for interconnection of open systems is the provision of the network service to transport layer entities in end nodes. The transport layer was the first layer in which standards were defined specifically for OSI as existing X.25 Recommendations were adopted for the lower layers.

## The session layer

The lower three layers of the OSI reference model are concerned with moving data through a network. The addition of transport layer protocols enables a reliable data transfer service to be provided over unreliable networks. There is nothing magical about this ability to detect and recover from errors; it is provided by cooperation between transport layer entities in recording and acknowledging successful receipt of messages and retransmitting those that failed.

The upper three layers are concerned with providing functions that enable application programs to exchange information in a controlled and efficient manner and in such a way that it can be interpreted by the recipient. The combination of reliable transfer of data, disciplined dialogue and interpretation of information is what characterizes a sophisticated communications architecture.

The upper layer functions in an OSI stack may usefully be compared with the functions that human experience and intelligence bring to a telephone conversation. The telephone network provides connectivity; the people provide control of the dialogue, resynchronization and interpretation of the information, sometimes including language translation. The session layer in an OSI stack is the first layer in which these functions appear.

Readers should by now be familiar with the process. The session layer is the user of the transport service discussed in the previous section. It requests, indirectly on behalf of its controlling application, connection to another session entity, transfer of data and release of the connection. It is not concerned with detecting and recovering from transmission errors as these are handled by the transport layer. The session layer is concerned with controlling the direction of data flow and ensuring that both partners in a dialogue maintain a common level of understanding. The latter requirement, in particular, is demanding and can result in a complicated session layer functionality and protocol. So far, nothing has been said about the *direction* of data flow on a connection between end systems. Some communication channels support simultaneous flow in both directions—they are called *two-way simultaneous* or *full duplex connections*. Others support flow in both directions but not at the same time—they are called *two-way alternate* or *half duplex connections*. Finally, there are *simplex channels*, which can be used in one direction only.

Although a connection may physically support two-way simultaneous flow, it may not be advisable for the users to take advantage of the facility. As to why this is so, take the example of the telephone conversation once more. It is possible for both parties to a telephone conversation to speak at the same time, but efficient exchange of information rarely results. Some convention is adopted to change the direction of flow, such as voice inflection or specifically asking a question. An equivalent mechanism is needed to allow for changes in direction on a data connection between two applications.

It is often necessary to transmit structured information over the telephone, such as a matrix of numbers (sales of 10 items for the last 12 months, perhaps). The sender may say to the receiver, 'Please set up a matrix of 10 rows and 12 columns and I'll give you the numbers by row'. (This, incidentally, is a presentation layer function that will be considered later.)

In transmitting 120 numbers, with possible repeat sequences, the sender may lose confidence that numbers are being entered in the right places in the receiver's matrix. At the end of row 3, say, the sender may offer a checkpoint by saying, 'That's the end of row 3' and wait for the receiver to agree or disagree. If the person does not agree, the parties need to restart from a point at which a previous checkpoint was requested and agreed. Again, a similar mechanism is needed for synchronizing distributed application processing where undetected loss of synchronization may have disastrous results.

To continue with the telephone analogy, it is common practice to call someone for a particular reason and then to take advantage of the call to raise a quite different subject. The change of subject is prefixed by a remark such as 'While you're on the phone . . .' or an explicit 'Let us change subject . . .'. At this point there is an implicit, or maybe explicitly stated, agreement that the previous subject is closed and that subsequent information relates to the new subject. The same facilities are required, and need to be formally defined, for data transfer between applications where establishing a connection may be costly and time-consuming. The facilities required are similar to those needed for synchronization but the concern now is with synchronization between subjects, or activities, rather than within a particular activity.

The implementation of these dialogue control functions on the telephone relies heavily on human experience and some commonly accepted conventions. The same functions must be provided by a data communications system that is intended, as an OSI system is intended, to support application-to-application communication for a variety of reasons and in a variety of distributed configurations. They are provided in an OSI stack by the session layer.

The mechanism used by the session layer to provide dialogue control is the use of *tokens*. The word 'token' has a variety of meanings, one of which, given in the *Concise Oxford Dictionary*, is 'serving as proof of authenticity'. It is used in the session layer standards to indicate the right to request certain elements of the session service. Four tokens are defined, although not always implemented. The means by which a token is represented is not defined but is an implementation decision. Some terminology needs to be introduced here to clarify the description of the four tokens.

A token is available (for use) if the functions that use it are provided by a particular implementation of the session layer. An available token may be assigned to (held by) a particular user or not assigned to either user. The services that appear to transfer a token actually transfer assignment of the token and hence the right to use the associated service (these associated services are described later). The four tokens defined for the session layer are as follows:

- *Data token*: the user to which the *data token* is assigned has the right to request transmission of data, that is to issue an *S-Data request*. The other user must wait until it has the token before it can send data.
- *Release token*: the user to which the *release token* is assigned may issue an *S-Release request* to initiate orderly release of the session connection between two users.
- *Sync-Minor token*: the user to which this token is assigned may issue an *S-Sync-Minor request* to synchronize processing within a particular dialogue.
- *Major or activity token*: the user to which this token is assigned may issue an *S-Sync-Major request* to synchronize processing of different dialogues on the same connection.

It is probably becoming apparent that the session layer can be a complicated layer. This should not come as a surprise as it is responsible for providing in a machine functions that are provided in human conversation by rather subtle aspects of human behaviour.

To enable implementations of the session layer to be provided without unnecessary complexity, the standards allow many of the functions and primitives to be optional. Functions are grouped into subsets, called *functional units*. The mandatory functions of connection establishment, data transfer, orderly release of the connection and abortive release either by the user or the provider constitute the kernel functional unit. Most of the optional functional units are concerned with dialogue control and, in particular, with providing services to enable users to manage tokens. There are three of these:

- *S-Token-Please*: this primitive enables a user to request assignment to itself of a particular token and the token is specified as a parameter.
- *S-Token-Give*: this primitive is issued by a user to re-assign the token to another user, enabling that user to access the service controlled by the particular token.
- *S-Control-Give*: reassigns all available tokens simultaneously.

The session service is rich in primitives, which reflects the complexity of its role in maintaining synchronization within a dialogue and controlling different serial activities on the same connection. It is possible here to give only a simple example.

The S-Sync-Minor primitive allows a user to request that a synchronization point (checkpoint) be placed in the dialogue. The checkpoint is allocated a number by the service provider. It is the user's responsibility to decide *when* to take a checkpoint and *what* information to record. If the dialogue subsequently loses synchronization, it can be restored to a known position by use of the S-Resynchronize primitive quoting a particular checkpoint serial number.

Finally, in this brief look at the session layer, it should be emphasized that it is the *application* that exercises the control provided by the session service. Requests for a checkpoint or for reassignment of a token, for example, come directly from the presentation layer but indirectly from an application. The parameters for session service primitives, such as the token to be reassigned, are supplied by the application and must be passed on by the application layer and the presentation layer. This, in turn, means that these parameters appear in the application layer and presentation layer primitives, although they have meaning only to the session service.

## The presentation layer

Messages exchanged between data processing systems are strings of bits. In order to extract useful information from a bit string its syntax needs to be known. The role of the presentation layer is perhaps best approached by imagining that it is not present so that applications pass their messages to and receive their messages from the session layer. The session service, and the transport and network services on which it relies, ensure that controlled, reliable exchange of messages can take place. Each application must code its messages in a way that is understood by every other application with which it communicates.

Such a scheme imposes an unacceptable contraint on application-to-application communication. It does not allow an application to express information in a syntax suitable for use in the local system, hand it over to the delivery vehicle and have it understood by a remote application with a different local syntax. Syntax transformation is needed that, as it is part of the process of communication, should not be left to the applications to provide. It is provided in an OSI stack by the presentation layer.

Consider a situation in which two people, A who speaks only French and B who speaks only English, wish to converse. They may do so through an interpreter who speaks both languages. In the more general case, A may use an interpreter who speaks French and German and B may use an interpreter who speaks German and English. Messages are exchanged between the interpreters in German and translations to the local languages are done at each end. The mechanism involved in this example is closely analogous to the part played by the OSI presentation layer.

The presentation layer allows an application to express information in a natural way suited to the local processing environment. The syntax of this information is formally described to the presentation layer. It is called the *abstract syntax* and is agreed between the users of the presentation service. ISO has developed a standard notation for describing the structure of user information. It is called *Abstract Syntax Notation One (ASN.1)* and is widely used in OSI protocol standards.

The problem remains of encoding the user data as a bit string. This is handled by the presentation layer. There are many ways in which it can be achieved and it is the responsibility of the presentation layer to negotiate the particular method to be used with its peer entity in the remote system. In a companion standard to ASN.1, ISO has defined the encoding rules for expressing data formatted in accordance with ASN.1, as a bit string. The syntax governing the message in transit is called the *transfer syntax*. Data transformations such as *encryption* or *compression* are examples of transfer syntaxes that may be required and that must be negotiated by the presentation layer.

In many simple examples of application-to-application communication, the application designers will agree the message syntax and not require the services of the presentation layer. The layer must, nevertheless, be included in the stack if application layer services are used but becomes merely a vehicle for providing the session service to the application layer.

## The application layer

The purpose of an OSI stack, and of the standards that define its services and protocols, is to enable application programs to communicate with each other. An implementation of an OSI stack enables an application to initiate and terminate a connection to a remote application, to control the quality of the connection, to send and receive normal or expedited data, to control the use of the connection, to recover from loss of synchronization and to ensure that messages are expressed in a syntax intelligible to the recipient. These functions imply complicated cooperative processing between local and remote elements of the communication system.

A full implementation of an OSI system enables an application programmer to request these sophisticated services secure in the knowledge that the communication system will provide connectivity to any other application supported by an OSI implementation. In short, the applications are *open to each other*. In many instances, the OSI stacks will negotiate a quality of service that they are able to supply and which is acceptable to the users.

The services that make open communication possible are provided to an application by the application layer in a full OSI implementation. It has been mentioned previously that a partial stack is permitted with one or more of the upper layers omitted, subject to the condition that if the stack is truncated at layer n (where n<7), all layers below n must be present. In this section a full implementation is assumed and the application layer services are examined.

The application layer is unique in that it provides services directly to applications rather than to another layer of the stack. It is these applications that control the use of the communications system. Layer n requests a service from layer n − 1 because it has itself been requested to provide a service by layer n + 1. Initially the request was generated by an application. This implies that the information needed at each service boundary in the stack is provided by the application to be used in the appropriate layer.

As the use of distributed systems has grown, many needs have emerged that require applications to communicate with distant applications in order to process a piece of work. Some examples are the processing of a transaction, such as a financial payment, the transfer of files from one computer to another, the sending of messages for later retrieval by the recipient, the interactive use of a remote computer and the batch entry of data to be processed remotely. Each of these processes has some communications requirements that are common to all of them and some specific to the particular application. This difference is reflected in the services defined for the OSI application layer.

**Common Application Service Elements (CASEs)**

A *Common Application Service Element (CASE)*[1] provides a service that is needed by all applications. An obvious example is the provision of a connection to another application. A connection between two applications provided by the application layer is called an *association* and the functions that provide it form the *Association Control Service Element (ACSE)*. The service caters for the establishment and normal release of an association and also for abnormal release by either the user or the provider of the service.

An important difference between association control and the connection services provided by other layers lies in the way in which the source and destination are identified. In other layers they are identified by address. For example, a request by the transport layer for a network connection supplies as parameters the addresses of the source and destination *Network Service Access Points (NSAPs)*. Users of the ACSE, on the other hand, are identified by *name, title* and a *directory function* is used to map the title to a *Presentation Service Access Point (PSAP)* address to be used as a parameter for the resulting presentation connection request. Many other parameters, required by lower layers, need to be provided to establish an association. They include the quality

---

[1]The terms CASE and SASE are no longer in common use but remain convenient distinctions.

of service requirements, the initial assignment of the tokens used by the session layer, an initial synchronization point serial number and the abstract and transfer syntax definitions.

The *Reliable Transfer Service Element (RTSE)* is a common element, allowing a user to establish and release an association (using the ACSE), to transfer data without error and to control the assignment tokens. The reader may be forgiven for thinking that reliable transfer of data is the role of the transport layer. This is so in that the transport layer recovers from errors in the network. It is, of course, unable to recover from errors resulting from total failure of an end system. RTSE provides this level of recovery.

Many interactions between applications consist of a request by one application for an operation to be performed by a remote application and for the return of some reply. OSI defines the *Remote Operations Service Element (ROSE)* to cater for this need. An operation is invoked by the *RO-INVOKE* service, quoting a predefined *Operation-ID*. The *RO-RESULT* and *RO-ERROR* services provide for the return of a result or an error response.

Another common use of distributed processing is to update a remote database. It is essential in such applications that a change to the database be made fully or not at all—an ill-defined partial change is not acceptable. Such actions that either succeed fully or fail completely, leaving the database in its original state, are called *atomic actions*. Atomic actions require a commitment from the processor making the change that it is ready and able to do so. Situations may arise in which a request to update a database is received from several sources concurrently, making commitment a complicated process. In all cases, simple or complicated, the ability to restore the database to its original state, in the event that commitment cannot be made, is required.

Services to control a remote task that may fail during an atomic action are defined by the *Commitment, Concurrency and Recovery (CCR)* CASE. These services make use of the synchronization facilities provided by the session layer.

The common service elements defined in the application layer have been explained briefly here. Detailed descriptions may be found in the works listed in the Bibliography. A CASE may be used directly by an application, by another CASE or by an element of the application layer that is provided for a specific type of application. Two of these specific elements are examined briefly.

**Specific Application Service Elements (SASE)**

A *Specific Application Service Element (SASE)* provides services to facilitate the implementation of an application for a specific purpose. A SASE is orientated towards a specific purpose as distinct from, say, association control, which all applications need.

Perhaps the most common use of a network is to provide electronic mail by the use of a store-and-forward *Message Handling System (MHS)*. Such a system is also called a *Message-orientated Text Interchange System (MOTIS)*. The most commonly implemented set of international standards, after X.25, is the X.400 series—the CCITT's defined standards for message handling. A similar set of standards is defined by the ISO 10021 series.

An electronic mail user accesses the MHS through an application called a *User Agent (US)*, UAs are connected to the message transfer system, which consists of an interconnected set of *Message Transfer Agents (MTAs)*. In topological terms, the UAs are end nodes and the MTAs are boundary nodes or intermediate nodes.

A number of application service elements provide MHS services:

- Message Transfer Service Element (MTSE)
- Message Submission Service Element (MSSE)
- Message Delivery Service Element (MDSE)
- Message Retrieval Service Element (MRSE)
- Message Administration Service Element (MASE).

The MTSE is the element responsible for moving messages between MTAs. It makes use of the *Reliable Transfer (RTSE)* and *Association Control (ACSE)* services discussed above. *MSSE* and *MRSE* enable a UA to submit messages to and retrieve messages from an MTA and make use of the *Remote Operation (ROSE)* service.

The *File Transfer, Access and Management (FTAM)* service element enables an application to perform operations on a file of data located anywhere in the network. Transfer is the movement of an entire file between end systems. Access is the reading, writing, addition or deletion of records in a remote file.

Management provides such operations as creating a file, changing its attributes and opening and closing a file.

FTAM is a complicated service with a large number of primitives. As in the session layer, the primitives are grouped into functional units. The choice of functional units in a particular FTAM implementation results in a number of different service classes, such as the access class (reading and writing records) or the management class (reading and modification of file attributes).

## 6.6 Summary

This chapter, it is hoped, has given readers a feel for the way in which the OSI reference model provides a framework for the development of systems in support of application-to-application communication. The rigour and precision of the service and protocol definitions deserve fuller treatment than it is possible to provide here. Whole topics, of considerable interest, such as system management and security services, have had to be excluded. They are covered in detail in books which are listed in the Bibliography.

Implementations of OSI have been slow to materialize. The world of networking is still dominated by proprietary systems and, in particular, by SNA. There are, however, many signs that manufacturers recognize the growing demand by their customers for open systems—a demand reinforced by government pressure and legislation. Many observers believe that, by the year 2000, OSI will be the dominant means of connecting systems.

*If this observation turns out to be true, and there are increasing signs that this will be the case, the WNB's strategy will be soundly based. Open systems interconnection between distributed applications in branches, regional and head offices and on customer premises is the way the WNB will run its business and provide services to its customers. OSI application-layer services will support applications for file transfer, funds transfer, transaction processing or electronic data interchange with customers, suppliers and other financial institutions (the use of conditional clauses and the future tense in the previous section should not go unnoticed).*

# CHAPTER 7  Systems Network Architecture (SNA)

## 7.1 Introduction

In Chapter 4, the concept of layered communications architectures was introduced and some examples were briefly discussed. This chapter is a more detailed description of the most widely implemented proprietary architecture—IBM's *Systems Network Architecture (SNA)*. It was introduced in 1974 to provide a framework in which IBM's products could be developed so as to facilitate communication between them. Since that time it has achieved a dominant position in the field of networking, such that by the start of the 1990s, three out of four networks conformed with some aspect of SNA. This penetration is expected to fall, however, as implementations of non-proprietary architectures become available.

Early implementations of SNA nodes provided connections between simple terminals and a single host computer in a star network. This led to the view that SNA was a remote access vehicle whereas an architecture such as OSI provided for connection between peer systems. This distinction no longer holds, if it ever did, as SNA has developed to provide application-to-application communication between a wide variety of systems. The hierarchical control structure of an SNA network has, however, survived although the architecture is developing in the direction of genuine peer-to-peer networking.

SNA, like any other aspect of IT, is rich in new terms and acronyms. This review of SNA begins by introducing some of them.

## 7.2 SNA terminology

SNA identifies certain functions that are necessary or desirable for reliable communication between systems. A component that includes these functions is an *SNA node* and it may be connected to other SNA nodes to form an SNA network. Provision is also made for connecting non-SNA equipment to an SNA network, although such provision is strictly outside the architecture. An SNA node may, of course, contain functions other than those concerned with networking.

It has been suggested previously that there is a case for distinguishing between the lower layer functions of a communications architecture and the upper layer functions. The lower layer functions are present in every node and are responsible for ensuring that messages move from node to node with integrity. They are typified by the X.25 Recommendation or the functions that result in the OSI network service. In SNA they have a special name—*path control*. The path control functions in all the nodes of an SNA network together make up the *path control network*.

Upper-layer functions provide functions to users, be they programs or people, in end nodes. They also have a special name in SNA—*Network Addressable Units (NAUs)*. As the name suggests, they are units (of function) that have network addresses and to which messages can be sent.

There are three types of NAU. The most familiar is the *Logical Unit (LU)*. A LU is a set of upper layer functions, with an address, that provides the facilities needed by users to communicate with other users. An SNA node may contain a number of LUs. Several LU types are defined by the architecture to cater for different types of end-user device.

One of the notable features of SNA is the provision of functions that enable the network nodes to be managed—activated, deactivated, monitored and so on. One of the key elements in SNA network management is the architectural definition of a *Physical Unit (PU)*. A PU is also a set of upper layer functions, with an address to which control messages may be sent. One PU is implemented in every SNA node to enable it to be physically controlled.

A set of LUs and PUs form a *domain*, which is controlled by the third type of NAU, the *System Services Control Point (SSCP)*. There is one SSCP in each control domain that acts as a focal point for connecting users and for management operations within its domain. The SSCP is formally defined to lie within its own domain, which consequently consists of a set of NAUs comprising one SSCP, a number of PUs and a number of LUs. A large network will generally consist of a number of domains in order to share the management load.

The purpose of any data network is to enable users to establish connections to other users and to send messages to each other. In an SNA network, these connections are established and messages exchanged between LUs acting on behalf of users. An LU is often referred to loosely as the *user's port* into the network. An SNA connection between two NAUs is called a *session*. In addition to LU-LU sessions on behalf of users, other sessions are defined for control purposes.

These basic terms are illustrated in Figure 7.1, which shows a network comprising several domains with LU-LU sessions established both between LUs within the same domain (single-domain sessions) and between LUs in different domains (cross-domain sessions). Each domain has its own SSCP and all the NAUs are attached to and connected by the path control network.

# Systems Network Architecture (SNA)

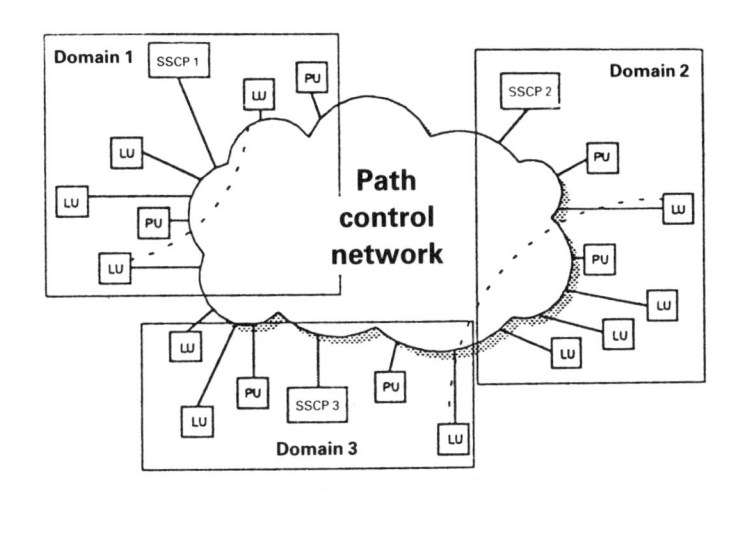

*Figure 7.1  SNA multidomain network*

We have so far described an SNA node as having path control (lower layer) functions and NAU (upper layer) functions without being more specific about the layering. SNA is a layered architecture, in common with X.25 and OSI and others yet to be covered.

The path control functions in SNA consist of the *data link control layer*, and the *path control layer*, equivalent, to layers 2 and 3, respectively, of X.25 or OSI. SNA does not define the physical layer but is prepared to use layer 1 standards from other sources, such as the CCITT.

The SNA NAU is divided into the *transmission control layer*, the *data flow control layer* and an upper layer whose terminology and structure have changed as SNA has developed (discussion of it is postponed until later in this chapter).

Some comparative remarks about X.25, OSI and SNA are appropriate at this point. The SNA path control network performs the same functions as X.25 in delivering messages to a destination identified by the user. Both fulfil this role by defining protocols at each of their respective layers. There is, however, no point in asking a normal SNA path control network to deliver an X.25 packet or an X.25 network to deliver a normal SNA message. Each will be rejected as having a protocol error. There are, however, means of achieving both, which we will describe later—hence the use of the word 'normal'.

Turning to the upper layers, it is tempting to compare the upper layers of OSI with those in an LU. They are, after all, there for the same purpose—to enable users to communicate. However, the temptation

115

was resisted in Chapter 4 and will be resisted here, for a number of reasons.

The OSI reference model is layered not only in its protocols but in its services. For example, it is possible to write an application that makes use of OSI services at any of layers 4 to 7. Such an application must do without or provide for itself the functions of the 'missing' layers. A similar application cannot be written to use an SNA LU.

Although an SNA NAU (and, in particular, an LU) is layered, it is layered for protocol purposes rather than to provide services. The transmission control and data flow control layers of an LU do not provide a progamming interface to the user. It is only at the uppermost layer of an LU, and then only in one (very important) instance, that an LU may be programmed in this sense.

## 7.3 LUs and LU-LU session types

SNA defines an LU as a set of layered functions, outside the path control network but addressable by it, that provides users with a means of accessing the network and using its facilities. The handset performs the same role in a telephone network.

The equipment that users might wish to attach to an SNA network ranges from simple terminals with a keyboard for input and a printer or screen for output to complex mainframe computers. Sessions will be needed between any two such machines or, more precisely, between the LUs that represent the users.

The architecture takes into account the widely differing capabilities of the potential end systems by defining a number of types of LU-LU session. In order to take part in a session of a particular type, a machine needs to incorporate the functions required to support such a session.

SNA nodes were first implemented at a time when networks were used mainly to provide access to a mainframe from remote terminals having keyboard input and printer or screen output. The remote machines were built with the necessary fixed function and were not programmable. Session types were defined in support of such communication. It was, however, recognized that there was, or would be, a need for applications in programmable machines to communicate on behalf of users or become users themselves. Other session types were assigned for this purpose.

LU-LU session types 0 to 7, with the exception of 5, are defined by SNA with type 6 having a number of flavours. Session type 5 was reserved for a use that has never materialized. In this chapter, the focus is on types 0, 2 and 6.2. A session type essentially defines the subset of NAU functions required to support a session of that type.

Session type 2 is defined for communication between an application and a VDU. The IBM 3270 Information Display System was, and largely remains, the workhorse of SNA networking. It communicates with a mainframe application on a type 2 session.

The 3270 is an example of a clustered system in which screens and printers are attached to a control unit that is itself attached to the network. The control unit is the SNA node and contains a PU and a separate LU for each attached device. The LU-LU session is established between the control unit and the application. Communication between the control unit and the display or printer is outside the scope of SNA. It has become customary to refer to a 3270 as '*an LU2*', meaning a device capable of engaging in an LU-LU session of type 2.

With the increasing availability of personal microprocessors, the use of application-to-application communication through a network is becoming the norm. Session types 0 and 6 are defined by SNA for this purpose. The latter has increased in importance to the extent that it is the *only* session type that is likely to be implemented in future SNA nodes. Its importance in the world of SNA is sufficient to warrant a section to itself (see Section 7.10).

A mainframe application may need to communicate with many types of device, ranging from simple terminals to other mainframes. Consequently, it needs access to LUs supporting many or all of the different session types. Manufacturers generally provide operating systems and subsystems that implement the necessary SNA functions. For example, IBM provides the Information Management System (IMS) and Customer Information Control System (CICS).

It is worth noting here that the OSI reference model is designed with application-to-application communication in mind. It thus requires an intelligent device for its implementation and is unsuitable for supporting dumb terminal communication. With the growth in programmable terminals it may be expected to play an increasing role in practical networking. IBM recognizes this and so affords equal status to OSI and LU6.2 protocols in its systems application architecture.

## 7.4 Control sessions

An SNA domain consists of a set of resources (LUs and PUs) controlled by a single SSCP. The SSCP is able to activate a resource so that it can be used, deactivate it in the event of problems occurring, determine its status, monitor its activity and so on. In order to perform these control functions, the SSCP needs to be able to exchange messages with each of the resources for which it is responsible. It is generally prompted to do so by a (human) network operator through an operator interface and command language.

In order for the SSCP to exchange messages with another NAU, a session must exist between them. These sessions are called *control sessions* and comprise SSCP-LU and SSCP-PU sessions. They are established when the network is initialized and remain established while the network is active. The establishment and maintenance of sessions with a substantial number of other NAUs requires processing and storage capacity in the machine in which the SSCP is implemented and is one reason for defining separate domains and sharing the load. The use of domains itself requires an additional session type (the SSCP-SSCP session) to enable cross-domain sessions to be established.

So far four session types have been identified:

- LU-LU sessions for user-to-user communication
- SSCP-LU and SSCP–PU sessions for resource control
- SSCP-SSCP sessions for cross-domain control.

PU-PU sessions are also defined and will be discussed later. LU-PU sessions are not allowed as they imply a facility for a user to send messages to a PU and, hence, exercise control over the physical network.

## 7.5 Session establishment

As mentioned above, control sessions are established during the network initialization process and remain permanently set up, enabling the SSCP to exchange control messages with its dependent resources at any time. User sessions between LUs are established on demand.

LU-LU sessions are established through the SSCP. The process, called session binding in SNA, is somewhat analogous to making a telephone call via the operator. By contrast, OSI and other architectures have the equivalent of direct dialling. This hierarchical dependence on the SSCP is seen as a weakness in SNA. At times when the SSCP is busy, session establishment can take some time. Also, when the SSCP is unavailable, no new sessions can be established.

The normal LU-LU session establishment process is illustrated in Figure 7.2. In order to provide a simple description of the process, some of the control messages that flow during session establishment are omitted from the figure, and from the following description. The originating LU sends a control message (an *INIT request*) to the SSCP on the SSCP-LU session, naming the target LU and including any user data appropriate at this time, such as a user identifier and password. The SSCP has a directory of all its resources, enabling it to convert the name to an address. It sends a control message (a *CINIT request*) to the target LU, which includes the address of the originator. It also includes the somewhat obscurely named *bind image*—information about the originating device that is held by the SSCP.

If it is able and willing to accept the session, the target LU sends a *BIND* request message directly to the originator. The message contains information, derived from the bind image, which will determine the

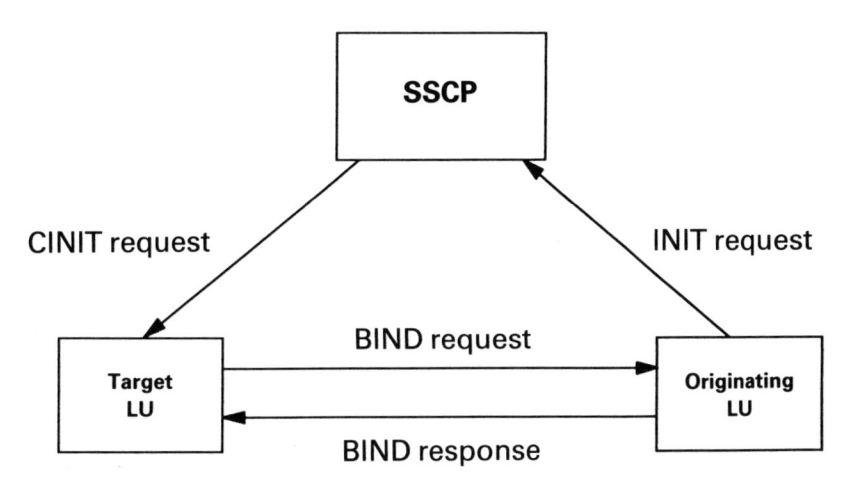

*Figure 7.2  Single-domain session establishment (simplified)*

parameters of the LU-LU session. If the originating LU accepts these parameters it sends a positive *BIND response* to the target LU and the session is established. A certain amount of negotiation of the session parameters is permitted. Failure to agree results in a bind failure. Once the session is established, messages flow directly between the originating and target LUs.

The above description applies when both LUs are in the same domain. If, however, they are in different domains, each is controlled by, and in particular has control sessions with, its own SSCP. Each SSCP holds information, such as addresses and capabilities, about the resources under its control. A modified session establishment procedure is required for cross-domain sessions.

It is highly desirable that this modification should be transparent to the LUs so that each continues to exchange the *same* control messages with its *own* SSCP. The cross-domain establishment procedure is shown (simplified) in Figure 7.3. The difference between this and the single-domain case is that the SSCP-SSCP session is used to enable the originating LU's SSCP to inform the destination LU's SSCP that a session has been requested.

## 7.6 Some more terminology

Some further terms, specific to SNA, are now introduced. These enable us to describe the addressing and routeing structure of an SNA network. Within an SNA domain, there are various types of node. One in particular—the node containing the SSCP—has the special function of providing the focal point for controlling the domain. Other nodes act as switches to enable a physical path to be established between pairs of NAUs when a session is requested. Yet other nodes provide physical attachment points for users.

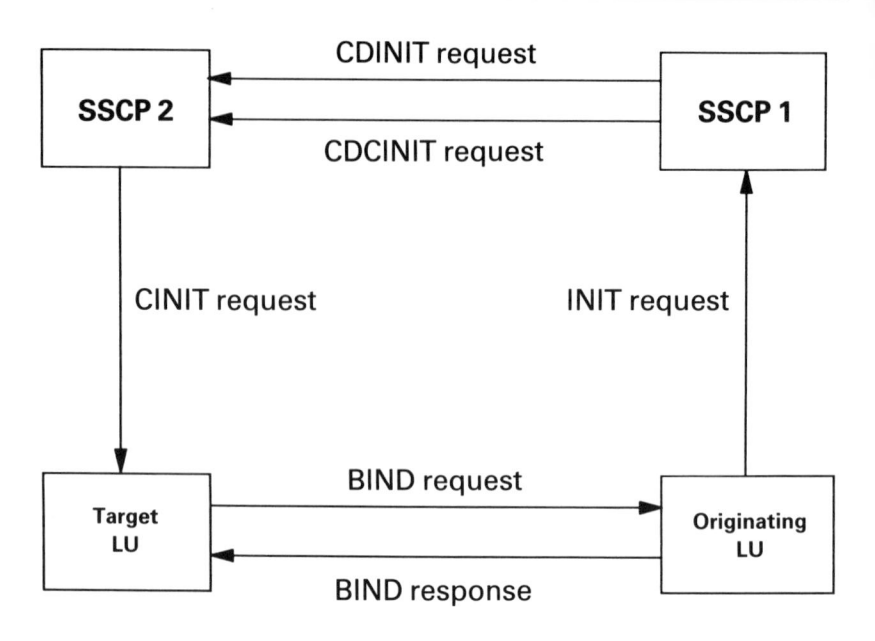

*Figure 7.3  Cross-domain session establishment (simplified)*

The different node types are distinguished by defining different PU types. PU types 1, 2 and 2.1 represent SNA nodes that provide for the connection of one or more terminals, such as displays or printers, to the network. These PUs are sometimes called *peripheral nodes*.

The *PU type 4 (or PU4)* is a switching node whose main role is to route a message to the next node and ultimately to its destination. A *PU type 5* is a switching node that also contains the SSCP function. Two types of PU4 are provided. A switch that is connected only to other switches is an *intermediate node* as it appears in the network topology at an intermediate point on the path through the path control network. A switch to which PU types 1, 2 or 2.1 may be connected and that therefore appears at the boundary of the network is a *boundary node*.

Remember that the PUs are the units of SNA upper-layer functions that enable the SSCP to exercise its control function over the physical network. The different PU types correspond to the different types of 'boxes' that make up an SNA network. By contrast, the LUs are units of function that enable users to access the network. These functions are also implemented in the network nodes.

A domain of an SNA network is divided into a number of *subareas*, each with a unique numerical address. A subarea consists of a switch (a PU4 or PU5), together with the peripheral nodes, if any, attached to it. This division is made for addressing purposes.

The address of an SNA NAU consists of two numbers: the subarea address and the element address. The subarea address identifies the subarea that contains the NAU and the element address identifies the particular NAU within the subarea. The scheme is analogous to the use of area codes and local numbers to identify a particular telephone. Subareas are connected by *Transmission Groups (TGs)*, where a TG consists of one or more physical links between the subarea nodes. The path control functions of SNA enable a multilink TG to be treated as a single link. Each TG attached to a subarea node has a number.

A session between two NAUs is established to enable messages to flow between them. Each session is allocated to a particular route through the network. The route is described in two ways. The *Virtual Route (VR)* is a logical connection between the first subarea on the route and the last subarea. The concept of a virtual route allows various characteristics of the route, such as throughput, response time, priority or security, to be specified without specifying the route explicitly. The *Explicit Route (ER)* is the sequence of subareas and transmission groups that make up the physical route. Every virtual route is mapped onto a specific explicit route. The VRs and ERs are also numbered.

A message destined for an SNA NAU must, as always, contain the address of the destination. It also contains the address of the origin. The address consists of two parts, a subarea address and an element address. The former contains the number of the subarea to which the destination NAU is directly attached. The latter contains the number allocated to the destination NAU within that subarea. The routeing of messages through the network by the subarea switches is achieved by examining the destination subarea number. For example, a message destined for subarea 5 is examined by each switch on its route. All switches other than number 5 forward it to the next node by reference to routeing tables. At switch number 5, the element address is used to route the message to the destination NAU. At this point the address changes to a simpler form. Figures 7.4 and 7.5 illustrate the new terms introduced here.

## 7.7 The path control network

In this section, the role of the path control network is considered. Unlike some of the SNA terminology, its name suggests its role—to control paths through the network in order to enable messages passed to the network to be routed to the correct destination. This role is similar to that performed by the lower layer functions in the other network architectures that have been described. It may be compared, but with care, with an X.25 network.

A packet presented at the interface to an X.25 network will be delivered to the destination DTE. The corresponding unit of information in SNA is called a *Path Information Unit (PIU)*. In each case, control information is appended to the message, in the packet header in the X.25 case

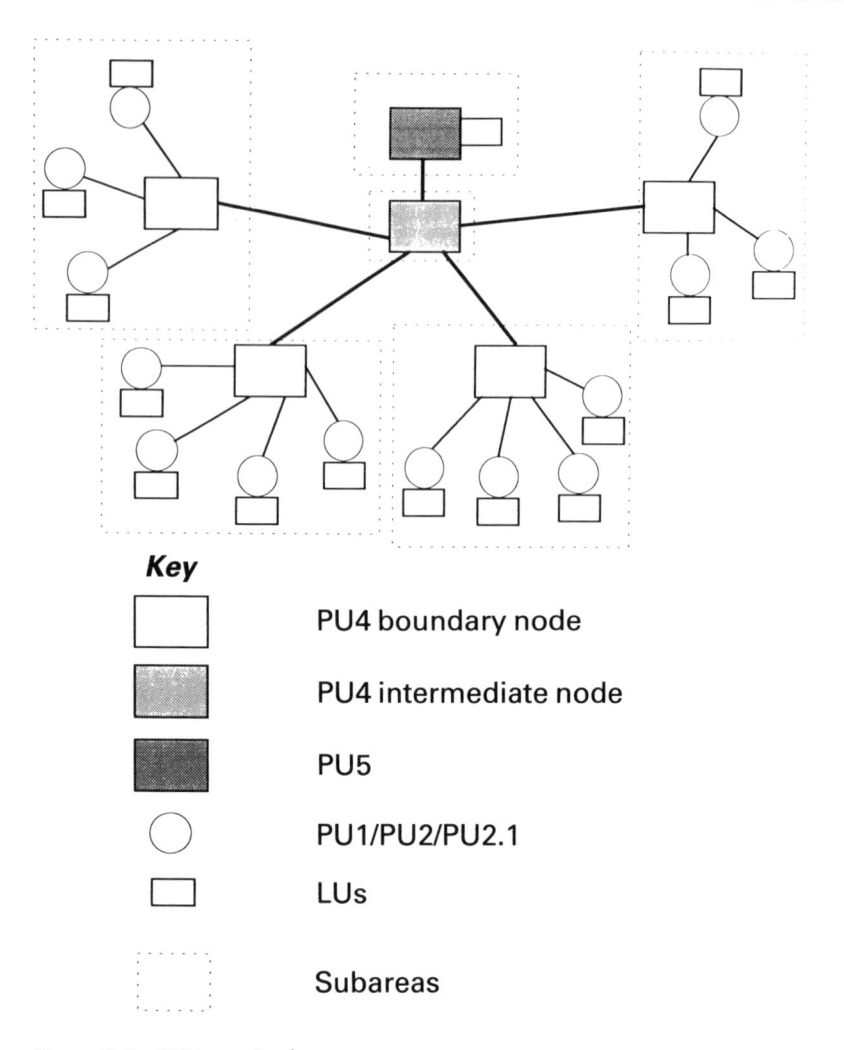

*Figure 7.4 SNA terminology*

and in the *transmission header* in the SNA case. The lower layer functions that use this information must be present in every node on the route to the destination.

Some major differences between X.25 and SNA must be noted here. It has been stressed previously that the X.25 Recommendation governs only the interface between DTE and DCE and *not* the internal functioning of the network. The SNA path control network functions, on the other hand, are present in *every* node. In the X.25 case it is often possible to separate physically, as well as logically, the lower layer functions, but this is not possible in an SNA network where the networking functions, although logically distinct, are not physically

# Systems Network Architecture (SNA)

**Key**

☐ Subarea

◯ NAU

⊏══⊐ Virtual Route

──▶ Explicit Route

◀┄┄┄▶ Session

═⊖═ Transmission Group

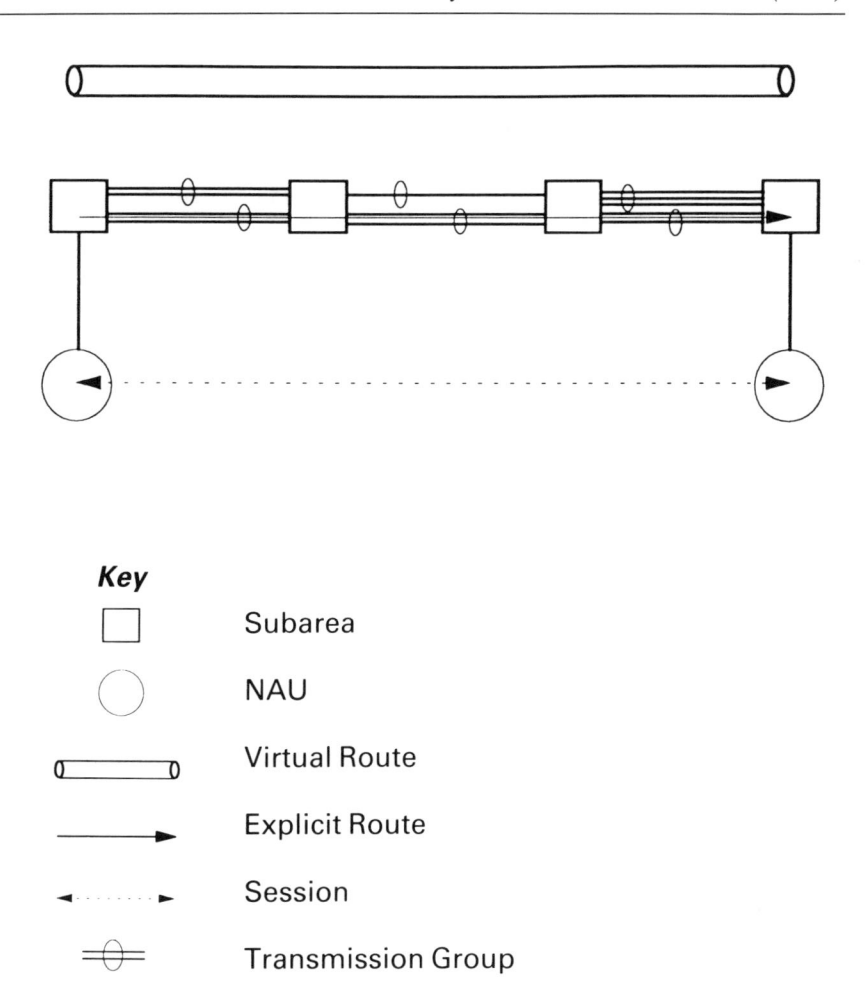

*Figure 7.5  Sessions and routes*

separable from the nodes in which they are implemented.

The SNA path control network consists of the data link control layer and the path control layer. SNA does not define the physical layer, but relies on CCITT Recommendations. The protocol at the data link layer is *Synchronous Data Link Control (SDLC)*, a variant of *High Level Data Link Control (HDLC)*. (HDLC is reviewed in some detail in Chapter 10 and so is not discussed here to avoid repetition). Rather, the focus is on the third layer, which is unique to SNA and where many of its strengths, and some of its weaknesses, lie. The path control layer contains three sublayers. They are, from lowest to highest, *transmission group control, explicit route control* and *virtual route control*.

**Transmission Group control**

A *Transmission Group (TG)* is a group of physical circuits between two subarea nodes that may be treated as one logical circuit. PIUs allocated to this TG may travel along any of the physical circuits. This facility improves the throughput and reliability of the TG but at the cost of some complexity in TG control.

TG control manages a queue of PIUs awaiting transmission to the next node. The queue is served by the one or more physical circuits that make up the transmission group. Each physical circuit is subject to SDLC data link control. The transmission vehicle is an SDLC frame with the PIUs carried as data in I-frames. The data link layer provides a service to TG control that ensures error-free delivery to the next node.

Several PIUs may be carried in one frame and one of the functions of TG control is to perform the blocking and unblocking. The TG may consist of physical circuits with different speeds or different error rates and PIUs may arrive out of sequence. Another function of TG control is to restore the sequence. Addresses in the subarea-to-subarea network have a different format to those in the subarea-to-element network. TG control is responsible for the format conversion.

**Explicit Route control**

An *Explicit Route (ER)* consists of an ordered set of subareas and TGs that represent the physical path between the origin subarea and the destination subarea. When a session is established, it is allocated (by the SSCP) to a particular virtual route (VR) as information regarding the characteristics of the route (secure, low response and so on) is associated with a VR. VRs are predefined when the network is configured. At the same time, each VR is mapped onto a specific ER. The ER number is carried in the transmission header of each PIU flowing on the session.

When a PIU arrives at a subarea node that is not its destination, it is the job of ER control to determine the next node and the appropriate TG and pass the PIU back to TG control for onward transmission. ER control thus performs the basic routeing function normally associated with the network layer or its equivalent.

Routeing in SNA is deterministic, that is it works according to predefined routeing tables. ER control uses the destination and ER number fields in the transmission header to determine the next subarea and the correct TG. In a large network, the definition of routeing tables is a complicated task.

**Virtual Route control**

The *Virtual Route (VR)* is a logical 'pipe' between origin and destination subareas. The pipe may be a 'fat pipe' for high throughput, it may be a 'low-delay pipe' for interactive sessions or a 'secure pipe' for data protection. The mapping of the VR onto an appropriate ER reflects the particular requirements of the pipe. The VR control sublayer of the path control network is responsible for functions that apply at the VR level.

Flow control is called *pacing* in SNA. It occurs at two levels: for a session and for a VR. VR pacing controls the flow between the end subareas of a route, that is through the path control network. Session-level pacing controls the flow between NAUs and is an upper-level function (this is discussed further later).

VR pacing uses a window technique similar to that used in HDLC/SDLC. The pacing window is the number of PIUs that may be sent down the pipe before an acknowledgement is received from the other end. An acknowledgement, or pacing response, consists only of a transmission header. Each VR is defined with minimum and maximum pacing window sizes. At the start of a session, the pacing window is set to the minimum value. It may be increased, subsequently, by setting a bit (the *change window indicator*) to 0 in the transmission header. If a node on the route is congested, it changes the setting of the indicator to indicate that the window should not be opened. A similar mechanism allows the pacing window to be closed.

## 7.8 SNA messages

The message generated by one NAU and sent to another via the path control network is either a request or a response to a request. SNA uses the term *Request/Response Unit (RU)* to refer to this message. Before passing the RU to the path control network for transmission to its destination, the origin NAU adds a *Request/Response Header (RH)* that contains protocol control information used by the upper layer functions that make up the NAUs. The message then becomes a *Basic Information Unit (BIU)*. The path control layer also needs information to play its role of end-to-end routeing and flow control. This information is carried in a transmission header added to the BIU resulting in a *Path Information Unit (PIU)*. A large BIU may be broken down into smaller units (segmented) for transmission through the path control network. One or more PIUs are carried from node to node in SDLC frames, with the SDLC protocol ensuring controlled and error-free transmission from node to node. The relationship between these messages is shown in Figure 7.6.

To illustrate SNA's use of protocol control information some of the fields in the transmission header of a PIU are examined as it moves through the path control network. The header is shown in Figure 7.7, but a full description is beyond the remit of this book.

The format of the transmission header changes as the PIU moves from the origin NAU to the destination NAU. In particular, it changes at the boundary subarea. Much of the information needed to control the PIU as it moves along the route is no longer needed. The transmission header becomes much simpler for the last leg to the destination element. Figure 7.7 shows a format 4 transmission header used between subarea nodes. The format identifier (FID) defines the type of header and the header in Figure 7.7 is known as a FID4 header.

```
┌─────┬──────────────────────────────┐
│ FMH │                              │
└─────┴──────────────────────────────┘
                 RU


┌────┬──────────────────────────────────┐
│ RH │              RU                  │
└────┴──────────────────────────────────┘
◄──────────────── BIU ─────────────────►


┌────┬────┬────────────────────────────┐
│ TH │ RH │           RU               │
└────┴────┴────────────────────────────┘
◄──────────────── PIU ─────────────────►


┌────┬──────┬──────┬──────┬────┐
│ LH │ PIU  │ PIU  │ PIU  │ LT │
└────┴──────┴──────┴──────┴────┘
◄──────────── BTU ─────────────►
```

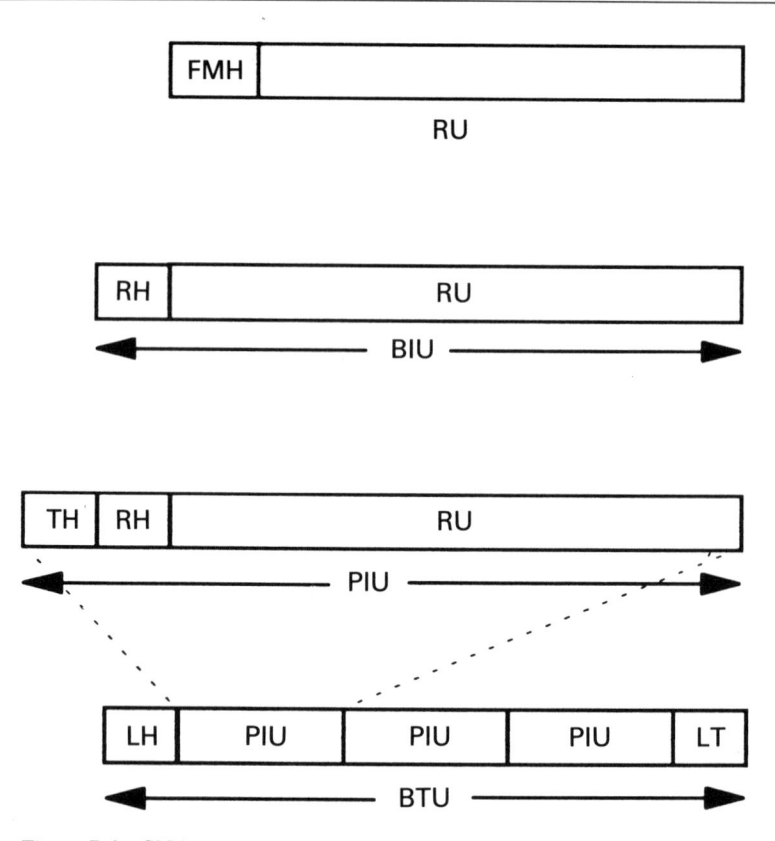

*Figure 7.6   SNA messages*

The header contains the origin and destination addresses, each consisting of a subarea number (32 bits) and an element number (16 bits). It also contains the number (*ERN*) of the explicit route to which the session has been assigned. The destination address and the ERN are used at each subarea node to determine, by reference to the node's routeing table, the next node on the route and the transmission group by which it is reached.

The 2-bit *Mapping Field (MF)* enables first, middle and last segments of a BIU to be distinguished and reassembled by virtual route control at the destination. The data count field is used to handle situations where several PIUs have been blocked into one BTU. It contains the length of each PIU, enabling the next one to be located.

A number of flags (single-bit indicators) are carried by the header to provide VR pacing—the mechanism controlling the flow of PIUs along the logical connection between the boundary subareas. The mechanism depends on a pacing window that defines the number of PIUs which may be sent by the originating subarea before waiting for an acknowledgement from the destination. The window may be adjusted between defined limits to enable congestion along the route to be handled.

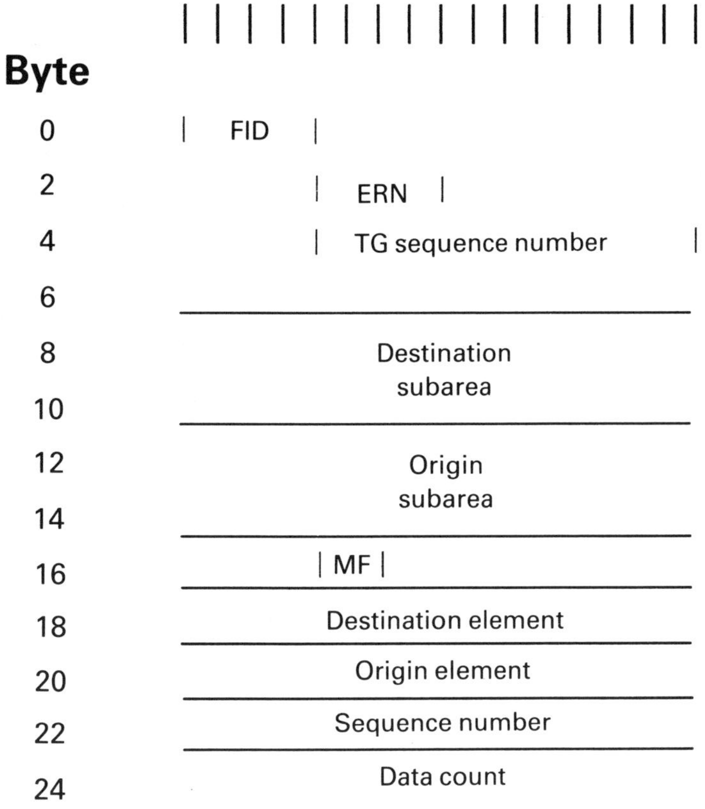

# Systems Network Architecture (SNA)

```
Byte
 0     |  FID  |
 2              |  ERN  |
 4              |  TG sequence number           |
 6     _____
 8                    Destination
10                      subarea
       _____
12                       Origin
14                      subarea
       _____
16                     | MF |
       _____
18                 Destination element
       _____
20                   Origin element
       _____
22                  Sequence number
       _____
24                    Data count
```

*Figure 7.7   FID4 transmission header*

The VR control elements at each end of the VR keep a pacing count. This is initially set to the minimum value of the pacing window and is decremented each time a PIU is sent. If it reaches 0 before a pacing response is received, transmission is suspended and resumed when the pacing response is received. The 'windowfull' of PIUs sent while the window is open constitutes a pacing group.

The first PIU of a pacing group has a flag (the *pacing request indicator*) set to one to indicate that a pacing response is expected if the flow of PIUs is to be maintained. A pacing response is a PIU with no BIU, that is a message consisting only of a transmission header. A further flag (the *pacing response indicator*) is set to one in this header to indicate that the receiver can cope with another pacing group.

Maximum throughput is achieved on the VR when the pacing count is at its maximum rather than its minimum value. Each time a PIU is sent, VR control sets a flag (the *change window indicator*) to 0 to indicate its willingness to send as many PIUs as possible before waiting. If this indicator is still set to 0 when the PIU reaches its destination, a flag (the *change window reply indicator*) is set to 0 in the pacing response to indicate that the pacing window may be increased (by 1) up to its maximum value. Any node along the route that detects congestion by, for example, observing excessive queue lengths, resets the change window indicator to 1. This is reflected in the setting of the change window reply indicator in the pacing response with the result that the pacing window is closed (decremented by 1) until the congestion has cleared.

The pacing mechanism in SNA illustrates the importance of individual bits in protocol control information and the role of lower-layer protocols in ensuring that bits are not corrupted. This observation is, of course, not confined to SNA.

A number of fields in a FID4 header are concerned with ensuring that messages arrive in the sequence in which they were sent. Sequence control is applied at three levels: TG, VR and session. A TG connecting two subareas may consist of several physical links. TG control will schedule a PIU for transmission on any physical link that is available. Different link speeds, different PIU sizes or link errors with subsequent retransmission may result in PIUs arriving out of sequence. Each PIU is assigned a sequence number that is carried in the transmission header. PIUs arriving out of sequence are held by TG control until the sequence can be restored.

VR control in the nodes at each end of a VR also maintains a count of the number of PIUs sent and received on the route. The send count is copied into the transmission header and compared at the destination with the receive count. If these do not match, the PIU is discarded. A third sequence number field is passed to the path control network by the transmission control layer and used by the LUs to maintain sequences across the session.

In this and the previous sections the SNA path control network and the path control protocol embodied in the transmission header have been described. The purpose of this network is to transmit messages between network addressable units. Now let us look at the functions that these units provide.

## 7.9 The upper layers of an SNA node

Many people would take the view that when a network has delivered a message from source to destination without error it has done its job. Let us consider the process of establishing a connection between source and destination in three network architectures with which we now have some familiarity.

An X.25 DTE will build a call request packet on behalf of the source and the destination DTE will deliver it as an incoming call packet. It is up to the user (some function above the packet layer of X.25) to decide how to respond. This function is not defined by X.25. Similarly, the OSI network service will accept an N-Connect request from the service user at the source and present an N-Connect indication to the service user at the destination. The service user is the OSI transport layer, if it is available. If not, it is some function outside the scope of the OSI model. In both the X.25 and OSI cases, the user of the layer 3 service may be an application. Three layers only are required for communication. The reliability of this communication is governed by the reliability of the three-layer network. Any deficiencies in quality must be made up by the using applications.

SNA takes a different view. The architecture defines functions above the path control layer and SNA nodes implement them, in various forms and subsets, whether the user likes it or not. Users of an SNA network are represented by LUs and sessions are established between LUs at the request of one user and with the agreement of the other. The process of session establishment (described in Section 7.5) is performed by the LUs, in conjunction with the SSCP, acting on behalf of users.

This description of connection or session establishment is an example of upper layers providing functions that would otherwise be left to the discretion of the user. In X.25 no such functions are defined, in OSI they are defined but not necessarily used and in SNA they are mandatory. We now go on to examine the purpose of these mandatory SNA functions that collectively constitute a NAU.

## Transmission control

The lowest functional layer in a NAU is the transmission control layer, which consists of two sets of functions: the connection point manager and session control components. For each session in which the NAU is engaged, there are logically distinct instances of these two components. Together they make up the *Transmission Control Element (TCE)* for that session.

As indicated in Section 7.8 the basic message unit exchanged between NAUs is a *Request/Response Unit (RU)*. An RU may originate in or be destined for the session control component of the TCE or one of the upper layers of a NAU. All outgoing and incoming RUs flow through the connection point manager, which acts as the focal point for session traffic.

The connection point manager is responsible for building and checking the Request/Response Header (RH), routing RUs to the appropriate destination within the NAU, maintaining message sequence, controlling session-level pacing and encrypting or decrypting data if required.

A Request Header is shown in Figure 7.8. The Response Header is similar with some indicators omitted. The *Request/Response Indicator (RI)* indicates whether the RU is a request or response. The 2-bit category field determines the destination of the RU—session control, function management, data flow control or network control (a component of the transmission control layer present only in PUs). The three

```
                |   |   |   |   |   |   |   |   |
Byte

0        RI  RU CAT   u   FI SDI BCI ECI
1        DR1   u DR2 ERI   u    u QRI  PI
2        BBI EBI CDI   u CSI EDI PDI   u
```

**Key**

| | |
|---|---|
| RI | Request/Response Indicator |
| RU CAT | Request/Response Unit/Category |
| FI | Format Indicator |
| SDI | Sense Data Indicator |
| BCI | Begin Chain Indicator |
| ECI | End Chain Indicator |
| DR1 | Definite Response Indicator |
| DR2 | Definite Response Indicator |
| ERI | Exception Response Indicator |
| QRI | Queued Response Indicator |
| PI | Pacing Indicator |
| BBI | Begin Bracket Indicator |
| EBI | End Bracket Indicator |
| CDI | Change Direction Indicator |
| CSI | Code Selection Indicator |
| EDI | Enciphered Data Indicator |
| PDI | Padded Data Indicator |
| u | Unused |

*Figure 7.8  Request header*

response indicators indicate the type of response required for this RU—none, only if an error is detected or always.

The *Enciphered Data Indicator (EDI)* is set if the RU is encrypted. Data is enciphered in 8-byte blocks and the *Padded Data Indicator (PDI)* is set if it has been padded to an integral multiple of 8 bytes. Encryption is performed according to the *Data Encryption Standard (DES) algorithm*. (Some other protocol indicators are described later).

RUs have associated sequence numbers that are assigned by data flow control (the layer above transmission control) but checked by the receiving connection point manager. Session pacing is also the responsibility of the connection point manager. The mechanism is similar to that used at the VR level, but a fixed window is used. The pacing indicator is set in the RH of the first request of a pacing group. It is set in a response to indicate that another pacing group may be released by the connection point manager.

The other component of a TCE is session control. Its primary responsibility is to initiate and terminate sessions. The architecture defines a set of control RUs for this purpose. Control RUs are used to activate and deactivate SSCP-LU and SSCP-PU sessions and to bind and unbind LU-LU sessions. They are used to start and stop the flow of data RUs in a session and to enable recovery from errors, particularly loss of sequence.

In order to participate in a session, a NAU needs a TCE specifically for that session. What happens when a session initiation command is received? There is no TCE to handle the command as the session does not yet exist. The answer is that a special component of transmission control, common session control, is invoked. It recognizes the commands ACTPU (to activate an SSCP-PU session), ACTLU (to activate an SSCP–LU) session and BIND (to activate an LU-LU) session. On receipt of these commands, common session control will establish a TCE for the session.

## Data flow control

In previous sections the mechanisms for controlling the rate at which data flows on a link between two nodes, on a VR or on a session, have been described. The data flow control functional layer in an SNA NAU is not concerned with the rate of flow; it is concerned with the form and discipline of the flow between two NAUs.

The simplest form of control provided at this layer enables the direction of flow to be controlled. A session may be established in one of three send/receive modes. Full-duplex mode enables requests and responses to flow in both directions simultaneously. Half-duplex mode only allows transmission in one direction at any one time and has two flavours. Half-duplex flip/flop puts the onus on the sender to reverse the direction of flow by setting the *Change Direction Indicator (CDI)* in the RH. Half-duplex contention mode allows either NAU to send, with one NAU designated (at session establishment) as the winner in the event of a contention. Note that these control modes are not related to the ability of network links to operate in duplex or half-duplex fashion.

It is sometimes desirable to treat a series of requests in one direction as a single unit, although they are transmitted separately. The data flow control protocol in SNA allows for several RUs to be chained together. Any response then relates to the chain as a whole rather than to individual RUs. Furthermore, error recovery operates on the chain as a single unit. The position of an RU in a chain is indicated by two bits in the RH—the *Begin Chain Indicator (BCI)* and the *End Chain Indicator (ECI)*. If both are on, the RU is the only one in the chain.

A further feature of the protocol at this layer enables the sender to determine the type of response to a chain of RUs. A definite response chain requires a *positive response* when the last RU in the chain has been successfully received and an *exception response* if the chain is broken. An exception response chain dispenses with the positive response. A no response chain does not require a response of any kind.

The use of chains and response control enables broken chains to be purged and recovery action applied to the chain as a whole. It may be necessary to apply recovery not just to a unidirectional chain but to a set of bidirectional requests and responses that together constitute a transaction which must be completed satisfactorily or purged. The appropriate protocol is the bracket protocol controlled by *Begin Bracket* and *End Bracket Indicators (BBI* and *EBI)* in the RH. Once a bracket is started, only RUs that belong to the bracket may be sent, preventing other RUs from interfering with the transaction.

The data flow control functions in a NAU are responsible for all of these control mechanisms. In addition, the layer is provided with a set of control commands. Examples are Quiesce at End of Chain (QEC—a request to suspend data transmission), Shut Down the transmission prior to session termination (SHUTD) or terminate a chain that is incomplete due to error (CANCEL).

## Function management

A description of the uppermost layer of an SNA NAU raises a slight problem in that the functional components of the layer have changed as the architecture has evolved. Furthermore, the terms used to refer to these components have also changed. This is particularly true of the most important type of logical unit, LU6.2. A description of this type is given in the next section. In this section, the architecture of the upper layer prior to the development of LU6.2 is described.

The formal name of the layer is NAU services, although it is often called the function management layer. It contains two types of function: function management data services and NAU services managers. Other terms used are end-user services, session presentation services, session network services and application-to-application services. The reader may begin to understand the slight problem referred to earlier. For the moment the term function management will be used to refer to this layer.

In discussing the connection point manager in the transmission control layer it was mentioned that it routes an incoming RU to one of four destinations within the NAU as determined by the category field in the RH. The possible destinations are session control and network control within the transmission control layer, the data flow control layer and the function management layer. Let us approach the function management layer by means of the messages that are destined for it.

There are two types of message that originate in and are routed to the function management layer: messages used for control purposes and messages that contain user data. The control messages (more in this layer than in the lower layers of the NAU) are handled by the network services component of the function management layer. End-user messages are handled by the end-user services component.

In Section 7.4 five types of session were described that may exist between NAUs in an SNA network. Four of them (SSCP-LU, SSCP–PU,

SSCP-SSCP and PU-PU) are for control purposes and carry control messages. Network services handles control messages routed by the connection point manager to the function management layer and these are examined first.

There are three categories—session services, configuration services and management services (sometimes called maintenance and management services). They are present in every NAU and form a distributed control system centred on the SSCP. Each has a defined set of control RUs that it sends or receives. The network services in LUs and PUs may be thought of as the local agents of the SSCP.

Session services provides functions and commands for establishing LU-LU sessions. Session establishment was outlined in Section 7.5 and Figures 7.3 (single domain) and 7.4 (cross domain). The INIT-SELF, CINIT, CDINIT, CDCINIT and SST commands are all drawn from the session services repertoire and processed by the network services functions in the SSCPs and LUs involved in the process.

Configuration services enable an SSCP to control the physical resources (the PUs and the links between them) in its domain. Included in the command repertoire are commands to activate/deactivate links, to download a control program to a remote node, dump storage at a node and transfer the dump to the SSCP.

Management services enable the network to be managed dynamically from the SSCP. Facilities include activating traces, displaying storage, executing tests and recording and retrieving maintenance statistics. Again a set of commands is provided by the architecture. A recent development has defined a special RU—the network management vector transport RU—to enable a number of management functions to be activated by a single message.

So far in this section the three layers that make up an SNA NAU have been discussed largely in terms of their control functions, which enable the network to be activated and managed and sessions to be established between users. The establishment of LU-LU sessions and the flow of messages on them is, of course, the purpose of the network. The control functions are provided to assist in fulfilling this purpose reliably. Finally let us look at the Request Units that are sent and received by users on LU-LU sessions.

These RUs are handled by the end-user services functions in the function management layer. The first thing to note is that these services depend on the type of session whereas network services (session, configuration and management) do not depend on the type, or indeed the existence, of LU-LU sessions.

The simplest functions in end-user services are those concerned with the layout of the data carried in an RU when it is presented to the user on a display screen or on paper from a printer. These functions are the session presentation services. The destination and presentation of the data in an RU are controlled by a combination of data stream selection, header information and string control bytes.

The data stream determines the way data and control information is coded into a bit string. SNA uses a number of streams. The 3270 data stream (defined before SNA) is used in session types 2 and 3 (and may be used in types 0 and 6) to control the appearance of data on a screen. It contains codes embedded in the data that control such attributes as position, highlighting and colour. The SNA data stream is used in session types 2 and 4 (it may also be used in types 0 and 6) and intermixes control codes with the data to provide for formatting operations such as spacing, tabs and new lines. The 5250 data stream is used in type 7 sessions with devices of the IBM 5250 family and is similar to the 3270 stream.

The RU may include a *Function Management Header (FMH)* preceding the user data. It will come as no surprise to learn that there are several types of FMH. Different FMHs are used for different session types that involve a choice between several possible destinations for the RU or where the recipient is an application program. They are consequently used for session types 1, 4 and 6. Types 2, 3 and 7 do not require FMHs as there is a single destination and formatting is defined by the data stream. In session type 0, the function management protocol is user defined.

The three layers of an SNA NAU have now been detailed—transmission control, data flow control and function management. Subsets of functions from each of these layers are involved whenever the NAU is in session with another NAU. This group of functions, drawn from each of the three layers in a NAU, is called a *half session*. A session may be thought of as two associated half sessions, one in each NAU, coupled via the path control network.

The choice of functions to make up a half session is not made arbitrarily. Specific subsets are defined by the architecture for each layer. These subsets are numbered and called *profiles*. The *Presentation Services (PS)* profile defines session presentation services functions. PS profiles numbered 0, 1, 2, 3, 4, 6 and 6.2 are defined. This is the origin of the LU numbering scheme. The *Transmission Services (TS)* profile defines functions in the transmission control layer. TS profiles numbered 1, 2, 3, 4, 5, 7 and 17 are currently defined. The *Function Management (FM)* profile defines the operation of the data flow control layer and some aspects of the function management layer. FM profiles numbered 0, 2, 3, 4, 5, 6, 17, 18 and 19 are in use.

The choice of profiles to be used for a session is made when the session is established. The session control request unit, ACTLU/ACTPU for establishing SSCP-LU/PU sessions or BIND for establishing LU-LU sessions, contains the numbers of the profiles to be used. These numbers essentially determine the protocols to be used in the upper layers and, hence, whether the NAUs can successfully communicate.

An LU type is defined in terms of its PS, TS and FM profiles. For example, LU2 has PS profile 2, TS profile 3 and FM profile 3. The functions associated with these profiles must be supported by both partner implementations for an LU-LU session type 2 to be established. Subsets are also defined in the layers that constitute the path control network. They are expressed by the format of the transmission header and give rise to the different types of PU (PU1, PU2, PU2.1, PU4 and PU5).

## 7.10 Application-to-application communication and LU6.2

SNA was originally defined in the late 1960s and early 1970s at a time when networks were used to enable users to access remote applications from simple terminals. A requirement for applications to communicate with each other developed as networking became more sophisticated and equipment more powerful. This requirement was reinforced by the development of microprocessors and the explosive growth of applications to run on them. The distribution of processing between a number of machines became possible and the need for them to communicate in an application-to-application sense followed. Together with this is a need for the developer of a communicating application to be able to call on the services of a communications system with the same ease as calling on a local file management system.

The LU types originally defined for SNA, and their implementations in various node types, were not suitable for application development and communication. They were aimed at dumb terminal to mainframe application communication and the interface to the telecommunications access method required the programmer to have a high degree of understanding of the architecture. The architecture was, however, sufficiently flexible to allow application-to-application communication to be added within its existing framework.

In considering the additions to the architecture necessary to support communication between applications, it becomes apparent that the layer most likely to be affected is the one nearest to the user—the function management layer. Receiving data from, or presenting data to, an application program, might be expected to differ from receiving data from a keyboard or presenting it on a display screen or printer. The distribution of a transaction between a number of applications might be expected to differ from the processing of a transaction by a single application.

In the simpler types of LU-LU session (types 1, 2 and 3), used for terminal-to-application communication, there is master–slave relationship between the application and the terminal. A peer relationship is more suitable to application-to-application communication. An early form of peer-to-peer communication was provided by LU4, but the development by IBM of full application-to-application capability derives from LU6 and, in particular, the variant known as LU6.2. It is on this type that all developments of SNA in the 1980s and beyond are based.

The architectural vehicles for this development are easily identified. They are essentially the FM profile, which determines the functions of the data flow control and function management layers, and the FM headers, which carry protocol control information between the session partners and the control RUs. At an architectural level, most of the work necessary to add program-to-program communication to SNA lies in the definition of new instances of these architectural building blocks. The work to implement these functions in SNA products is far from simple.

The basic function of LU6.2 is to support communication between applications. These applications are referred to as *transaction programs*. Transaction programs communicate on conversations that take place over a session between the supporting LUs. Once a session is established between the LUs, it may be used for a number of conversations, one after the other, between the same pair or different pairs of transaction programs. All the requests and responses that flow during a conversation are grouped together as a bracket.

A notable feature of LU6.2 is the inclusion in its definition of a set of verbs that enable the writer of a transaction program to request services from the LU. This verb set is analogous to the definition of a set of OSI service primitives. Indeed, the service provided to an application by the LU6.2 verb set is very close to the service provided by the OSI transaction processing service. This is the only instance of an application programming interface incorporated in the architecture. Another feature of LU6.2 is the definition of a basic and mandatory subset of verbs and several optional subsets. OSI adopts a similar approach through its functional units.

The basic set of verbs enables a transaction program to:

- allocate (start) and deallocate (end) a conversation
- send and receive data
- request and provide confirmation that messages have been received successfully
- request a partner to change from send to receive state in order to change the direction of the conversation
- indicate to a partner that an error has been detected.

These are sufficient for many instances of application-to-application communication. LU6.2, however, is designed to support distributed processing situations in which a transaction involves many applications and multiple conversations. The *syncpoint* option provides application programmers with a mechanism that keeps track of all changes to protected resources such as databases. A new set of services—the syncpoint services—is required in the upper layer of the LU and a logfile in which changes are recorded.

The mechanism is controlled by the application programmer through the *SYNCPT* and *BACKOUT* verbs. One of the transaction programs initiates synchronization by issuing the *SYNCPT* verb. The other programs involved in the transaction act as agents and are informed that a checkpoint has been initiated via a return code from the *RECEIVE-AND-WAIT* verb. Each program that receives such a return code itself issues a *SYNCPT* request. The result is that the resource managers in each of the LUs involved in the transaction record the state of protected resources. If a program is unable to complete its part in the transaction, it issues the BACKOUT verb rather than SYNCPT and restores the state of its resources to the previous checkpoint. This backing out process percolates through the set of cooperating transaction programs and the system is restored to a consistent state. Although the mechanism is simple from the point of view of the application programmer, as it should be, it involves a complex exchange of control messages between the participating LUs.

The OSI reference model and SNA have often been described as taking quite different approaches to networking. OSI is, and always has been, about the interconnection of peer systems able to support application programs. Early implementations of SNA provided for the connection of terminals to mainframe applications in order to meet user requirements as perceived by IBM at the time. Architecturally, however, SNA was always positioned to provide application-to-application communication when the need (again as perceived by IBM) arose. The outcome was the architectural definition of LU6.2, its implementation in a wide range of products from IBM and other manufacturers and its adoption by IBM as its main networking vehicle. The similarity between the OSI transaction processing service and protocol and the LU6.2 verb set and protocol is a major milestone along the road to system interoperability.

Having established an SNA platform for application-to-application communication, IBM defined, during the 1980s, a number of application-level protocols based on this platform. The *Document Interchange Architecture (DIA)* defines a protocol for the transmission of documents between the nodes of an office system. A related architecture, the *Document Content Architecture (DCA)*, although not strictly concerned with communication, enables a document to be described and presented to a user. It operates at two levels. One is *Revisable Form Text (RFT)*, which, in addition to the text itself, contains descriptions of the text as it would appear on paper or on screen. It includes information such as typeface, page size, margins and tab settings. Both the text and the descriptive contents of an RFT document can be edited. The other is *Final Form Text (FFT)*, which consists of the text and embedded control characters that, when sent to a particular output medium controller, result in a formatted display of the document. The combination of DCA and DIA enables a document to be created, edited, distributed and presented to a user. The underlying communications vehicle is LU6.2.

In order for two users to communicate across an SNA network, the LUs that support them must be in session. This imposes an unacceptable constraint on office systems that should enable a recipient to receive a document asynchronously. The *SNA Distribution Services (SNADS)* provide this capability. A SNADS network consists of a number of transaction programs, called *Distribution Service Units (DSUs)*, that are connected by LU6.2 conversations. These DSUs are transaction programs that are part of an LU. Such built-in transaction programs are called service transaction programs and are analogous to the Specific Application Service Elements (SASE) in the OSI application layer. They provide a specific service to application programs that, in the case of DSUs, is the service of store-and-forward document distribution.

## 7.11 Peer-to-peer networking in SNA

One of the criticisms levelled against SNA is its dependence on the SSCP for the establishment of sessions between LUs. This contrasts with the OSI model where two systems are able to establish a connection without the intervention of a third party. In addition, the early history of SNA, with its emphasis on terminal-to-mainframe communication, encouraged a distinction between the *primary LU* and the *secondary LU* in an LU-LU session. Both of these characteristics of SNA are incompatible with the communication between peer applications made possible by LU6.2. The difficulty was recognized by IBM and measures taken to resolve it by the definition of a new type of PU, PU2.1, in conjunction with the definition of LU6.2.

A control domain of a traditional SNA network consists of a single PU type 5 that houses the SSCP for the domain, a number of PU type 4 nodes to provide switching capability and peripheral PU type 2 nodes supporting clusters of LU type 2 nodes. This structure is appropriate for terminal-to-mainframe connectivity. If the peripheral devices are powerful microprocessors providing LU6.2 services to application programs, establishing sessions via the SSCP is inappropriate when the application programs may be in personal computers in the same building.

The solution lies in devolving some of the responsibilities of the SSCP to PUs in the peripheral network. For this purpose PU2.1 is defined so that it contains a subset of SSCP functions and forms a *Peripheral Node Control Point (PNCP)*. The PNCP allows sessions to be established between LUs that are defined to the PNCP *without* involving the SSCP. This mechanism allows peer-to-peer networks of large numbers of small systems to be built using PU2.1 and LU6.2 as the architectural platform. These concepts are embodied in the *Advanced Peer-to-Peer Networking (APPN)* architecture.

In a traditional SNA network, each peripheral node (PU1 or PU2) is attached to a single boundary node (PU4) and supports a star cluster of LUs. In an APPN topology the peripheral networks have a mesh structure of PU2.1s. This mesh may or may not be connected to a traditional backbone network. If it is operating stand-alone, the PU2.1 functions provide session establishment services and automatically update their knowledge of the network topology as new nodes are added. Connection to a backbone network is made through one or more PUs that behave as PU2.0 nodes in their communication with the backbone switches.

## 7.12 Summary

This completes the survey of SNA, providing a basic knowledge of its workings, benefits and shortcomings. The architecture, and the products based on it, have had a major influence on the science of networking. The gradual movement of SNA towards achieving interoperability with other architectures should be welcomed by those dedicated to open communication.

*IBM mainframe processors have dominated the data processing world for some time, particularly in data-intensive areas such as banking. These processors are intended to be nodes in an SNA network and communication between them and other nodes is intended to conform to SNA protocol. Organizations such as the WNB have traditionally used SNA networks and applications that require such networks, resulting in a situation in the late 1980s when upwards of 70 per cent of private WANs were based on SNA.*

*This period will probably turn out to be the zenith of SNA, and from the late 1990s onwards, a gradual decline in the proportion of SNA networks, and indeed other proprietary networks, as users move towards open systems, will become apparent. Manufacturers, including IBM, recognize this trend and are themselves increasingly providing open products. The 1990s will be a period of coexistence between proprietary and non-proprietary systems.*

*The implementation by the WNB of an X.25 network brought an immediate need for such coexistence between SNA PUs and LUs as they were expecting to communicate over an SNA path control network, but needed instead to communicate over an X.25 network. IBM had already foreseen this need and developed the Network (Control Program) Packet Switching Interface (NPSI)—an optional feature in its PU4 imple-*

mentation that provides an SNA mainframe with an X.25 DTE appearance. NPSI is an early example of coexistence by protocol conversion between proprietary and non-proprietary architectures.

Sending SNA Path Information Units (PIUs) in X.25 packets (so-called SNA over X.25) is less efficient than sending user data in X.25 packets or PIUs over the SNA path control network, because of the need to generate and transmit additional protocol control information. This disadvantage is more than offset by the ability to build a hybrid network. It is also worth noting that the reverse process of X.25 over SNA is also possible. Another PU4 option is the X.25 SNA Interconnection (XI) feature, which enables an SNA boundary node to present an X.25 DCE appearance. Because of the definition of X.25 as an interface, any node presenting an X.25 DCE appearance not only looks like, but *is*, an X.25 DCE. A set of such switches not only looks like, but *is*, an X.25 network.

# CHAPTER 8 Local Area Networks (LANs)

## 8.1 Introduction

A walk through the business area of any city in the developed world and a glance through an office window, apart from being impolite, will reveal a significant development in the use of computers—almost every desk has one. Coupled with this desktop revolution is a substantial development in the use of communication technologies. It is hoped that it will be demonstrated in this chapter that this has been an evolution rather than a revolution.

A desktop computer is a major aid to productivity in the processing of information. Workers in commercial and industrial establishments, in academic and government institutions and in their own homes can create documents, manage databases or perform complex numerical analysis. What do they do with all this information? The answer, frequently, is that they send it to somebody else.

Data networks provide for the exchange of information between machines often acting on behalf of people. The data networks of the 1970s enabled a user to transmit instructions and data to a remote computer, have the computer process the data according to the instructions and return the result. The number of bits exchanged between the machines was relatively small. The data networks of the 1980s and 1990s enable a user to transmit substantial amounts of data that have been processed at the user's desk. It is often necessary to send this information to a person in the same building for review or additional processing. These two factors, the amount of data to be transmitted and the proximity of users, have resulted in a whole new networking world—the world of LANs. It is the only world that many network users know.

A LAN is a network serving an area of limited geographical spread—a building or a group of buildings in close proximity to each other. A Wide Area Network (WAN) has unlimited geographical coverage. Network structures intermediate between LAN and WAN are also defined, in particular the Metropolitan Area Network (MAN). Is it possible to accommodate these real world developments in a layered architectural approach to networking?

The traditional view of a WAN, for trains, mail, voice, data or whatever is that of a switch, or a set of switches, to which user nodes are connected. Connectivity between user nodes, which is the purpose of the network, is achieved at the circuit or message level. Such a network generally requires point-to-point connections between its nodes, although, in many cases and for economic reasons, a multipoint configuration is used to enable a number of user nodes to share a physical link to a switch. It will be seen shortly that a mechanism which enables several users to share the same physical link assumes critical importance in a LAN.

Providing a connection between two users in the same local area may well be accomplished by connecting both to a switch. Private telephone exchanges operate in this manner. The caller signals the switch to provide a circuit to a specified receiver and the switch notifies the receiver by sending a ringing signal. A different approach is taken in most local area data networks. The nodes on a LAN (often called *stations*) are all connected to the same physical cable. Two ways of laying the cable are in common use: the *ring LAN*, where the cable forms a closed ring, and the *bus LAN*, where the cable has a linear topology and ends that are terminated electronically to prevent the reflection of signals.

Sharing a physical medium between multiple users is not peculiar to LANs. It was mentioned earlier that it is common in multipoint access to a WAN. It occurs in telephone 'party' lines and is, of course, common practice in road and rail networks. In all cases, some means of controlling simultaneous attempts to access the medium by one or more users is needed. On the roads and the railways it is provided by signals or relies on observation by the driver. On a data network it is provided by the *data link control protocol*.

Connecting all users to the same medium enables a connectionless mode of operation to be used on LANs that relies on intelligence in the receiving station to filter out its own messages. Conventional telephones do not have this intelligence—if all the telephones in an office were connected to the same line, they would all ring when any one of them received a call.

The limited length of cable in a LAN enables high-bandwidth media to be used that would be prohibitively expensive in a WAN unless provided by a common carrier and shared by many users.

In summary, the use of a high-bandwidth medium shared by a number of stations provides an efficient and cost-effective means of exchanging large amounts of data between users in a limited geographical area. Let us now examine the protocol developments that have resulted in the explosive growth of LANs.

The most significant of these developments has occurred, as might be expected, at the data link layer. It is this layer that is responsible for ensuring that messages are passed reliably from one network node to the next. On a shared medium it has an extra role to perform to ensure that simultaneous attempts to access the medium by more than one station are prevented or, at least, detected and corrected. Such an attempt results in a collision just as it does on the road. The consequences are a message or a vehicle that is unrecognizable.

Potential collisions are not new in data networking. It was, and remains, common practice to connect a number of low usage terminals to a WAN via a multipoint link. In Chapter 10, High Level Data Link Control (HDLC) protocol is discussed in some detail, so it is sufficient to say here that the normal response mode of operation of HDLC designates one of the stations on a multipoint link as the primary station and all others as secondary stations. The primary station controls access to the link by polling each secondary station according to a predefined polling list. A secondary station that has data to transmit when it is polled is given exclusive use of the link.

Although polling is used in some small LANs, it is an inappropriate solution for a high-speed LAN that connects intelligent peer terminals in that it makes inefficient use of the bandwidth and has an inflexible priority scheme that relies on the number of times a given terminal appears in the polling list.

The structure of the data link layer for LANs was developed by the IEEE in its Project 802. The standards proposed by this project were subsequently adopted by ISO as the 8802 series of international standards. These standards describe the operation of the data link layer by considering it as two sublayers. The lower sublayer, the *Medium Access Control (MAC)* layer, is covered by a number of standards that reflect the different ways of handling collisions. The upper sublayer, the *Logical Link Control (LLC)* layer, is common to all MAC protocols.

## 8.2 Medium Access Control (MAC) layer

On a LAN, as on any other data network, the bits that constitute a message are represented by electrical signals propagated through the physical medium between nodes. If two stations on a LAN transmit simultaneously, or sufficiently closely in time, their signals will overlap (collide) and the information content of both will be destroyed. The sender may well be unaware that a collision has occurred. Two techniques are used to overcome the effect of collisions. One ensures that they never happen, while the other ensures that, when they do happen, they are detected so that corrective action can be taken.

**Token ring**

The concept of a token will be familiar from the description of the session layer of the OSI model. Possession of the appropriate token entitles a system to exercise the function associated with the token. A similar concept is used to control access to the physical medium in a LAN.

How are tokens used in a ring LAN? As this concerns the data link layer, the unit of data exchanged between stations is called a *frame*. A token is a special 24-bit frame that circulates continuously, passed from one station to the next, when the LAN is idle. When a station has a message to transmit, it waits for the token to arrive, captures it and sends its message. No other station can transmit until the token is restored. The destination station copies the message, marks it as 'read' and sends it on round the ring. It is recognized and removed by the original sending station, which then restores the token. Consequently, one message only can be on the ring at any one time. The technique is simple and elegant, although some complexity is inevitably introduced by the need to make the technique reliable.

Although designed for peer-to-peer communication, one station on a token ring is special. It is the *active monitor station*. Every station is able to assume the role of ring monitor. The first one to join the ring, by powering up, gets the job. All other stations, as they join, adopt standby mode. The first task of the monitor is to generate the token. It then sends, at regular intervals, an *Active Monitor Present (AMP)* frame to indicate to other stations that the monitor is alive and well.

Having assumed control of the ring, the monitor station has a number of other jobs. A token ring is critically dependent on there being one, and one only, token. The monitor regenerates the token if it gets corrupted and removes duplicates that may appear as a result of some error. It also removes frames that are circulating permanently. If all is well, a frame should circulate only once. The sender sets a bit in the frame header (the *monitor bit*) to 0 when it sends a frame. The monitor changes the bit to 1. When the frame has been copied by the recipient, it should be removed by the sender. Consequently, the monitor should never receive a frame with the monitor bit set to 1. If it does, it removes the frame.

The standby stations also have a role to play in managing the ring. Each station expects to see an AMP frame and a token at a regular intervals. If either of these frames fails to appear within a certain time, the standby station prepares to take over the monitor role by starting to send *Claim Token (CT)* frames. Other stations may do the same thing, resulting in contention for the medium—the very thing the token mechanism is supposed to prevent. This situation is avoided by each station examining the source address of any CT frame that it receives. If the station's own address is higher than that in the incoming CT, it removes the frame and sends one with its own address. If it subsequently gets this frame back, indicating that no other station has made a stronger claim, it assumes the role of active monitor and starts sending its own AMP frames. If subsequently an AMP frame appears that it did not originate, the station reverts to a standby role to avoid the disaster of two active monitors on the ring.

All this activity requires a control protocol and, as usual, control information is carried in a frame header and trailer. The frame format is shown in Figure 8.1.

The frame is contained (almost) within 8-bit delimiters. The access control field contains the monitor bit, which has already been mentioned, and the token bit, which is set to 0 to indicate that the frame is a

## Local Area Networks (LANs)

| Header | Data | Trailer |
|---|---|---|

**Header**

| Delimiter | Access control | Frame control | Destination address | Source address |
|---|---|---|---|---|

Bytes  1   1   1   2 or 6   2 or 6

**Trailer**

| Frame check sequence | Delimiter | Frame status |
|---|---|---|

Bytes  4   1   1

**Token**

| Delimiter | Access control | Delimiter |
|---|---|---|

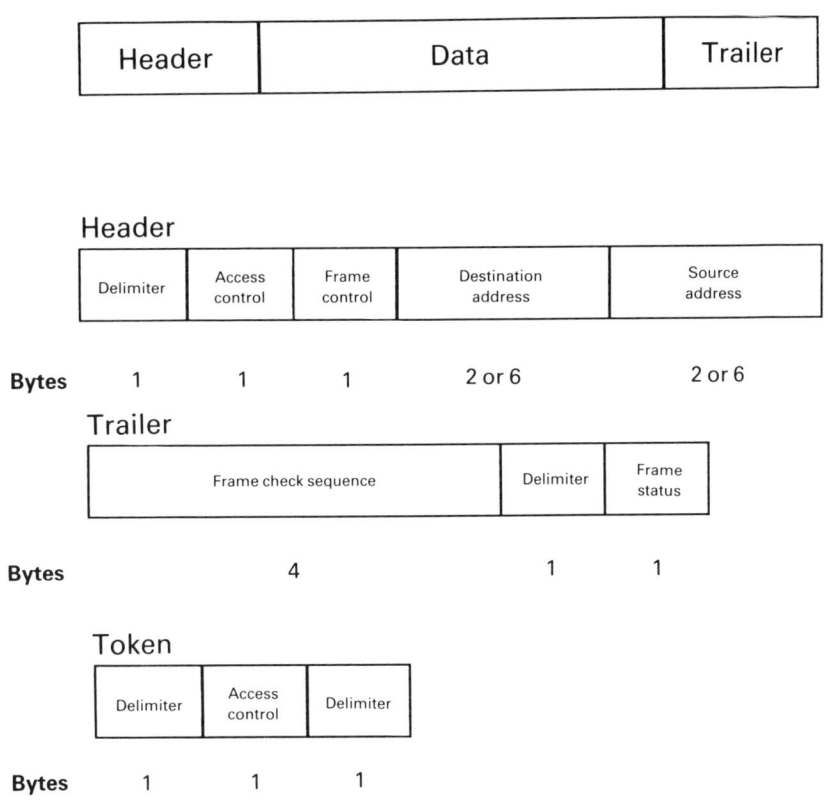

Bytes  1   1   1

*Figure 8.1   Token ring MAC frames*

token. The token itself consists only of the access control field and the delimiters. (The other bits are discussed later.) The frame control field determines whether the frame is a ring management frame (such as an AMP) or a data frame carrying user data. The address fields are self-evident, although it is worth noting that the 'all 1s' destination address is used, as is the convention, to broadcast a message (such as AMP) to all stations. The data field contains either user data or ring management information. The frame check sequence contains the 32-bit checksum to enable bit errors to be detected. The last field, following the end delimiter and not included in the checksum, is used to indicate to the sender that the frame has been recognized and copied by the recipient.

When a station captures the token and inserts a data frame, the network is not available to any other station until the token is restored. In the absence of a priority system, the token will be used by the first station that detects it and has a message to send. Other stations, perhaps with urgent messages, will continue to wait. The network should be able to offer something better than this 'first come first served' service.

The access control field in the frame header is used to implement a simple priority system. The monitor and token bits in this field were mentioned earlier. The remaining six bits provide the priority scheme. They are divided into three *reservations bits (RRR)* and three *token priority bits (PPP)*. Initially both subfields are set to 0, the lowest priority.

A station waiting to send a message sets RRR in a passing data frame to the priority of its message—a value n between 0 and 7. When the token is regenerated by the sender of this data frame, it sets the PPP bits to n and resets the RRR bits to 0. The token may now be used only by stations with a message of priority equal to or greater than n. Other stations with messages of lower priority may reserve it for use next time round. Stations that raise the priority of the token are responsible for restoring it to its original value.

The token ring MAC protocol is fully described in IEEE 802.5 (ISO 8802.5). It is the access control system preferred by IBM in its LAN products.

## Carrier Sense Multiple Access/Collision Detection (CSMA/CD)

An alternative, and quite different, technique for dealing with collisions on a shared medium is defined by IEEE 802.3 (ISO 8802.3). It originated with the Ethernet research project at the Xerox Palo Alto Research Centre. Ethernet, or Ethernet-like, implementations are used on the majority of LANs.

Whereas the use of a token prevents collisions by effectively disabling the network while a message is in transit, CSMA/CD allows a station to transmit when it believes that the network is not in use. If this belief subsequently proves to be ill-founded, a collision will occur and messages will be corrupted. CSMA/CD enables each station whose message has been corrupted to detect the fact and retransmit its message. The name implies that it is a technique for allowing multiple access (to the physical medium) and enables collisions to be detected. Carrier sense indicates the way in which a station decides whether to transmit.

Two techniques are used to transmit bits on a LAN. Baseband LANs carry digital signals while broadband LANs use analog modulation of a carrier signal and require modems. Any station on a LAN is able to detect an incoming message—that is part of its reason for being there. On a baseband LAN, it detects a message by detecting voltage changes on the cable corresponding to the coding of digital information. On a broadband LAN, it detects modulation of the carrier. The term 'Carrier Sense' in CSMA/CD refers to the detection of a message by either process.

A station with a message to transmit first 'listens' to the cable. If it detects a message, it refrains from transmitting until the medium appears to be idle. Because of the finite speed of transmission through the cable, it may appear to be idle when, in fact, a message has been transmitted but has not yet reached the listener. The result of this misconception is a collision and the corruption of both messages.

A transmitting station continues to monitor the medium for incoming signals during its transmission. It is able to detect a collision by the appearance of unexpected voltage levels. If a collision is detected, the station stops transmitting, sends a jamming signal to ensure that the collision is detected, and waits for a random time before retransmitting.

The collision detection technique in CSMA/CD imposes some limitations on the network parameters. Consider two stations, A and B, at the extremities of a bus LAN. Station A transmits a message that takes time to reach B. B also has a message to send and does so just before A's message arrives, believing the medium to be idle. B detects a collision almost immediately and sends a jamming signal that travels towards A. In order for A to recognize that its message has been corrupted, it must still be transmitting when B's jamming arrives. Consequently, the minimum message size, and the maximum length of the LAN, must be

| Field | Bytes |
|---|---|
| Preamble | 7 |
| Delimiter | 1 |
| Destination address | 2 or 6 |
| Source address | 2 or 6 |
| Length | Variable |
| Data | Variable |
| Padding | Variable |
| Frame check sequence | 4 |

*Figure 8.2* *CSMA/CD MAC frame*

such that collisions can be detected in the worst case described above. For example, on a 10 megabits per second Ethernet, the minimum packet size is 64 bytes and the maximum length 1.5 km.

Figure 8.2 shows the format of a CSMA/CD MAC frame. The 7-byte preamble field, containing alternate 1 and 0 bits, enables transmitter and receivers to establish bit synchronization. The start of frame field (10101011) marks the beginning of the frame. The address fields are generally 6 bytes, although the standard allows for 2-byte addresses. As the frame must have a minimum length, it may be necessary to pad the data field. A length field indicates the number of bytes of actual data. The frame is completed by a 4-byte check sequence.

The CSMA/CD protocol is somewhat simpler than that needed on a token ring. The use of a special frame, the token, on a token ring LAN results in a rather more complicated protocol to ensure that the token is always present and to allow a degree of priority. On a lightly loaded network, CSMA/CD is more efficient as there is no need to wait for the token. As traffic increases, the use of a token ensures that a station can transmit with confidence when it has the token and the necessary priority.

## Fibre Distributed Data Interface (FDDI)

In Chapter 2 (see Section 2.4) the high data rates that can be achieved using the wide frequency spectrum of an optical fibre were described. Optical methods of transmitting data are playing an increasing part in both WANS and LANS. In this section, a medium access control mechanism and a physical interface defined specifically for optical media are detailed. This is the FDDI. It was first proposed in order to connect mainframe computers to their peripheral input/output devices. It was subsequently developed to provide connectivity between LAN stations and between lower-speed LANs. Its journey to the status of ISO standards (ISO 9314 multipart standard) has been shepherded by the ANSI X3T9 Committee.

Some of the specification parameters of FDDI are:

- medium — 62.5/125 µm optical fibre
- access method — token passing
- maximum packet size — 4500 octets
- data rate — 100 Mbits/second
- signalling rate — 125 MBaud
- signal encoding — 4B/5B
- maximum ring perimeter — 100 km
- maximum station separation — 2 km
- maximum number of stations — 1000 physical layers.

It will be seen from these parameters that FDDI uses a token-passing technology for medium access control, but at a data rate that is an order of magnitude above that in use on metallic rings. It will also be seen that FDDI networks can cover a large area and support a large number of high-speed stations. The optical fibre is defined by the diameters of its core and cladding. The original specification for multi-mode fibres has been extended to allow single-mode implementations. This enables larger station-to-station separations for MANs. For the signal encoding, 4 bits of data are encoded into groups of 5 bits for signalling (hence 4B/5B), resulting in a signal transmission rate of 125 MBaud.

FDDI is similar in a number of ways to the more common 8802.5 token ring standard discussed above. The most obvious similarity is the concept of token possession in order to control access to the medium. There are, however, significant differences that cater for the 'bigger and faster' specification of FDDI.

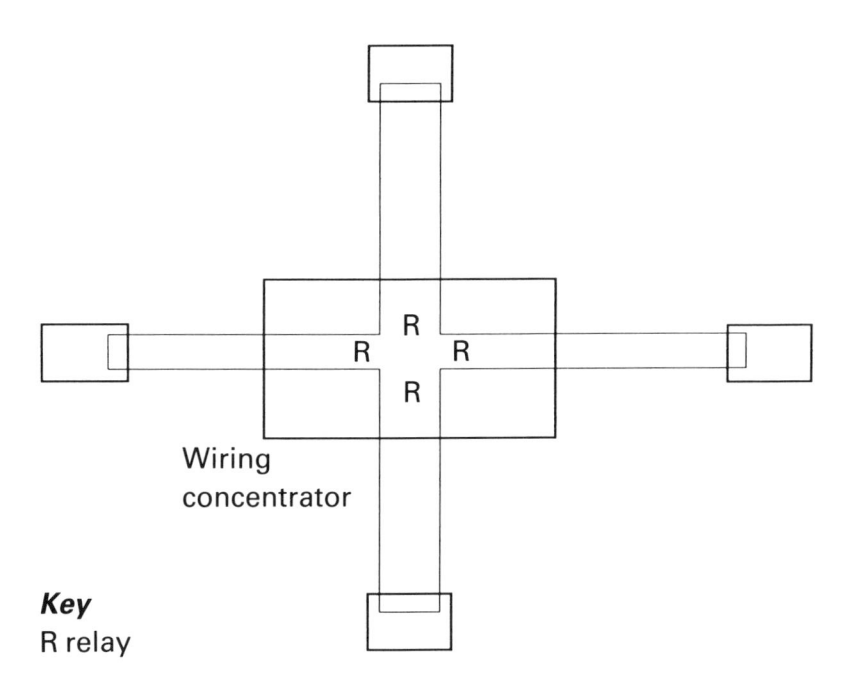

**Key**
R relay

*Figure 8.3   Token ring wiring*

Transmission through a ring, via its attached stations, depends on the ring not being broken and all stations being switched on. The configuration of a conventional token ring, although logically a ring, is physically wired in a star topology, centred on a wiring concentrator. This is shown in Figure 8.3. The lobe connection to each station is maintained by a relay in the concentrator, energized by power from the attached station. If the station fails, or the lobe circuit is broken, the relay switches to bypass the defective lobe.

Such a configuration is unsuited to the larger FDDI ring. The physical topology of an FDDI ring is shown in Figure 8.4.

**Key**

☐   Dual attachment station

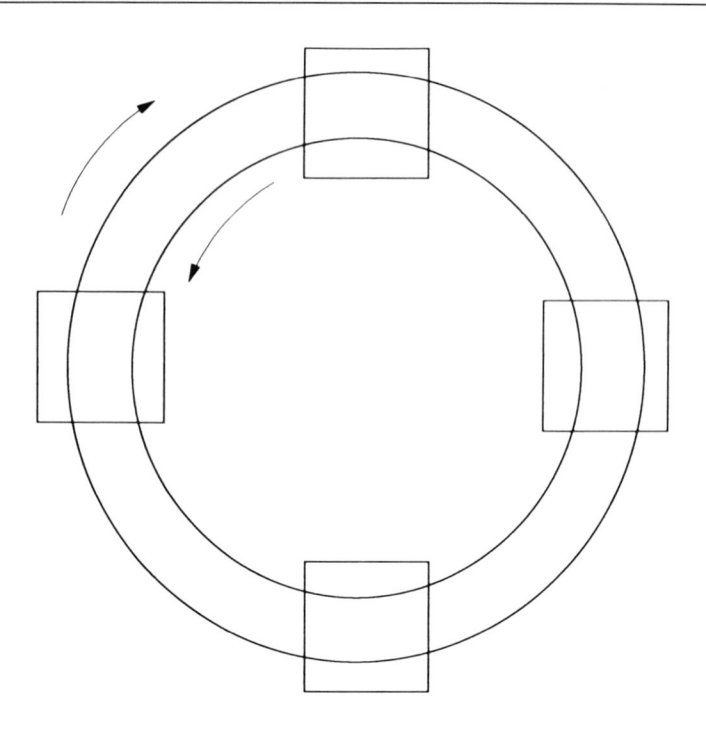

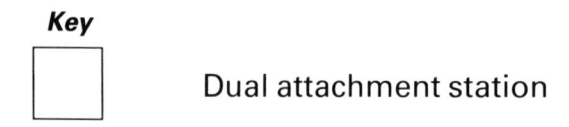

*Figure 8.4   FDDI dual counter-rotating ring*

It consists of two concentric rings in which data circulate in opposite directions, and is known as a *dual counter-rotating ring*. In normal circumstances, only one ring is used, although the standards allow for the simultaneous use of both rings. If a break in the fibre is detected, stations on either side of the break connect the primary ring to the secondary ring to form a single, elongated ring, enabling connectivity to be maintained. The stations are called *dual attachment stations*. Wiring concentrators are also used to support physically smaller configurations using (cheaper) single attachment stations. Failed stations may be bypassed using optical relays that connect the incoming and outgoing fibres directly.

The FDDI MAC protocol differs from the 8802.5 protocol in two respects. The first concerns the point at which the token is regenerated. On a token ring LAN, it is regenerated when the transmitting station detects its frame returning, having been copied by the recipient. On an FDDI LAN, a token is produced by the transmitting station immediately it has finished transmission. Many frames may consequently be on the LAN at any one time. To remove its own frames, and not those of other senders, a transmitter examines the source address.

The second difference lies in the mechanism for assigning priority to stations. 8802.5 uses the reservation and priority bits in the access control field of the token, as described in Section 8.2. The priority scheme in FDDI is based on timers.

A large FDDI ring may have many different types of station attached. The standards allow for two types of traffic—asynchronous and synchronous. Asynchronous use of the network is intended for stations whose transmissions are unpredictable in time, while synchronous use is for stations that engage in predictable dialogues with other stations. Synchronous stations are given a *Synchronous Allocation (SA)* of time (a time slot), the length of which may be different in different stations.

The greater the level of activity on the LAN, the longer is the time interval between the token being detected at a particular station. A target time is defined—the *Target Token Rotation Time (TTRT)*—and stored in each station. Each station bids a value for TTRT when the network is initialized. The lowest value is chosen, being the bid from the station with the most urgent need for network capacity, and stored in each station.

Each station maintains a *Token Rotation Timer (TRT)*, which is initialized to TTRT and counts down, and a *Late Counter (LC)*, which is initialized to 0 and counts up. TRT is reset each time a token passes, while LC is incremented each time TRT expires. A token is *late* if LC is greater than 0 when it arrives and *early* if LC is still 0, indicating that TRT has not expired.

If the token is early (LAN not busy), the station saves the remaining TRT value as a *Token Holding Time (THT)*, resets TRT and restarts the TRT timer. It may now transmit synchronous frames, if any, for a time SA, and/or asynchronous frames for a time THT. If the token is late (LAN busy), LC is reset to 0, TRT continues to run and synchronous frames only may be transmitted for a time SA. The scheme ensures that synchronous bandwidth is always available to each station that needs it in proportion to its SA value. Any spare capacity is available for asynchronous traffic.

The structure of an FDDI MAC frame is shown in Figure 8.5. The number associated with each frame is the length in 4-bit symbols and, hence, twice the length in octets. Note that the information field contains an integral number of symbols but not necessarily an integral

**Frame**

| PA | SD | FC | DA | SA | DATA | FCS | ED | FS |
|----|----|----|----|----|------|-----|----|----|
| 16 | 2  | 2  | 12 | 12 |      | 8   | 1  | 3  |

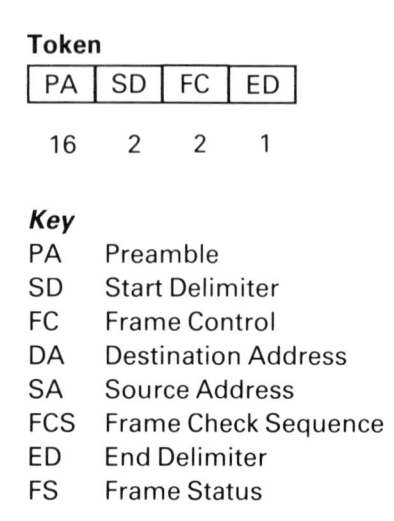

**Token**

| PA | SD | FC | ED |
|----|----|----|----|
| 16 | 2  | 2  | 1  |

**Key**
PA   Preamble
SD   Start Delimiter
FC   Frame Control
DA   Destination Address
SA   Source Address
FCS  Frame Check Sequence
ED   End Delimiter
FS   Frame Status

*Figure 8.5   FDDI MAC frames*

number of octets. The address fields are essentially those defined for the token ring. The control field contains bits indicating the type of frame, distinguishing synchronous frames from asynchronous frames, indicating the use of extended addressing, indicating a restricted token and indicating a void frame. Special symbols are used as delimiters.

A further development of the interface, known as FDDI II, enables an FDDI network to support circuit-switched applications in addition to packet-switched ones. It is thus suitable for voice and video applications in *Integrated Services LANs (ISLANs)* and *Integrated Services Metropolitan Area Networks (ISMANs)*—large-scale, multipurpose networks providing communication within cities.

## 8.3 Logical Link Control (LLC) layer

The MAC layer just discussed—the lower of the two sublayers into which the data link layer is divided—is concerned with controlling access to a shared physical medium. It does not provide for the controlled, error-free transmission between two stations once control of the medium has been established. These are the functions normally associated with the data link layer. On a LAN they are provided by the *Logical Link Control (LLC)* sublayer. In terms of a layered model, this layer provides service to the network layer and is itself a user of the MAC service. The LLC protocol is common to all types of LAN.

In Chapter 5 the HDLC protocol and its manifestation as LAPB in the X.25 Recommendation was described. In Chapter 7 it was indicated that SDLC, SNA's layer 2 protocol, is a variant of HDLC. It should come as no surprise, then, that LLC is closely based on the same protocol.

HDLC provides for both balanced and unbalanced configurations. In a balanced configuration, no distinction is made between stations and either may transmit asynchronously. In a WAN, it is restricted to point-to-point links. In an unbalanced configuration, one station has primary status and the other stations have secondary status. Two modes of unbalanced operation are defined. In asynchronous response mode, despite the primary–secondary relationship, any station may transmit at any time and a contention resolution mechanism is required. In normal response mode, secondary stations may transmit *only* when polled by the primary station. Both modes of unbalanced operation may be used on point-to-point and multipoint links.

A LAN is essentially a multipoint balanced configuration for which HDLC does not make provision. One of the purposes of the MAC layer is to fill this gap.

The LLC protocol, then, becomes a subset of HDLC with a number of interesting variants.

The most obvious variant is the presence of both source *and* destination addresses in the LLC header. On a point-to-point link, the source is known. A multipoint link in normal response mode essentially becomes a point-to-point link when a secondary station responds to a poll, although the address field always contains the secondary address. On a LAN, both addresses are carried in the header. LLC uses extended send and receive counters, reflecting the higher speed and low error rate of LAN media. Consequently, the control fields in information and supervisory frames are 16 bits long. The LLC standard allows for the provision of three types of service to the network layer.

The *Unacknowledged Connectionless Service (LLC-1)* is a simple 'datagram' service. The service consists only of the DL-UNITDATA request and indication primitives. It uses the *Un-numbered Information (UI)* frame to carry user data. No acknowledgement, flow control or error detection is provided.

The *Connection-orientated Service (LLC-2)* consists of the usual three phases—connection establishment, data transfer and connection release. A connection is established by the *Set Asynchronous Balanced Mode Extended (SABME)* command, with an *Un-numbered Acknowledgement (UA)* response. It is released by a *Disconnect (DISC)* command with UA response. Information frames carry user data. Flow control and error detection are implemented using the send and receive counters and a fixed window.

The *Acknowledged Connectionless Service (LLC-3)* is effectively LLC-1 supplemented by acknowledgement of the receipt of a packet. An un-numbered frame, the *Acknowledged Connectionless (AC) Information* frame, is used to convey both data and acknowledgement. This frame is not defined by HDLC.

## 8.4 The network layer and above

The normal role of a network layer is to enable a message to be routed from its source through one or more intermediate nodes to its destination. On a single LAN, with all stations attached to the same medium and each station able to examine all messages, this routeing function is not required.

It is common, however, to connect a LAN to a WAN via a router node. Network layer protocol information must then be included by the sending LAN station for use at the router to provide routeing information to the WAN. Most WANs are connection orientated and it would seem reasonable to provide a connection-orientated network service to LAN stations wishing to communicate with the outside world. This does not necessarily imply that LLC-2 must be used at the data link layer, although the lack of flow and error control in LLC-1 may result in problems at the network or higher layers.

Above the network layer is strictly outside the network proper and in the world of end-to-end protocol. Any such protocol may be used or none at all. Application-to-application communication may be achieved using the upper layers of the OSI suite of SNA LUs, particularly LU6.2. The most common end-to-end protocol in use on LANs is probably the *Transmission Control Protocol (TCP)* layer of the TCP/IP protocol suite, to be described in the next chapter.

## 8.5 Bridges, routers and gateways

An inevitable consequence of the spread of LANs was the need to connect a LAN to another network. Different departments on the same site may have separate LANs with most of the messages being intradepartmental, but with an occasional need for interdepartmental traffic. There is then a requirement for interworking between LANs. A station on a LAN may wish to communicate with a remote station across a WAN and so requires LAN to WAN transmission. In principle, a connection between two stations can be made across series of LAN-WAN interconnections, but, in practice, the number of hops may be limited by performance considerations or the need to meet a time-out imposed by end-to-end protocols.

The terminology in the world of internetworking is, unfortunately, not well established—a 'router' to one person is a 'gateway' to another

## Bridges

person. Here, a terminology based on the level in the OSI protocol stack, at which any conversion required takes place, has been adopted.

The simplest form of interconnection is a *bridge* between two LANs that are not geographically separated and both of which conform to the same MAC protocol, as shown in Figure 8.6. The bridge is a special station connected to both LANs.

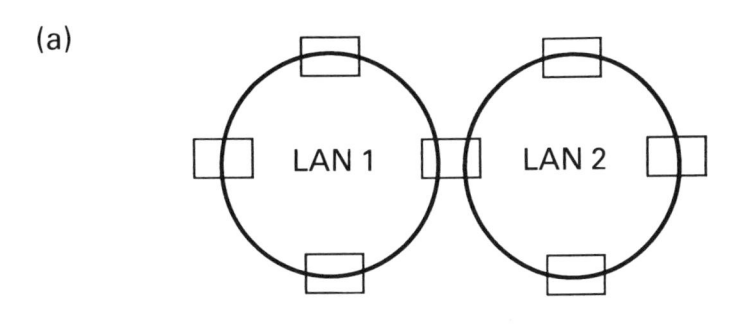

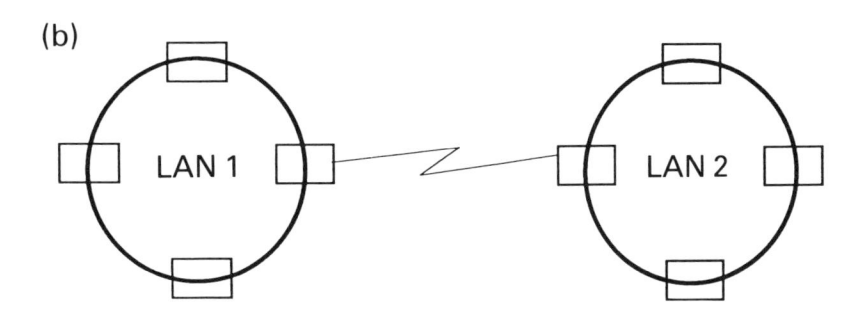

*Figure 8.6  LAN bridges (a) local bridge (b) remote bridge*

The bridge maintains two tables of MAC addresses—one for LAN 1 and one for LAN 2. It examines all messages on both LANs and forwards across the bridge those messages destined for the other LAN. Such a bridge is sometimes called a *MAC relay*. It operates at layer 2 as it relies on the MAC address to determine whether or not to forward the message across the bridge. The data content of the frame, which includes protocol control information for the LLC and higher layers, is unchanged.

It has so far been assumed that the two networks to be connected are geographically close so that the bridge may be connected to both networks. Such a bridge is called a *local bridge*. The concept of a bridge may be extended to cover cases where the two networks to be connected are geographically separated. The result is a *remote bridge*, consisting of two half-bridges, one on each network, connected by a telecommunications link. This link may be a point-to-point link or a circuit through a WAN, such as an X.25 network. When the local half-bridge decided that a message needs to be forwarded across the bridge, it encapsulates it in the appropriate wide area protocol and sends it to the remote half-bridge. At no point is the content of the message above the MAC layer changed or even examined.

Most bridges provide a connection between two similar LANs, say, two token rings or two CSMA/CD networks. In such cases no changes are needed at the MAC layer and the bridge performs a pure relay function. In order to connect a station on a token ring to a station on a CSMA/CD network, however, conversion of the MAC headers and trailer is necessary. This is not a simple process as it involves, among other things, a recalculation of the frame check sequence as the content of the frame over which the FCS is calculated has changed. Despite this, such a device is often still called a bridge, although others would call it a router and some would even call it a gateway!

Even a simple local bridge between two networks has a routeing decision to make: it must decide, based on its address tables, whether or not to forward the message. Complicated networks may be built using local and remote bridges. For example, a LAN may have more than one bridge and a bridge may be connected to more than one LAN. Alternative routes may then exist between two stations. Routeing then becomes much more complicated and is beyond the scope of this book.

## Routers

In the previous section bridge routeing was mentioned in the sense of deciding whether or not to forward a packet to a different LAN. Here, the general problem of connecting a LAN station to a WAN and hence to a range of external resources either on other LANs or directly connected to the WAN is considered. A typical situation is shown in Figure 8.7.

The device that connects a LAN to the WAN now has a routeing decision to make, in the sense of choosing between a number of different stations on different networks. As always, the decision is made based on protocol information provided by the source station. This information is provided via an *Internet Protocol (IP)*. The device that uses it is called a *router*. The analysis of the communication between A and B in Figure 8.7 is an interesting exercise in the use of layered protocol suites.

Station A is attached to token ring LAN X. It can send messages directly to other stations on X, including the router. These messages have LLC headers, defined by ISO 8802.2, and MAC headers, defined

*Local Area Networks (LANs)*

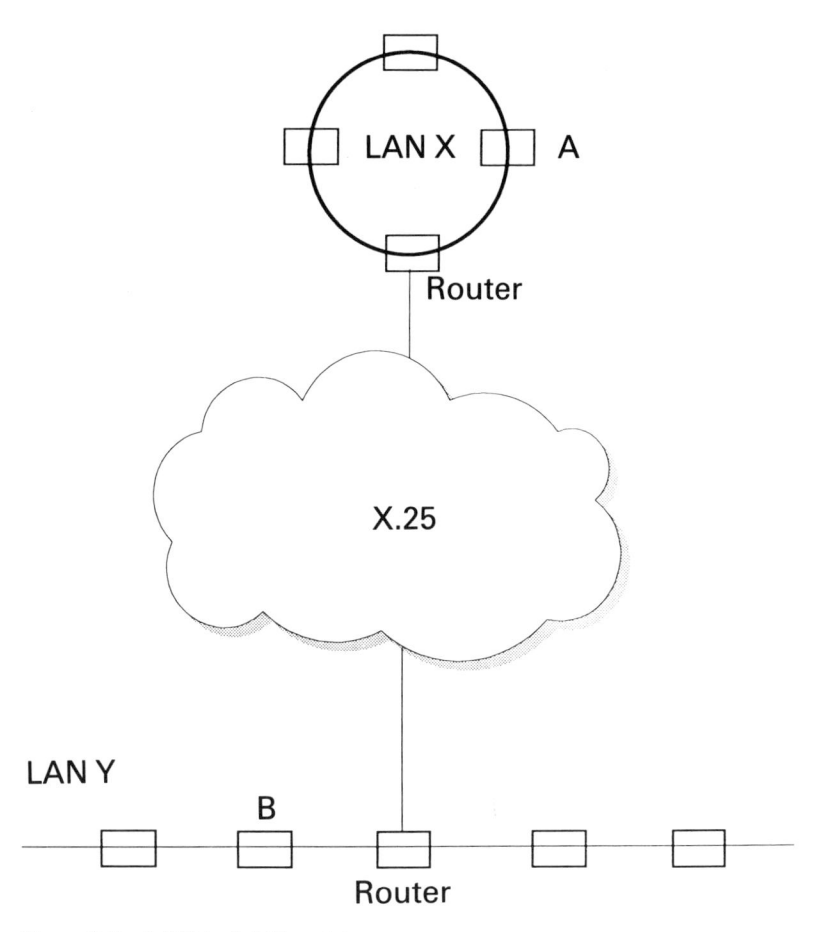

*Figure 8.7  LAN-to-LAN routeing*

by ISO 8802.5. Some of them are destined for station B on LAN Y. The data content of these messages must include information enabling LAN Y and station B to be identified. This information is contained in the internet protocol in the form of an address consisting of two parts: a network address and a station address. The most common internet protocol is that defined as part of the TCP/IP suite. The two routers themselves are X.25 DTEs. The source station must also, of course, supply any end-to-end protocol information required for communication between A and B.

**Gateways**

A bridge operates at layer 2 as its decision whether or not to forward a frame is based on layer 2 protocol information, the MAC address. A router operates at layer 3, basing a routing decision on an IP address consisting of network and station identifiers. In both these cases, the protocols above the layer at which the device operates must be compatible to allow useful communication between the end systems.

In many instances, it is necessary to provide communication between applications that are served by quite different protocol suites. Examples would be application-to-application communication between OSI and a proprietary architecture or between two proprietary architectures. The protocol must be fully converted, at all levels, to extract the user data and relay it to the target application.

Such a relay device, operating at layer 7, is properly called a *gateway*, although the term is used for devices that operate at lower layers. The gateway implements both sets of protocols and includes an application that accepts user data from one stack and relays it on the other and is thus a complicated communication system in its own right.

With the increasing use of TCP/IP to achieve interworking between different architectures, routers have become widespread. A growth in the use of gateways may also be expected if OSI is to replace, or at least interwork with, proprietary protocols for application-to-application communication.

## 8.6 Summary

Many people's experience of networking is confined to using a workstation on a LAN. It is possible to be given the impression that either this is not counted as networking or is treated as something very different from 'real' (that is wide area) networking. The intention in this chapter was to emphasize the many similarities between LANs and WANs and the few, but important, differences. The special protocols for LANs provide for controlled data flow between stations. Various upper layer protocols may be implemented by those stations to support application-to-application communication. The next chapter covers a suite of upper layer protocols commonly used on LANs.

*The branches and other offices of the WNB are staffed by a number of people, many of whom need access to data processing applications. The bank's policy of putting applications where they are most useful and can be supported results in some of these applications being provided by local servers and others by remote servers. LANs are the way to provide access to local servers, while WANs are the way to provide access to remote servers. The nature of the WNB's business requires that its staff have access to both. Consequently, the WNB's user-to-user network is either an on-site LAN or a LAN-WAN or LAN-WAN-LAN internet.*

*In keeping with its open systems strategy, the WNB's LANs conform to ISO standards, in particular 8802.3. The decision to use CSMA/CD bus LANs was largely governed by the availability of products in the mid 1980s when LANs were provided in branches and, somewhat later, in dealing rooms. Routers connect these LANs to the X.25 WAN. Work stations with 'open' (that is popular) multitasking operating systems and windowed graphical interfaces have started to appear.*

CHAPTER 9

# Transmission Control Protocol/Internet Protocol (TCP/IP)

## 9.1 Introduction

In Chapter 6 the services and protocols defined under the general umbrella of the OSI reference model were considered. These services and protocols allow application-to-application communication between a pair of open systems—systems that generate and recognize messages formatted according to the standard protocols at all layers of the model. In Section 6.5, some of the common and specific elements of the application layer that provide for different types of application-level communication were described. In Chapter 7 the provision of application-to-application support by the LU6.2 session type in SNA was outlined. In this chapter another protocol suite generally known as *TCP/IP* is discussed.

The TCP/IP family originated in work commissioned in the late 1960s by the Advanced Research Projects Agency (ARPA) of the US Department of Defense. This resulted in an experimental packet-switched network called *ARPANET* that enabled hosts to be connected by a network of packet switches called *Interface Message Processors (IMPs)*. The host-to-IMP protocol included many of the concepts subsequently incorporated in the X.25 Recommendation.

During the 1970s and early 1980s, ARPANET expanded to embrace a large number of research establishments. The *Internet Protocol (IP)* was further developed and TCP added to the suite. Military research establishments split from the ARPANET to form a separate network called *MILNET*. Other specialized and restricted military networks were added, including the *NSFNET*, funded by the National Science Foundation to connect super-computer centres. These networks are connected to form the internet. The term 'Internet' (with the capital 'I') is used to refer to this network and has effectively replaced the ARPANET, while the term 'internet' (with the lower-case 'i') refers to *any* set of connected networks. By 1990, the Internet had expanded to include over 3000 networks and 200 000 end systems. All of these systems use TCP/IP, and its associated protocols, for communication.

Why is TCP/IP so popular? There are many answers to this question: the protocols are non-proprietary, they are relatively simple and easy to implement and are consequently widely available in products from many manufacturers, the development of the protocols is adequately funded and staffed by people in research institutions with a strong motivation to develop ways of communication, the protocols work in most cases without attempting to be all-embracing, the terminology used to describe the TCP/IP suite is not pedantic, and sometimes even amusing, which is more than can be said for OSI. Some time in the 1990s it is anticipated that the fun will be over and OSI will gradually replace TCP/IP. We wait to be convinced.

The architectures that have so far been studied—SNA, OSI and the LAN standards—are intended to be applied to homogeneous networks in which every node conforms to the architecture. In an SNA network, or set of networks, all nodes are SNA nodes. In an OSI network, all nodes are open. All stations on a given LAN use the same lower-layer protocols. The early ARPANET was similarly homogeneous. Connections between different architectures require protocol conversions at some level. The TCP/IP suite has, however, come to be associated with internetworking—the ability to connect a computer on one network to a computer on another network where the architecture of the two networks is different. The connection may well be established via intermediate networks, each conforming to a different architecture.

One way, and probably the simplest way, to describe a network is as a set of connected switches. Each switch makes a routeing decision, based on protocol information carried in the message, to determine the next switch and, ultimately, the last switch, before delivering the message to its destination. In a homogeneous, single-architecture network, the connections between switches are simple point-to-point links. In an internet, they are complete networks. Thus, an internet is a set of switches, or routers, connected to each other by networks of various types. The IP carries the internet routeing information; it is a network layer protocol in OSI terms. The TCP is a transport layer protocol; it provides reliable end-to-end transmission of messages between machines. Other protocols in the suite provide the functions of layers 5, 6 and 7 for specific types of application-to-application communication.

## 9.2 The Internet Protocol (IP)

Note that despite the use of an upper case 'I', we are talking here about the *internet* protocol!

Readers who have stayed the course will by now recognize that routeing decisions are made in layer 3. The X.25 packet layer, the OSI network layer and the SNA explicit route sublayer are all concerned with determining the next leg in the passage of a message from source to destination. The information used to make this decision is the address of the destination, carried in the layer 3 header.

The format of these address fields depends on the architecture. The original X.25 standard allowed for an address consisting of up to 14 decimal digits. Identifying an OSI network destination requires up to 40 decimal digits, necessitating an extension to the CCITT's X.25 Recommendation in 1984. An SNA destination is identified by a combination of a 32-bit subarea address and a 16-bit element address. In all cases, the address identifies a destination within a single network, although X.75 and *SNA Network Interconnect (SNI)*, respectively, make provision for connecting two X.25 or two SNA networks together.

In an internet, the destination is a particular computer on a particular network. It might be expected that IP addresses are split into a network address and a host[1] address and this is indeed the case.

A message relies on the internet layer for transmission to its destination. The internet service is connectionless. There are thus no connection establishment and connection termination phases but only a data transfer phase. The unit of data in the internet is a datagram consisting of a header and the message to be transmitted.

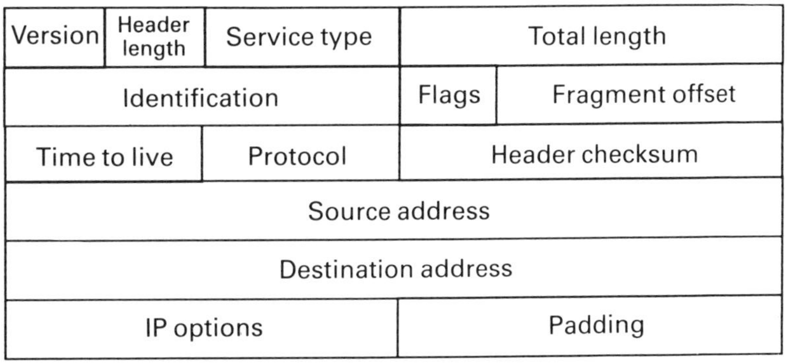

| Version | Header length | Service type | Total length | |
|---|---|---|---|---|
| Identification | | | Flags | Fragment offset |
| Time to live | | Protocol | Header checksum | |
| Source address | | | | |
| Destination address | | | | |
| IP options | | | Padding | |

*Figure 9.1   Internet datagram header*

An internet header is shown in Figure 9.1. It is an integral multiple of 32 bits consisting of the following fields:

- *version (4 bits)*: this field indicates the version of the IP protocol used to create the header and, hence, the format of the header
- *header length (4 bits)*: total length of the header—necessary as it may contain different options
- *type of service (8 bits)*: the field indicates the way in which the datagram should be handled by routers through which it passes. The priority of the datagram may be specified together with the delay, throughput and reliability of the connection. These parameters are equivalent to quality of service parameters in OSI and class of service in SNA

---

[1] Any machine with an IP address is called a 'host'.

- *total length (16 bits)*: this is the total length of the datagram
- *identification (16 bits)*: the total length field allows a maximum datagram size of 65 536 bytes. Most networks will not carry this amount of data in a single packet or frame. A datagram may cross several networks before it reaches its destination. It may therefore be necessary to fragment a datagram. The identification field is a unique number assigned to each datagram and enables fragments to be associated with their parent datagram. Once a datagram has been fragmented it stays fragmented until it reaches its destination
- *flags (3 bits)*: one bit is used to indicate that a datagram should not be fragmented since some implementations may not support re-assembly. If a router needs to fragment a datagram with this flag set, it discards the datagram and returns an error message to the originating host. A second bit is used to indicate the last fragment and the third bit is unused
- *fragment offset (13 bits)*: this field contains the offset (in units of 8 bytes) of the data in the fragment from the start of the data in the datagram
- *time to live (8 bits)*: specifies how long (in seconds) the datagram is allowed to remain in the internet delivery system, with a maximum of 255 seconds. It is decremented by each router through which the datagram passes by an amount depending on traffic congestion—when the count reaches 0, the datagram is discarded
- *protocol (16 bits)*: the protocol field indicates which upper layer protocol was involved in creating the datagram and, consequently, which protocol should receive it, for example, TCP is assigned the decimal number 6, while the OSI transport protocol is number 29
- *checksum (16 bits)*: an error detection checksum covering only the fields of the header
- *source/destination addresses (32 bits each)*: IP addresses are divided into a network identifying number and a host identifying number and three address formats are used distinguished by the contents of the first two bits: class A addresses allocate 7 bits to the network and 24 bits to the host and are used to address the small number of networks that have many thousands of hosts; class B allocates 14 bits to the network and 16 bits to the host; class C allocates 21 bits to the network and 8 bits to the host, enabling many small networks to be addressed. IP addresses are written as four decimal numbers, representing the contents of the 4 bytes of the address, separated by decimal points, such as 136.1.3.12
- *options (variable length)*: this field allows a number of optional operations on a datagram which are used mainly for testing purposes and afford a method of extending the protocol, including route recording, time stamping and the ability to specify a particular route.

An internet consists of a number of IP routers that use the address in the header to route the datagram to its destination. Source and destination hosts are connected to routers, and routers are connected to each other, by networks. These networks carry datagrams encapsulated in the appropriate protocol. For example, an X.25 network will carry a datagram between routers as data in an X.25 packet; a token ring network will carry a datagram from a station to the router in a frame.

A router may fragment a datagram, if allowed, in order to get it across the next network. The next router will not, however, reassemble it, even if it could be passed on in its entirety. This is left to the receiving host. Each router verifies and recalculates the checksum as the header is modified by each router—the time to live field, at least, is changed.

In OSI terms, the internet protocol provides a layer 3 service (the terms 'protocol' and 'service' are not so clearly separated as in OSI documents). As far as an IP router is concerned, the underlying network is providing the layer 2 service of getting a message to the next node. A number of other protocols are associated with the internet protocol.

The *Internet Control Message Protocol (ICMP)* defines the format of control messages that are sent by hosts or routers to indicate to the sender that a problem has occurred. For example, that a datagram could not be delivered. These control messages are sent using IP and strictly belong to layer 4.

Internetworking raises interesting problems of address resolution. A host accessible via an internet essentially has two addresses: its IP address and the address by which it is known in the network to which it is physically attached. The final IP router in the internet must be able to translate the incoming IP address into a local physical address. It may achieve this using a statically configured address mapping table or by dynamically building a cache of addresses.

The *Address Resolution Protocol (ARP)* is included in the TCP/IP suite to facilitate dynamic address resolution. When an IP datagram is received, the router broadcasts an ARP message to all stations on its network. The ARP message contains the target IP address, whose hardware address is sought, and is carried as data in a frame appropriate to the type of target network. A station, which recognizes the IP address as its own, responds with its hardware address, which is then cached by the router for future reference.

ARP relies on a station knowing its IP address and being able to store it in secondary storage. This is not always the case, particularly with diskless machines. A further protocol, *Reverse Address Resolution Protocol (RARP)*, enables such a machine to broadcast a message asking for an IP address, including its own. The message is answered by a *RARP server*. At least one such server is required on any network that uses RARP.

The IP enables a host on one network to communicate with a host on a different network, possibly via a number of intermediate networks. Each network involved in the process may conform to a different protocol. Networks are connected by routers that are able to receive data conforming to one data link protocol and retransmit it on a different data link protocol to the next router. At the internet level, the route from source host to destination host is a sequence of IP routers. This is superimposed on a sequence of routes across separate networks, each handled by the appropriate layer 3 protocol.

IP provides a connectionless service. It is intentionally kept simple and efficient and does not claim to be fully reliable. Datagrams may be lost or deliberately discarded and the protocol contains no mechanism for detecting lost data. This is because connection control and detection/recovery of lost data are considered to be the responsibility of layer 4 and the TCP.

## 9.3 The Transmission Control Protocol (TCP)

TCP, in conjunction with IP, enables a connection-orientated reliable transport service to be provided to users. These users are various upper-layer protocol ULP entities that, in turn, support applications. Users of TCP are able to assume that a reliable connection exists to another user without needing to be aware of the characteristics and quality of the underlying network(s). Justifying such an assumption requires a sophisticated and powerful protocol and TCP was designed to satisfy this requirement. Its success is reflected in its adoption as the basis of the OSI transport class 4 (see Chapter 6) and its use (without IP) on LANs, particularly those based on Ethernet.

TCP accepts the upper-layer protocol data as a continuous stream of octets—indeed, it is sometimes referred as a stream-orientated transport protocol. The data stream is blocked by TCP into units, called *segments*, that are then carried as data in a lower-layer packet, usually an IP datagram. A segment, as with any other protocol, has a header that carries the protocol control information, enabling the TCP layer to perform its role of ensuring reliable transport. The format of a TCP header is shown in Figure 9.2. Let us examine the TCP in the light of the use and content of the fields in the segment header.

| Source port | | | Destination port |
|---|---|---|---|
| Sequence number | | | |
| Acknowledgement number | | | |
| HLEN | | Code Bits | Window |
| Checksum | | | Urgent pointer |
| Options | | | Padding |

*Figure 9.2   TCP segment header*

*Transmission Control Protocol/Internet Protocol (TCP/IP)*

**Source/destination port**  Multiple applications, or upper-layer protocols, may use TCP concurrently. Each user is uniquely identified by a (protocol) *port number*. Thus the IP address identifies a particular machine and the port number identifies a particular user within that machine. The combination of IP address and port number is called a socket. Some port numbers, in the range 1 to 255, are assigned to commonly used applications. For example, X.400 is assigned to TCP port number 103 and an application using the *File Transfer Protocol* (FTP—see below) is assigned to port number 21. These ports are referred to as *well-known ports*.

A connection between two users is identified by the sockets at its ends. A TCP connection is full duplex with segments passing in both directions simultaneously. When a connection is opened, it is given a name (by TCP) that the user may subsequently use to refer to the connection. TCP associates messages with a connection, taking into account both source and destination sockets. This enables the same port on a given machine to take part in multiple, concurrent connections with different users. For examples, all incoming electronic mail, from different sources, is delivered through the same port (number 103 if it is X.400 based) and its source identified via the connection name.

**Sequence/acknowledgement number**  TCP numbers each octet that it transmits on a given connection. The initial sequence number is established, for each direction, when the connection is established. It need not be 1 nor the same for each direction. When a data segment is transmitted, the sequence number field in the header contains the sequence number of the first octet in the data field. The acknowledgement number field contains the sequence number of the octet that the sender expects to receive next. These numbers enable the TCP component to reassemble the data stream at its destination before passing it to the user. They also enable lost data to be detected and retransmitted.

**Header length**  This is a field containing the length of the header, in 32-bit units. This field is necessary to enable the start of the data field to be computed as the length of the header is determined by the options selected.

**Code bits**  TCP defines four segment types, all with the same header format. They are connection establishment, connection termination, data and acknowledgement segments and are distinguished by the setting of the control flags or code bits. The use of these flags is best illustrated by examining the flow of segments during connection establishment, data exchange and connection termination for two users, A and B.

Connection establishment is a three-way handshake. Usually one TCP component is the active partner, initiating the handshake, and the other is the passive partner, waiting for the handshake. Assume A is active and B is passive, although either may assume either role.

A sends a segment to B that has the SYN bit set, as one of the purposes of the handshaking exchange is to synchronize sequence numbers. The sequence number field contains the initial sequence number, x, for the flow from A to B. B responds with a segment with both the SYN and ACK bits set. The sequence number field is set to y, the initial sequence number from B to A, and the acknowledgement field to x + 1, as the next octet that B expects is number x + 1. Finally A sends a segment with an acknowledgement set and an acknowledgement field of y + 1. Note that SYN indicates that the segment contains an initial sequence number (and is therefore sent to establish a connection) and ACK indicates that the acknowledgement field contains a sequence number. Data may now be sent and acknowledged in each direction, using the ACK bit to indicate when a data segment also carries an acknowledgement.

When a user has no more data to send, it closes the connection in the outbound direction. This causes TCP to send a segment with the FIN bit set, indicating that no more data may be expected. The partner TCP acknowledges the FIN segment, but may continue to send data until it is also closed, resulting in a final FIN/ACK exchange.

TCP transmits information by treating the data submitted by a user as a continuous stream and dividing the stream into segments. This reduces the overhead that would result if small numbers of octets were transmitted each time the user issues a send request. There are, however, situations in which data should be sent immediately, particularly those involving interactive transactions. The user is provided with a 'push' option to force TCP to push data out of its buffer without waiting for it to fill. A mechanism is also required to force the receiver to make the data available to the destination application immediately they are received. This is achieved by setting the PSH flag in the data segment.

TCP does not provide an expedited data service as such. It does, however, enable a user to flag data for urgent delivery to their destination. The mechanism consists of the URG bit in the code field coupled with the urgent pointer field in the header. If the URG flag is set in a data segment, all octets in the data field up to the urgent pointer value are to be delivered immediately to the destination user, regardless of their position in the data stream.

Finally, the RST bit in the code field is used to abort the connection and immediately stop data transfer in both directions.

**Window**

The window field provides TCP with a flow control mechanism. It is a 16-bit number, set in an acknowledgement segment, indicating how many further octets the receiver is willing to accept. A window size of 0 temporarily stops the flow of data in that direction although the sender is required to continue sending segments periodically, and the receiver to send ACK segments, until the window is opened.

**Checksum**

A checksum calculation is performed by the sender, including header and data, and repeated by the receiver, to check the integrity of the segment.

**Options**           The options field is used to extend the protocol. The most common use of this field is to negotiate a maximum segment size during connection establishment.

The interface between a TCP user (an upper layer protocol) and the TCP layer is described in terms of a number of primitives—service requests and service responses. An example of a TCP service request is the active open, which enables a user to request a connection to another socket. The required request parameters are the source port, the destination port and the destination IP address with, optionally, precedence and security parameters. If the connection is successfully established, the TCP service provider returns a handle (the local connection name) used to refer to the connection in subsequent service requests.

Outgoing data is sent on the connection by invoking the send service, supplying as parameters the local connection name, the data and their length and, optionally, a push request or an urgent request. Incoming data are delivered to the user with an indication of the connection name, the data length and possibly an urgent flag.

## 9.4 The User Datagram Protocol (UDP)

The TCP, discussed in Section 9.3, provides a connection-orientated reliable transport service between two applications or upper-lower protocols. The protocol supports sequence numbering at the octet level, flow control by sliding, variable sized window and forced or urgent delivery. The sophistication of these features is reflected in the rather complicated structure of a TCP service provider. The protocol is well suited to the exchange of large amounts of data between two users, but less well suited to a brief exchange of short messages.

An alternative to TCP is provided by the *User Datagram Protocol (UDP)*. As its name suggests, it is connectionless and allows upper layer protocols to exchange datagrams. The IP also allows for the exchange of datagrams. The main contribution of UDP is to permit different destinations (different upper layer protocols) within a particular host to be specified in the datagram.

The UDP datagram header is shown in Figure 9.3. The source/destination port fields are used to identify specific applications on machines that are themselves identified by the underlying IP address. As in TCP, certain common services are allocated to specific port numbers. Two different applications, one using UDP and the other using TCP, may use the same port number. The two data streams are distinguished by the protocol field in the IP header (see Section 9.2), which is set to different values for different IP users (such as 6 for TCP and 17 for UDP).

The checksum in UDP is optional. However, as the IP checksum covers only the IP header, the UDP checksum is the only way of checking that

(a)

| Source port | Destination port |
|---|---|
| Message length | Checksum |

(b)

| | Source IP address | |
|---|---|---|
| | Destination IP address | |
| Zero | Protocol | Length |

*Figure 9.3  UDP headers (a) UDP datagram header (b) UDP/TCP pseudo-header*

data have survived the trip uncorrupted. Both TCP and UDP checksum calculations incorporate a feature not found in other protocols.

When calculating the checksum, both TCP and UDP create a pseudo-header that is included in the checksum calculation but not transmitted with the message. The format of the pseudo-header is also shown in Figure 9.3. The protocol field contains the same value as that in the IP header (6 for TCP and 17 for UDP). The length field contains the datagram or segment length, excluding the pseudo-header.

The purpose of the pseudo-header is to verify that the message has reached its intended destination. The destination is specified partly by the IP address in the IP header and partly by the port number in the UDP/TCP header. It thus uses information from two protocol layers. When a message reaches its destination, the IP layer must pass IP addresses to the TCP/UDP layer, in addition to the segment or datagram, to enable the checksum to be recalculated and delivery of an uncorrupted message to the correct destination verified.

## 9.5 Upper layer protocols

The IP enables internets to be created. An IP datagram is encapsulated in the appropriate data unit for transmission across individual networks that make up the internet. IP may be supplemented by other layer 3 protocols, such as ICMP, ARP and RARP, and used by layer 4 protocols such as TCP and UDP. They are all part of the flexible world of TCP/IP.

Within the TCP/IP community, OSI layers 5, 6 and 7 tend to be considered as a single entity, generically called the upper layer protocol.

The upper layer protocol is the user of the TCP or UDP service. It may be an application program that may itself provide the functions associated with these layers or may dispense with them. The application may, on the other hand, take advantage of the many upper layer protocols that have been defined, under the aegis of TCP/IP, to address specific application needs. They are analogous to the SASE of the OSI model (see Chapter 6). In this section, some of the more common upper layer protocols associated with TCP/IP are described.

## File transfer

The most common protocol associated with file access and transfer in a TCP/IP environment is the *File Transfer Protocol (FTP)*. FTP follows the client/server model with a TCP/IP internet providing connections between client and server. FTP components appear in both client and server systems.

FTP uses two TCP connections between client and server. The *control connection* is used to carry control commands and responses between client and server. These messages tell the server which file is to be accessed and the type of operation to be performed. The server system listens on a well-known port (number 21) for control connections from clients.

A second connection, the *data transfer connection*, is established dynamically if a file needs to be transferred between client and server. The server again uses a well-known port (number 20) for file transfer with clients. The client port number to be used is sent over the control connection. A client may request a file transfer between two servers by establishing a control connection with each server and then requesting a data transfer connection between the two servers.

A less sophisticated file transfer mechanism is provided by the *Trivial File Transfer Protocol (TFTP)* assigned to well-known port number 69. It provides a simple file transfer service using UDP as the underlying transport service. A file is sent in fixed 512-byte blocks, with each block being acknowledged by the receiver.

## Electronic mail

Electronic mail is the most widely used application in a distributed system. It is used for small notes, memoranda, reports and as an alternative form of file transfer. The TCP/IP suite includes standards for both the format of electronic mail messages and for the protocol governing the exchange of messages between server and client.

The message format standard is known as *822*, from the number of the standard. It defines the format of the message header as a number of lines, each containing a keyword followed by a colon followed by a value. Keywords include TO, FROM and REPLY-TO. The format of the body of the message is not specified and is free for the sender to choose.

The protocol for message exchange is the *Simple Mail Transfer Protocol (SMTP)*. The protocol defines a number of commands sent from client to server and a number of responses sent from server to client. Commands consist of a keyword, such as MAIL or RCPT (recipient), together with appropriate parameters, and responses consist of a three-digit number followed by text. For example, the number 220 in a response indicates that the server is ready for mail, 250 indicates acceptance of a command and 354 invites the client to start mail transfer. These numbers are used by the SMTP software to control the flow of messages. The associated text is largely to assist human understanding of the flow.

The simplicity of this protocol is typical of the upper layer protocols defined for TCP/IP and is in sharp contrast with the abstract, complex but all-embracing protocols defined for the upper layers of the OSI model. The approach taken by the two standards communities is quite different. TCP/IP defines a protocol to satisfy a particular need, such as electronic mail, and tries (but not too hard) to make it complete. If it turns out to be inadequate, another protocol is proposed. Sometimes, a protocol turns out to be more than adequate and so a 'simple' version is introduced—SMTP is a simplified version of an earlier MTP. ISO, by contrast, tries very hard to ensure that a protocol caters for all foreseeable situations. The result so far has been relatively widespread implementations of the TCP/IP protocols compared with OSI.

## Remote interactive access

Interactive sessions between a terminal and a remote application are a common use of a network. TCP/IP includes the TELNET protocol to support such sessions. The protocol is also based on a client/server model. The client process accepts input from the user's terminal and provides output. It is connected, via a TCP/IP connection, to a server process that interfaces to the remote application.

Many types of terminal and host are used for interactive computing, each with its own protocol. In order to allow for these different types, TELNET incorporates the concept of a *Network Virtual Terminal (NVT)*. Messages between client and server processes are all in NVT format. The client and server processes map this format into the format expected by the real users that they represent. The client process may also represent an application process. For example, the communication on the FTP control connection (see under file transfer above) conforms to TELNET NVT protocol.

A further feature of TELNET allows client and server to negotiate options that characterize the type of connection between them, such as half or full duplex operation, 7- or 8-bit data and line mode rather than character mode operation.

## Naming and addressing

In Section 9.2, the contents of the IP datagram header were described, in particular the way machines on an internet are addressed. Network users expect to refer to end points by name rather than by address and all network architectures provide a name-to-address translation facility.

# Transmission Control Protocol/Internet Protocol (TCP/IP)

In an SNA network, it is one of the responsibilities of the SSCP. ISO defines a directory service in the 8-part standard ISO 9594, which corresponds closely to the CCITT X.500 series of recommendations. TCP/IP includes the *Domain Name System (DNS)*.

DNS uses a hierarchical system that divides the set of entities to be named into subsets called domains. Each domain may be divided into further domains. For example, the Internet defines the following top-level domains:

- COM for commercial organizations
- EDU for educational institutions
- GOV for government organizations
- MIL for military organizations
- NET for network support centres
- INT for international organizations
- ORG for organizations not covered by the above specific names
- two-letter code for countries (such as GB, US).

Most users adhere to this system, which allows for both an organization-based hierarchy and a geographically-based hierarchy. For example, the ABC manufacturing company may register the domain ABC.COM to contain all its sites and then introduce further domains to contain subsets. Alternatively, it may register a number of domains such as ABC.US and ABC.GB. Top-level domains and immediately subordinate domains are administered by the *Internet Network Information Centre*. The ABC company, having registered the domain name ABC.COM, is then free to subdivide and administer that domain as it chooses.

The mechanism for mapping names to addresses is implemented as a hierarchical set of name servers that communicate over the internet. The ABC company will provide a server for the domain ABC.COM that is subordinate to the .COM server. When the UK Inland Revenue at CORP.UKIR.GOV wishes to send a message to the ABC company at TAX.ABC.COM, it gets the address, in theory, via the .GB IR, .GOV, .COM and .ABC servers. In practice, the number of servers is reduced, and their address stores increased, to reduce the number of server references. Furthermore, servers dynamically update their knowledge by caching recently used names and their addresses, so that they can supply the information without reference to the authoritative server. In this case, the client is warned that the information may be out of date.

DNS defines a protocol for communication between name servers and their clients. The protocol enables multiple questions and multiple answers to be carried in a single message.

**Network management**  TCP/IP includes the *Simple Network Management Protocol (SNMP)* to enable the configuration of an internet to be controlled and its status examined. The suite also allows for the use of the OSI *Common Management Information Protocol (CMIP)* over a TCP connection (so-called CMOT). Discussion of internet management is saved for Chapter 12.

## 9.6 The TCP/IP standards process

In this chapter, a few of the many services and protocols that have become associated with the internet suite have been described. Work on TCP/IP standards is carried out by working groups and coordinated by the *Internet Activities Board (IAB)*. The IAB includes two major groups, the *Internet Engineering Task Force (IETF)* and the *Internet Research Task Force (IRTF)*, each with a steering group to coordinate the activities of its working groups. The IETF, much the larger group, concentrates on short- to medium-term internet problems, while the IRTF undertakes longer term research activities.

The work of these bodies is published, by the Internet Network Information Centre, in a series of *Requests for Comments (RFCs)*. Every three months, the IAB publishes an RFC that lists the various TCP/IP standards and their status.

Any protocol in the TCP/IP suite has a state and a status. The state describes the progress of the protocol through the standardization process, ranging from *initial* (submitted for consideration) to *standard* (officially recognized as part of the suite). The status specifies the use of the standard. It may be *required* (mandatory), *recommended* (encouraged), *elective* (up to the user), *limited use* (not for general use) or *not recommended* (used mainly for obsolete protocols). Very few protocols have required status, although IP is included. All other protocols mentioned in this chapter, including TCP, have recommended status.

## 9.7 Summary

There is a pragmatist's view and a purist's view of the TCP/IP suite. The pragmatist points to the simplicity of the protocols, the ease of implementation and the availability and use of products. The purist also points to the simplicity of the protocols, but in order to emphasize their limited scope and contrast them with the all-embracing intent of the OSI layer protocols. Open communication would best be served by a compromise in which ISO and the IAB work towards a common goal, with more than one eye on users' needs.

*The WNB's approach to upper layer protocols has been more pragmatic than purist in that it has made more use of TCP/IP than of the upper layers of the OSI model. This approach has, again, been governed by the availability of off-the-shelf products and the need to communicate with other enterprises.*

# CHAPTER 10
# Integrated Services Digital Network (ISDN)

## 10.1 Introduction

In Chapter 2 the fundamental difference between the analog nature of sound, such as the human voice, and the digital nature of computer-processed information was described. Also described was a technique, *Pulse Code Modulation (PCM)*, for converting speech into digital form. PCM dates back to 1937 when its commercial exploitation was, at best, uneconomical. By the late 1960s, devices were becoming available that were able to provide PCM at reasonable cost. At about the same time, the ability of an optical fibre to carry enormous amounts of digital information was beginning to be recognized. The exploitation of these technologies has resulted in a quiet revolution in the world of telephony that will be felt by customers during the 1990s.

During the 1980s, telephone companies have been replacing their trunk circuits with optical fibres carrying digital signals and their telephone exchanges with computer-controlled digital switches. This infrastructure is largely complete in many countries. Interexchange telephone traffic is increasingly carried in digital form. Since data produced by a computer is naturally in digital form, the two types of information may be integrated on a common digital circuit. The result is the *Integrated Digital Network (IDN)* operated by many of the world's telephone companies.

In the meantime, telephone users have analog telephones and computer users or fax users have digital machines. They are often, and increasingly, one and the same person or business. What is needed to complete the picture, and to provide end-to-end digital communication, is the extension of the IDN to customer premises to provide an *Integrated Services Digital Network (ISDN)*. In its Recommendation 1.110, the CCITT defines an ISDN as:

> A network, in general evolving from a telephony Integrated Network, that provides end-to-end digital connectivity to support a wide range of services, including voice and non-voice services, to which users have access by a limited set of standard multi-purpose user-network interfaces.

In this chapter are described some of these services and interfaces in the light of the previous discussion of layered architectures, beginning with some of the new (or resurrected) terminology that inevitably accompanies new technology. Quotations are from the CCITT's Recommendations.

ISDN uses the term *bearer* to refer to the common physical channel over which various services are provided to the customer, using *time division multiplexing*. The bearer is the digital circuit provided by the telephone company to the customer's premises. The services that are provided to the customer fall into two categories.

A *bearer service* is 'a type of telecommunication service that provides the capability for the transmission of signals between user–network interfaces'. The service provides the user with an information channel from his or her own user–network interface to the user–network interface of another user. The channel may be circuit-switched or packet-switched. The interface to the channel is defined by the CCITT's Recommendations, such as X.25, covering layers 1 to 3 of the OSI model. Users are free to use whatever upper-layer protocols they choose to control communication on the channel.

A *teleservice* is 'a type of telecommunication service that provides the complete capability, including terminal equipment functions, for communication between users according to protocols established by agreement between Administrations and/or RPOAs'. *Administrations* and *RPOAs* are the telephone companies. Teleservices provide functions equivalent to the upper layers (4 to 7) of the OSI model and include Telephony, Telex, Teletex, Telefax and Videotex.

These services can be enhanced by supplementary services. A supplementary service is defined (not very usefully) as 'any service provided by a network in addition to its basic services'. Supplementary services are intended to provide optional enhancement similar to those provided by optional facilities in X.25 (see Chapter 5) and other X-series Recommendations. They include options such as closed user groups and calling line identification for both voice and data calls.

The ISDN equivalent of a customer's conventional analog telephone connection is a *basic rate* ISDN connection, which provides the customer with two 64-kbits/second information channels and a 16-kbits/second signalling channel. The information channels are *B channels* and the signalling channel is a *D channel*. A *primary rate* access, for larger customers, provides 30 B channels in Europe and 23 in North America, where digital trunk circuits run at 1.544 Mbits/second rather than the 2.048 Mbits/second used in Europe. In both cases, the D channel rate is 64 kilobits per second.

## 10.2 Lines and customer premises equipment

An ISDN basic rate connection defines two 64 kbits/second channels and one 16-kbits/second channel, all of them full duplex. The traditional connection between a customer and the local exchange is two copper wires twisted together, which the telephone companies would like to continue using for ISDN access. The line is artificially restricted to the

# Integrated Services Digital Network (ISDN)

minimum bandwidth required for intelligible speech to enable the maximum number of speech circuits to be carried by the trunk lines. Removing this restriction enables the much greater intrinsic bandwidth of copper wire to be used. Careful attention to controlling cross talk and random noise enables local telephone loops to provide the capacity for basic-rate access. Full-duplex operation is achieved by one of several techniques. *Frequency division duplex* separates the transmit and receive signals into different frequency bands. *Time division duplex* separates them into different time slots. *Echo cancellation* essentially subtracts the echo of the transmitted signal from the received signal, to reveal the part of the signal that is due to transmission from the other end. The details of these line optimization techniques are beyond the scope of this book. Their effect is to extend the IDN to the customer's premises and bring with it the ISDN.

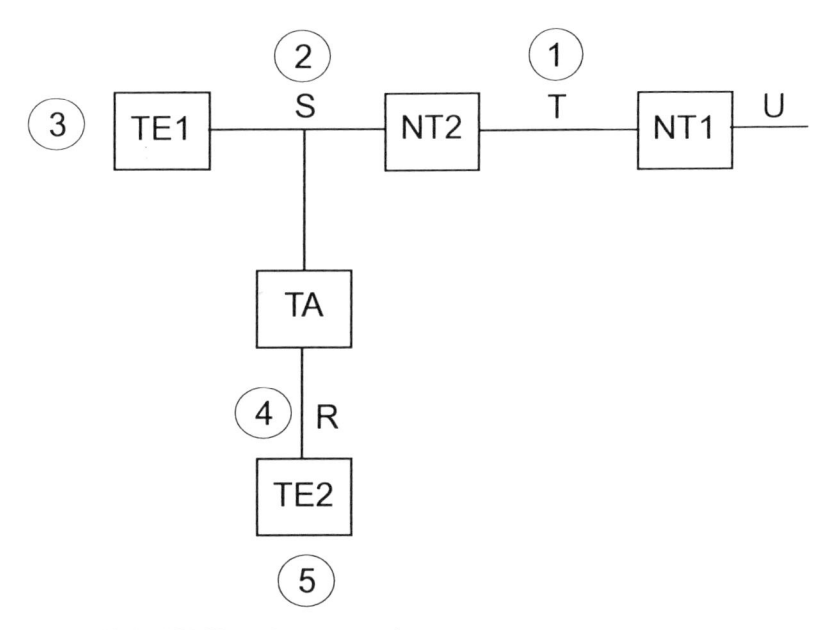

*Figure 10.1  ISDN service access points*

Figure 10.1 shows the points of access to the ISDN for customer equipment, such as digital telephones, fax machines and personal computers. Also shown are reference points at which physical interfaces are formally defined by the CCITT. The ISDN line is connected to *Network Termination 1 (NT1)* and provides an interface at reference point T. NT1 is normally owned by the telephone company. The *U interface* provides for ownership of NT1 by the customer. A further network termination (*NT2*) allows for connection of multiple terminals, for example on a PABX, a LAN or via a cluster controller. Terminals interface to *NT2* at the *S reference points*. In simple configurations, NT2 is not required and terminals connect at the T reference point. Up to

175

eight terminals (telephones, fax machines, PCs and so on) may be connected to a basic-rate ISDN line using a four-wire bus, sometimes called the *S/T bus*.

ISDN bearer services are accessed at points 1 and 2 via the T and S interfaces respectively. These interfaces are new to ISDN. Access to services defined by older recommendations, such as X.21 and X.25, is provided at access point 4 via a *Terminal Adapter (TA)*. *TE1* and *TE2* represent *Terminal Equipment* types 1 and 2. TE1 is a terminal, such as a PC with an ISDN card, that conforms to the S interface standard. TE2 is a terminal, such as a PC with an X.25 card, that connects via a terminal adapter to the S interface. These types of terminal equipment are required for teleservices that are accessed at points 3 and 5. In summary, NT1/2, TE1/2 and TA are groups of functions separated by defined interfaces—a concept with which we are now familiar. As ISDN equipment replaces X-series equipment, points 4 and 5, TA and TE2 and reference point R, will become less common.

## 10.3 ISDN services

A basic-rate ISDN connection provides two 64 kbits/second information (B) channels and a 16 kbits/second signalling (D) channel for making and receiving calls. The two information channels may be used simultaneously, providing full-duplex connections to any two of eight terminals. Some networks will also carry user packet data on the D channel. The impact on the user, apart from simultaneous access to more than one service, will be most apparent in the set of teleservices offered, which includes digital voice.

In the brief description of PCM in Chapter 2, it was indicated that a data capacity of 64 kbits/second is needed for good-quality encoding of a 3.1 kHz voice bandwidth. PCM encoded speech would not be noticeably improved in quality on an ISDN B channel. More recently, however, algorithms have been developed that enable a 7 kHz bandwidth signal to be transmitted on a 64 kbits/second digital line. These depend on a modified form of PCM known as *Adaptive Differential Pulse Code Modulation (ADPCM)*. The higher bandwidth significantly improves the quality of ISDN-transmitted speech and may soon enable CD-quality sound to be transmitted.

The most common PSTN service, after the telephone service, is fax transmission. This will obviously benefit from the higher rate possible with ISDN. The group 4 fax Recommendation has been developed by the CCITT for use on the ISDN. The group 4 Recommendation envisages a machine very different from the common group 3 machines. High resolution and a sophisticated compression algorithm make full use of the 64 kbits/second data rate. A full seven-layer communication protocol stack is defined. The link layer protocol is based on the LAPB version of HDLC and the network layer on an enhanced X.25 packet

## Integrated Services Digital Network (ISDN)

layer. Layers 4 and 5 conform to the OSI transport and session protocols and the upper layers are defined by the *Document Transfer and Manipulation (DTAM)* protocol and the *Open Document Architecture (ODA)*. It will be many years before such machines are in common use.

Other, currently low-quality services, will be significantly enhanced by ISDN techniques. Low-cost Videotex terminals are common. Photographic quality transmissions may be achieved using the ISDN and a high-performance compression technique known as a *Discrete Cosine Transform (DCT)*. Moving images may also be compressed for ISDN transmission, enabling videotelephone and videoconference services to be offered.

## 10.4 ISDN protocols

An ISDN basic-rate connection provides the user with B channels on which to exchange information with another user and a D channel to exchange signals with the exchange. New protocols have been defined for ISDN at the physical layer (layer 1) for both types of channel and at the data link (layer 2) and network (layer 3) layers for the D channel. They are all defined in CCITT Recommendations.

**The physical layer**

Layer 1 functions are responsible for transferring bits across the interface between NT and TE equipment (between the network and the terminal at the S or T reference points). It is defined by the CCITT's Recommendations 1.430 for basic rate and 1.431 for primary rate. It is used for full-duplex transmission on both B and D channels.

The physical layer functions assemble a bit string by time division mutiplexing input for the three channels. The bit string is transmitted as 48-bit frames with one frame lasting 250µs, resulting in a bit rate of 192 kbits/second. The structure of a frame is slightly different in the two directions. In Figure 10.2 the structure of the NT to TE frame is shown.

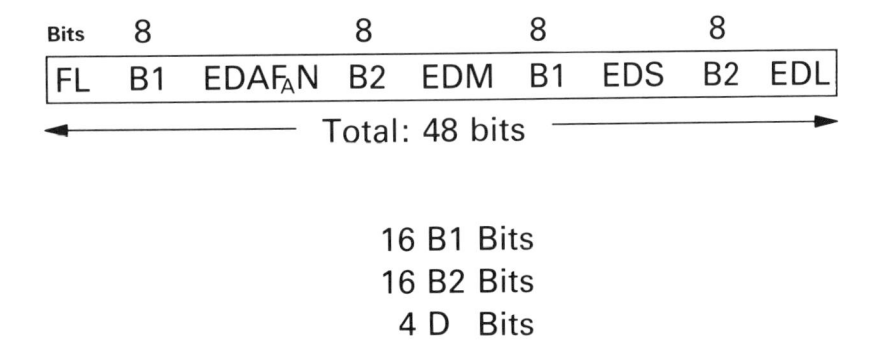

Bits  8        8       8      8

| FL | B1 | ED A F$_A$ N | B2 | ED M | B1 | ED S | B2 | ED L |

◄——————— Total: 48 bits ———————►

16 B1 Bits
16 B2 Bits
4 D Bits
in 250 µs

*Figure 10.2  ISDN layer 1 frame*

The frame begins, for the TE, at the left with a *framing bit* (F) followed by an L bit. *L bits* are used to balance the frame to prevent a dc buildup on the line. The *FL* combination marks the beginning of a frame. The main components are substrings of bits destined respectively for the current users of the two B channels (B1 and B2) and the D channel in each 250μs period, B1 and B2 each get 16 bits, equivalent to 64 kbits/second, and D gets 4 bits, equivalent to 16 kbits/second. The 4 bits marked *'E'* are on the E, or echo channel, on which bits arriving at the NT on the D channel are echoed back to the TEs. The echo channel is used in the collision detection mechanism, which is explained below. The remaining bits are an *Activation bit (A)*, used in the activation procedure, the $F_A$ and *N bits* used to ensure frame alignment, the *M bit*, used for multiframing, and a reserved bit *S* (the reader is referred to more specialized works, particularly *ISDN Explained* by Griffiths et al, for a discussion of the use of these bits).

A TE wishing to make a call sends a *call establishment message* to the D channel. There may be up to eight TEs, in a multidrop configuration on the S/T bus and, consequently, contention for the channel. The layer 1 D channel *contention procedure* ensures that each terminal gets an opportunity to transmit. It depends on the layer 2 protocol, which is a variant of HDLC (see below). In particular, it depends on the bit stuffing technique used to ensure that the frame delimiters (flags) are detected (see Chapter 5). A sequence of more than six 1 bits can never occur during transmission of information under HDLC. Between HDLC frames, binary 1 bits are transmitted.

A TE, when it wants to access the D channel, begins counting the number of 1 bits on the channel. If the count exceeds a predetermined value, which itself exceeds six, the channel is idle and the TE can use it. If a 0 bit appears, the counter is reset. After transmitting a frame of information (an HDLC frame), the predetermined count is incremented by 1 and, consequently, the TE needs to wait longer for its next turn, allowing other TEs with a lower threshold to access the channel. This simple technique combines access control with a priority system.

Collisions may still occur if two TEs have the *same* priority (are waiting for the same number of 1 bits). This is where the E channel comes in. A transmitting station compares each bit that it sends on the D channel with the next bit it receives on the E channel. If they are the same, it continues transmitting. This technique of 'listening' while talking was met with earlier—it is the CSMA/CD technique used in LANs. Once a TE has successfully established a call, it has exclusive use of the B channel to which the call is allocated.

**The data link layer**

Having acquired the D channel, a TE exchanges signalling information with the exchange. The data link protocol used to ensure that this information is not corrupted is a variant of HDLC, developed for use on the D channel, and called *LAPD (Link Access Protocol for the*

# Integrated Services Digital Network (ISDN)

*D-channel)*. Other variants of this have been mentioned previously, namely SDLC, the unbalanced normal response mode used in SNA, and LAPB, the asynchronous balanced mode forming level 2 of the X.25 interface. SDLC supports multidrop configurations, albeit by the inefficient technique of polling, while LAPB does not. The ISDN D channel requires multidrop operation as it may need to support up to eight TEs.

HDLC was described in some detail in Chapter 5 (see Section 5.3) so the discussion here is confined to the special features of LAPD. It uses extended sequence numbers so that the control field in the LAPD frame consists of two octets to contain the wider counters. It also uses extended addressing, requiring a two-octet address field (the structure of this field is shown in Figure 10.3). The *Service Access Point Identifier (SAPI)* field identifies the service for which the frame is intended. In Section 10.3 it was mentioned that some networks use the D channel to carry packets of user data. X.25 packets have a SAPI value of 16. A few of the other 64 service access points have been allocated values; most are reserved for future use.

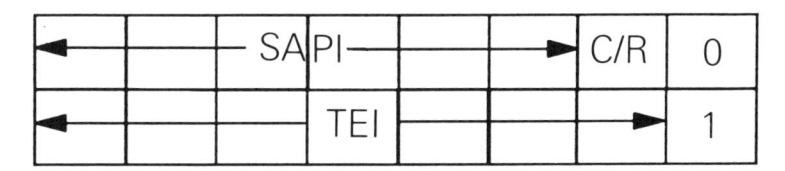

| | | SAPI | | | C/R | 0 |
|---|---|---|---|---|---|---|
| | | TEI | | | | 1 |

*Figure 10.3  The structure of the LAPD address field*

The *Terminal Endpoint Identifier (TEI)* field identifies the terminal to which the frame is addressed. The combination of SAPI and TEI identifies a particular service access point in a particular terminal. For example, if the SAPI has a value of 16, it is destined for an X.25 terminal. The terminal that recognizes its own TEI will accept the frame. As is conventional, the all-ones TEI (value 127) means a frame broadcast to all terminals that have a SAPI corresponding to that carried in the frame, such as all telephones on the S/T bus. TEI values in the range 0–63 are assigned by the user and must, of course, be different. A terminal with a TEI in this range may establish a layer 2 connection without negotiation with the network. TEI values in the range 64–126 are assigned by the network. They are conveyed to a management SAPI (value 63) in the TE, using the HDLC UI frame.

**The network layer**

The information field of a LAPD frame carries the layer 3 messages used to establish connections. The format of a message is shown in Figure 10.4. The protocol discriminator field enables ISDN call control messages to be distinguished from messages formatted according to other protocols that may also be used at layer 3 on the D channel. The value assigned to ISDN control is 16. The call reference value identifies

| Protocol discriminator |||||
|---|---|---|---|---|
| 0 | 0 | 0 | 0 | Length of reference value |
| Call reference value |||||
| 0 | Message type ||||
| Additional control information |||||
| |||||

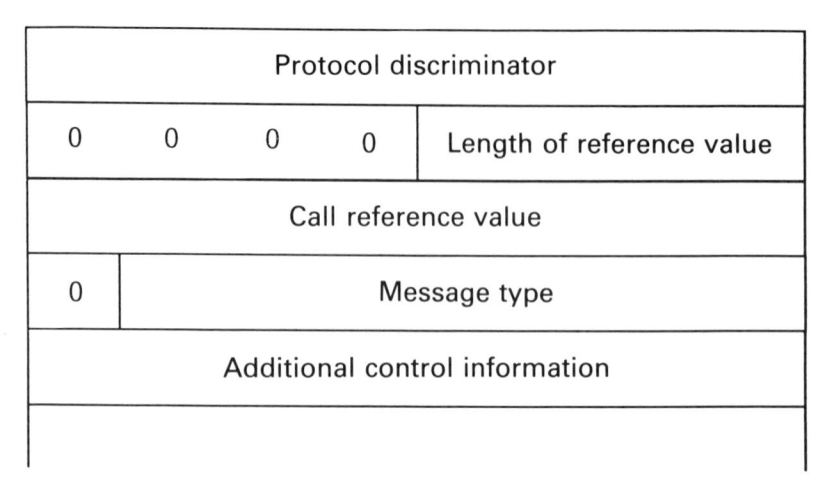

*Figure 10.4  ISDN layer 3 signalling message*

the call with which the message is associated. The message type field defines the type of control message and the additional information field, of variable length, carries other parameters needed to establish the call.

Many control messages are defined, each requiring different elements of additional information. The CCITT's Recommendation that specifies the ISDN layer 3 protocol (Q.931) consists of some 360 pages in the CCITT's 1988 Blue Book. A description of one of the messages and a few of the associated information elements, many of which are optional, follows.

The SETUP message is sent by a TE to its exchange to establish a call to another TE. The called TE receives a SETUP message from its local exchange. The additional information field in the message contains a mass of information to describe the type of call requested. One of the information elements (the bearer capability element) defines the characteristics of the required connection—circuit switched or packet mode, 3.1 kHz or 7 kHz audio, data transfer rate and so on. Another (the high-layer compatibility element) identifies the type of application necessary to support the call at the called address. Options include Telephony, group 4 fax, Teletex, Telex, X.400 message handling systems and OSI applications. Other elements enable the maximum transit delay to be specified and enable the calling TE to select the route (source routing). The facility element enables various supplementary services to be selected.

Many of these optional elements of information are similar to quality or class of service parameters specified when an association is requested by an OSI application or a session is requested by an SNA LU. The ISDN SETUP message is probably the most complicated message defined by any communications protocol. This is understable as it seeks to cater for all known and predicted means of, and reasons for, communication between people and applications.

## Common channel signalling systems

The ISDN three-layer protocol, which has just been discussed, enables a TE to pass messages to and from its local exchange, to establish and clear calls and to provide call progress information. This protocol is used only on the interface between the TE and the network, not between exchanges. In this respect, it is similar to the three-layer X.25 interface.

Communication between exchanges in the IDN is carried on a 64 kbits/second channel derived by time division multiplexing. In Europe, timeslot 16 is conventionally allocated as the signalling channel. In North America, it is timeslot 24. The protocol governing this communication is referred to as a *Common Channel Signalling (CCS)* system. The CCITT's No. 6 signalling system was used in early IDN development, but has been superseded by the CCITT's No. 7 system.

We should not, at this stage, be surprised to learn that the No.7 system has a layered structure. The lower three levels are collectively called the *Message Transfer Part (MTP)* and are responsible for the reliable transfer of messages over the signalling channel. The messages constitute the *User Part (UP)*. The UP for Telephony signalling is the *Telephone User Part (TUP)*, while the UP part for ISDN signalling is the *Integrated Services User Part (ISUP)*. When ISDN is in full flow, ISUP will replace other user parts. ISDN messages between the TE and the exchange are converted at the local exchanges into ISUP messages for transport by the MTP across the IDN.

## 10.5 Broadband ISDN

The provision of basic rate ISDN access is a major event in the development of telecommunication. It is expected to encourage the use of networks, by both business and private users, to access a range of teleservices. Two 64 kbits/second circuits may merely whet the user's appetite and their limitations may soon become apparent. Primary-rate access gives more of the same rather than the higher data rates needed for true video telephones, for videoconferencing or for television transmission. The provision of circuits able to carry more than B channel rates is the province of *Broadband ISDN*. This is known as B-ISDN to avoid confusion with the older narrowband, N-ISDN.

The channels defined by the CCITT for B-ISDN are the H channels. Currently identified are H0, H11 and H12. These channels are all related to the European or North American primary rates of 2.048 Mbits/second and 1.544 Mbits/second respectively. H0 has a rate of 384 kbits/second, equivalent to six 64/kbits/second circuits and is suitable for videoconference and high fidelity sound transmissions. H11 runs at 1.536 Mbits/second and H12 at 1.920 Mbits/second. They use all the timeslots of the North American and European primary rates respectively. H21 (around 34 Mbits/second), H22 (around 55 Mbits/second) and H4 (around 135 Mbits/second) are under discussion.

The availability of optical fibre circuits in the local loop to the customer potentially enables very high rates to be provided. Two interfaces to these high-speed circuits are proposed: one at 150 Mbits/second and one at 600 Mbits/second, enabling many channels of various capacities to be carried. These rates make the delivery of high-definition television possible alongside lower bandwidth services.

The problem of multiplexing these services on to the common bearer is addressed by two techniques. *Synchronous Digital Hierarchy (SDH)* is a form of time division multiplexing based on an American (ANSI) development to enable managed optical connections to be provided. A frame consisting of 2430 bytes is constructed and transmitted in 125µs, giving a data rate of 155.52 Mbits/second. A higher rate interface of 622.08 Mbits/second enables bytes from four different frames to be interleaved. The frame of 2430 bytes is represented as a 9-row by 270-column matrix in which the first 9 columns of each row (except row 4) contain control information and the remainder of the matrix (called the payload) contains user data. The matrix is transmitted in row order (consult specialized references for more details about the multiplexing technique). The second technique is part of the rapidly growing area of fast packet switching.

## 10.6 Fast packet switching

The X.25 interface (described in Chapter 5) provides a reliable means of transferring packets of data between DTEs. The interface was first proposed in the late 1960s and first recommended by the CCITT in 1976, when data circuits were not as reliable as they have since become. Consequently, it incorporates, particularly in the level 2 protocol (LAPB), facilities for ensuring that packets are not corrupted, lost or repeated and that they are kept in order. After delivering a packet safely across the interface, the data link level hands it to the packet level to perform its routeing function. Routeing a packet through a packet-switched network is a relatively complicated and time-consuming process.

Data circuits have not only become more reliable, they can also offer much higher bit rates than were possible in the 1970s. ISDN, in particular in its broadband implementations, promises data rates of hundreds of megabits per second. At the same time, terminals have become increasingly able to provide upper layer functions to support end-to-end error control. LANs, operating at tens of megabits per second, need to exchange information across WANs. High-speed circuits are of little use without high-speed switches. A number of techniques have been developed to reduce the time that a switch needs before it can forward a packet. All of these techniques retain the concept of transporting data in discrete units and these are described by comparing them with the three levels of X.25.

## Frame relay

Frame relay dispenses with level 3 altogether and substantially reduces the functions of level 2, while at the same time incorporating routeing functions at level 2. The data link (level 2) protocol is a modified version of LAPD, the D channel protocol that is described in Section 10.4. The most significant difference is that the control field has disappeared and, with it, the different frame types, the sequence numbers and the P/F bit that are so important in LAPD and LAPB (see Chapter 5, Section 5.3) for controlling transmission between network nodes. These controls are expected to be exercised by higher-level functions in the end systems, not by the network. The aim of the network is to relay frames to their destination as quickly as possible. The frame protocol information is therefore reduced to the minimum necessary to achieve this end. The protocol is described in the CCITT's Recommendation Q.922, issued on an interim basis in 1991. It draws on the full LAPD protocol described in Q.921 and consists only of the core functions of that protocol.

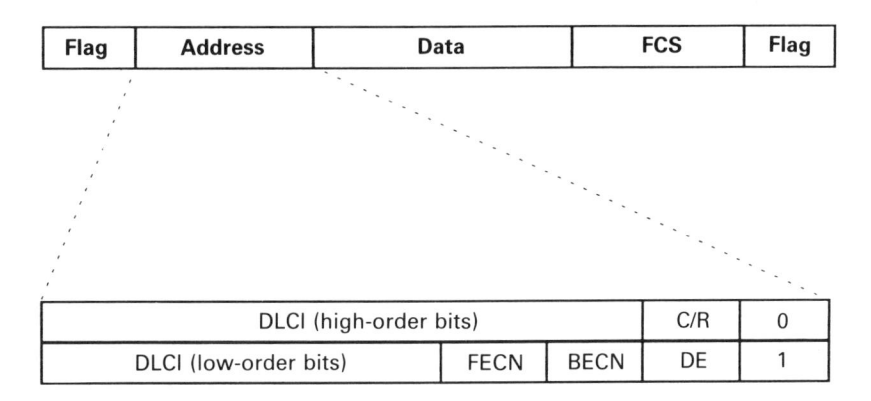

| Flag | Address | Data | FCS | Flag |
|---|---|---|---|---|

| DLCI (high-order bits) | | | C/R | 0 |
|---|---|---|---|---|
| DLCI (low-order bits) | FECN | BECN | DE | 1 |

**Key**
DLCI    Data Link Connection Identifier
C/R     Command/Response
FECN   Forward Explicity Congestion Notification
BECN   Backward Explicit Congestion Notification
DE      Discard Eligibility

*Figure 10.5   LAPD for frame relay*

Figure 10.5 shows a LAPD frame as defined for frame relay. It is a full LAPD frame less the control bytes. The flag and FCS fields have their usual function. Relaying of the frame depends on the 2-byte address field (extendable to 3 or 4 bytes) that contains the *Data Link Connection Identifier (DLCI)* of 10, 17 or 24 bits depending on the use of extended addressing. The DLCI is assigned when the call is established and is different at each end of the connection. It is analogous to the LCI in a conventional X.25 packet (see Chapter 5, Section 5.2). The DLCI allows different connections to be multiplexed on a single channel. The

DLCI is used by the frame relay switches to route the frame to its destination. Note that this is a level 2 function and no level 3 is required. The other bits in the address field are used to provide congestion indications, distinguish between commands and responses, indicate that a frame can be selectively discarded and indicate the extent of the address field itself.

The information field of the frame is of variable length and is of no interest to the network. It may contain virtually anything—X.25 packets, SDLC frames, HDLC frames, LAPB frames, full LAPD frames, LLC frames from LANs or IP datagrams. Each of these may, of course, encapsulate higher-layer protocol information and user data. A frame relay network is a fast and versatile means of transferring information. It is particularly popular for LAN-WAN-LAN internets.

## Frame switching

Frame switches also incorporate routeing at level 2. The protocol differs from frame relay in that it uses the full LAPD facilities, including the control field. A frame-switching network is thus able to provide node-to-node error control and flow control.

## Cell relay (Asynchronous Transfer Mode)

*Asynchronous Transfer Mode (ATM)* uses packet techniques to enable multiple channels, of differing rates, to use a single bearer. It is a particular example, defined for B-ISDN, of a technique known as *cell relay*. Other proprietary implementations of cell relay are also defined. Here attention is focused on ATM. The packets, which are called *cells*, are of fixed length (53 bytes) and consists of a 5-byte header and a 48-byte information field or payload. The header is particularly simple, as a switch would be unable to handle a data rate of 600 megabits per second if it were expected to perform complicated routeing processing on each cell. ATM differs fundamentally from TDM in allocating bandwidth to a channel dynamically, on demand, rather than allocating a fixed time slot to each channel, whether or not it has data to send. ATM does, however, impose a 5-byte overhead on every 48 bytes of data.

Despite its simplicity, the ATM cell header carries most of the information one would expect to see in a control field—route identification, flow control and error control. Routeing is performed at the ATM layer in a switch by reference to hardware implemented routeing tables. Level 3 of the B-ISDN reference model, the ATM adaptation layer, performs the break-up and reassembly of user data into cell payloads. Error checking, in keeping with the modern trend, is performed only on the header. More work remains to be done on the relationship between the lower layers of the OSI model and the lower three layers of the B-ISDN model.

Voice traffic is amenable to cell transport. A 64 kilobits per second digitized voice signal may be sent as 48 bytes of cell payload representing 6 ms of speech. The 'bandwidth on demand' characteristic of cell relay makes it ideally suitable to 'bursty' traffic, such as video transmissions that need large bandwidth when the picture changes.

The proposed standards for MANs (ISO 8802.6) are also based on cell relay. Cell relay and frame relay are emerging fast packet-switching technologies that, combined with the bandwidth of optical fibres, will make B-ISDN a reality and enable a wide range of services and a variety of internets to be accessible to homes and offices via a single socket.

## 10.7 Summary

The acronym ISDN has many pejorative interpretations, such as 'Information Subscribers Don't Need'. It is probably true that it will be many years before even N-ISDN is in common use. In the world of telecommunications, solutions in search of a problem have a habit of finding one.

*The main impact of ISDN on the WNB has been in the related area of fast packet switching. As X.25 has evolved, the bank's network has evolved with it. The latest step in this evolutionary process is the introduction of frame relay into the upper tier of the WNB's WAN. Cell relay may also be expected to be introduced in the future, together with the use of ISDN connections to branches. In its private voice network, the WNB has long made use of an ISDN-related signalling system—the Digital Private Network Signalling System (DPNSS)—between its voice circuit switches.*

# CHAPTER 11  Network security

## 11.1 Introduction

A communications network, public or private, local or wide area, is of critical importance to many businesses, particularly those with national or international scope. The reliable transfer of information between locations is essential to the operation and management of businesses. The organization of large companies is held together by their networks.

Many examples of the use of networks are increasingly familiar to the general public, particularly in the banking, travel and retail sectors. A company and its customers both readily accept transactions based on communication between computers. Goods and services are delivered and accounts debited and credited with little human intervention; cash appears through a hole in a wall. On a wider scale, governments and commercial organizations, often in a hostile or competitive environment, make far-reaching decisions based on the transfer of information between computers.

A company's network is an important tool in its operations. The tool needs to be available, and usable, when it is needed (these aspects are covered in Chapter 12). Of equal importance is the need to ensure that the tool is properly used. The proper use of a network is the subject of this chapter.

An information network delivers information from one point to another. This information may be in the form of speech, text or pictures. When processed by a computer, it is encoded in digital form. In various places, earlier in the book, protocols have been detailed that ensure that accidental corruption of data can be detected. How is it possible to detect intentional corruption of the data designed to introduce spurious operations? How can access to it in transit be prevented—it may well be confidential? How is it feasible to prevent unauthorized people using the tool (the network)? What does 'authorization' imply? The answers to these questions are the concern of network security.

## 11.2 Attacks and countermeasures

Attempts to use a network improperly are called *attacks*. They include making the network inoperative, use of the network by unauthorized people or equipment, reading information in transit through the network without changing it, changing information in transit, and capturing messages for retransmittal. Any of these attacks may damage the reputation or profitability of a business. In diplomatic and military circles, the effects may range from embarrassing to disastrous.

A prudent network provider will take countermeasures against attacks. Countermeasures cost money and may impose undesirable constraints on legitimate users, but failure to take countermeasures may also cost money due to the results of an attack. The provision of network security involves balancing the probability and cost of a successful attack against the cost of a countermeasure. Both sides of the equation are difficult to quantify with any precision. There is an unfortunate tendency for network providers to take the risk, particularly as it is not in the provider's interests to publicize a breach of security.

## Masquerade attacks

A device may be attached to a network permanently by a private link or temporarily by a dialled connection through the public telephone network. The network provider can exercise some control over leased connections but has much less control over dial-in devices. Such a device may establish a connection and perform unauthorized functions, ranging from eavesdropping to masquerading as a network host and, for example, authorizing funds for transfer. The provider requires a method of authenticating devices that are attached to the network.

Even if the device is legitimate, the network may wish to validate the identity of the person using it. Perhaps the most common type of computer fraud is the impersonation of a credit, debit or charge card holder by another person. Methods of authenticating devices and people are based on a common technique, that of the challenge and response. The more complicated case of personal authentication is considered first.

The person is required to respond to a demand to exhibit some physical characteristic or to show possession of some token or some knowledge. The challenging system holds a copy of the expected response that is compared with that offered by the person seeking authentication. Common physical characteristics used for authentication include general appearance, signature (appearance or dynamic structure), voice and fingerprint. The general appearance of a person is compared with an 'official' photograph, usually carried by the person. A signature is compared visually with a reference pattern, again usually carried by the person. The combination of possession of the token and the visual inspection is taken as proof of identity. The visual inspection is often cursory and such methods are not suitable for strong personal authentication.

Stronger methods using physical characteristics rely on a personal attribute such as fingerprint or retinal pattern. These patterns are recorded for each individual, digitized, expressed as a bit map and stored by the system. The pattern is measured when authentication is requested and compared with the stored reference pattern. Neither of these methods is socially very acceptable. A more user-friendly method is to examine the dynamic structure of a person's signature in terms of certain parameters, such as pressure, acceleration and lift-off points. Writing a signature is a largely unconscious act and the resulting dynamic structure is highly reproducible by the individual and difficult to forge. It is readily subject to digital representation and comparison and increasingly used in situations that call for reliable authentication. The reference pattern may be stored on a token and carried with the user so that authentication may be performed at the point of entry.

Voice characteristics are also suitable for user authentication as they are highly unique when expressed as digital patterns. On registration, the user is required to record perhaps 25 words from the system dictionary. When authentication is requested, the entry device displays words chosen randomly and asks the person to speak them until their identity is validated.

Methods depending on knowledge are familiar to network users in the form of passwords or Personal Identification Numbers (PINs). Again, they are often combined with a token such as an entry pass or an ATM card. They are considered weak due to the need to change the information frequently, resulting in the prevalent habit of writing down the (supposedly) secret information. They are sometimes augmented by a random request to supply some information, such as grandmother's maiden name, which can be remembered without recording it.

The point at which reference information—be it a photograph, a complex bit map or a simple number—is stored and processed by the system is of some interest. It is sometimes carried by the person, as noted above, and is made available to the system by means of some token-reading device. It is sometimes stored locally at the point of entry and sometimes at a central location. Local storage and processing enables authentication, which may involve a complex pattern comparison process, to be performed more quickly but may restrict the user's points of entry. Central storage and processing involves sending messages through the network, which takes time. Furthermore, they contain information that should be kept secret. Probably the best combination is an intelligent token (a *smart card*) coupled with local authentication processing.

Authenticating a *device*, rather than a *person*, uses a similar challenge-response technique. When an unknown device appears on the network and sends a message, the receiving device issues a challenge. It may, for example, generate a random number, encrypt it using a key that should be known by legitimate network stations and then send it to the unknown station. If the remote device knows the key, it can retrieve the random number, perform some operation on it (such as incrementing by one), re-encrypt it using the same key and return the result to the challenger. The device is accepted as authentic by virtue of its possession of the correct key, which must, of course, remain secret. Many variants of the technique are implemented, all of which establish authenticity on the basis of possession of secret information.

## Data secrecy and integrity

The methods outlined above are designed to prevent attacks on the network from unauthorized devices or users. They perform an access control function similar to the physical access control that might be exercised for a building and similar techniques are used. Many of them rely on information, such as passwords, PINs or keys, being kept secret from an unauthorized user. They also depend on information not being changed. If the system's copy of, say, a password is changed, a legitimate user will be unable to use the network. Denial of access to a legitimate user is also classed as a threat against which countermeasures should be taken.

There are many other examples in networking of the need to preserve the secrecy and/or the integrity of information. In the introduction to this chapter, it was intimated that networks are often used to carry information of commercial, diplomatic or military sensitivity. Measures must be taken to protect this information during its transit through the network.

Several types of attack may be made on data carried by unprotected channels, such as those leased from a common carrier such as a telephone company. A channel may be tapped, enabling an intruder to read messages but not modify their contents. Such an attack is called a *passive attack*. More sophisticated equipment may be used to capture messages, change their content and retransmit them to the intended destination. Captured messages may be retransmitted twice, without change, resulting in two funds transfers, say, from one message. These types of attack are *active attacks*. Methods of countering attacks on either the secrecy of data, its integrity or both are required. Such methods should be applicable to data either in transit or in storage. It has long been accepted that *cryptography* is the most suitable method for the protection of data and so this is considered in the next section.

It was mentioned earlier that security involves a compromise between the *risk* of not having it and the *cost* of providing it. Most networks make some provision for access control and data protection. Both involve not only cost but also processing overhead. Access control is usually mandatory while data protection may be offered as a user-selected option. It is possible to build highly secure networks. They depend on some information being kept secret and, ultimately, on people being trusted to keep secrets.

The ultimate dependence on people is inevitable. Insider attacks by people who know the secret are perhaps the most common form of computer fraud. Countermeasures to such attacks require dual, or multiple, control over sensitive operations on secret data so that no one person knows the whole secret and collusion is necessary to perpetrate a fraud.

## 11.3 Cryptography

Cryptography is the processing of data with the intent of hiding their meaning. It has been used since early times, indeed, transposition ciphers were known to the ancient Greeks and the Caesar cipher was supposedly first used by Julius Caesar. Such early cipher systems were operated by hand. As the science developed, mechanical and electromechanical methods were used to convert clear text into cipher text and vice versa. The subject, and the companion subject of cryptanalysis, have developed enormously with the use of electronic data processing.

A *cipher* transforms individual characters and symbols of the plain, or clear, text message into individual characters and symbols in the cipher text. A *code* transforms words and phrases into different words and phrases. The distinction shall not be dwelt on here, rather the word 'encryption' shall be used to cover ciphers *and* codes.

Fundamentally, cryptography is a subject for mathematicians and, in particular, number theorists. The authors do not qualify as such and neither, we assume, do many of our readers. In this section, therefore, an attempt has been made to provide a description of the techniques with minimal mathematical content. As a result our treatment may lack rigour.

The process of encrypting a message, transforming it from clear text to cipher text, should be relatively easy. On the other hand, the reverse process of converting cipher text to clear text should, under most circumstances, be effectively impossible. Effectively impossible, or computationally infeasible, means that, given the fastest available processor, a systematic and exhaustive analysis of the cipher text in an attempt to deduce the clear text takes longer than anybody is able or prepared to spend. Such a process is called a *one-way function*. Note, however, that what is computationally infeasible today may not be so in the near future with the continuing and dramatic increase in processor speed and developments in parallel processing.

The function must, of course, not be entirely one way. Under most circumstances it means without special knowledge. Given that special knowledge, the process becomes easily reversible, enabling the clear text to be retrieved. The special knowledge is sometimes called a *trap door* and the associated process a *trap door one-way function*, although the use of the term 'trap door' in this way is not universal. The special knowledge required is the key, which must be kept secret.

A *cryptographic algorithm* is a precisely defined process for encrypting and decrypting data. The input to the process is a message, or part of a message, in clear text. The output is the message, or part of the message, in cipher text. The process is controlled by a second piece of input, the encipherment key. Cipher text is converted back to clear text using the same algorithm with a decipherment key.

*Network security*

Computers process information—numbers, text, images and so on—in binary digital form. A block of such information, such as part of a message to be encrypted, is a string of bits. The key that controls the algorithm is a number, also expressible as a bit string. The algorithm itself is a series of bit string manipulations using logical operators. The output from the algorithm is a bit string that forms part of the message to be transmitted or stored securely.

The algorithm itself may be published or may remain secret. The use of a secret algorithm is limited to those entrusted with the secret. A public algorithm, on the other hand, may be used by anyone, including an attacker. However, it should be impossible (computationally infeasible) for the attacker, even knowing the algorithm, to produce plain text from cipher text.

An obvious brute force approach would be to try all possible keys in an effort to find one that converts the cipher text into meaningful plain text. A key of n bits has $2^n$ possible values. If it takes m units of time to execute the algorithm for one of these values on the fastest available processor, $2^n \times m$ should satisfy the 'longer than anybody is prepared to take criterion'. Key length is an important parameter in determining the strength of a cryptographic algorithm. Of course, if it is suspected that the key is known to unauthorized people, the system is compromised and the key must be changed to limit the damage.

Many network operators change keys regularly as an extra precaution. This, in itself, brings its own problems for those algorithms that require both participants in an exchange of information to use the same key. How do they both get to know the key? It can be sent through the network, but only if protected by being encrypted. How does the remote user get to know the key encryption key that encrypts the key to be used for data transmission? There is no satisfactory answer to this series of questions other than to distribute keys by means (such as a human courier) that do not involve transmission through the network (key management is discussed in more detail later in this chapter).

## Symmetric cryptographic algorithms and DES

Symmetric algorithms use the same key for encryption *and* decryption. The key must be kept secret, particularly if the algorithm itself is in the public domain. A key used for encrypting data from A to B may also be used for encrypting data from B to A—hence the system is symmetrical.

The most common algorithm used for data protection during the growth of data networking in the late 1970s and 1980s was the *Data Encryption Algorithm (DEA)* defined by the *Data Encryption Standard (DES)*. It is still widely used, but is likely to be superseded by more flexible asymmetric algorithms.

In 1972, the US National Bureau of Standards (NBS) invited manufacturers to submit proposals for a public encryption algorithm. The NBS repeated the invitation in 1974. In response, IBM submitted an algorithm based on the Lucifer algorithm that the corporation had developed earlier and implemented in several of its products. The algorithm was evaluated by the National Security Agency (NSA) of the US Department of Defense and submitted for public discussion before being adopted as a Federal Information Processing Standard (FIPS publication 46) in 1977.

The DES algorithm is illustrated in Figure 11.1. The figure shows the process by which a 64-bit input block of plain text is enciphered to produce a 64-bit output block of cipher text. The process starts with an

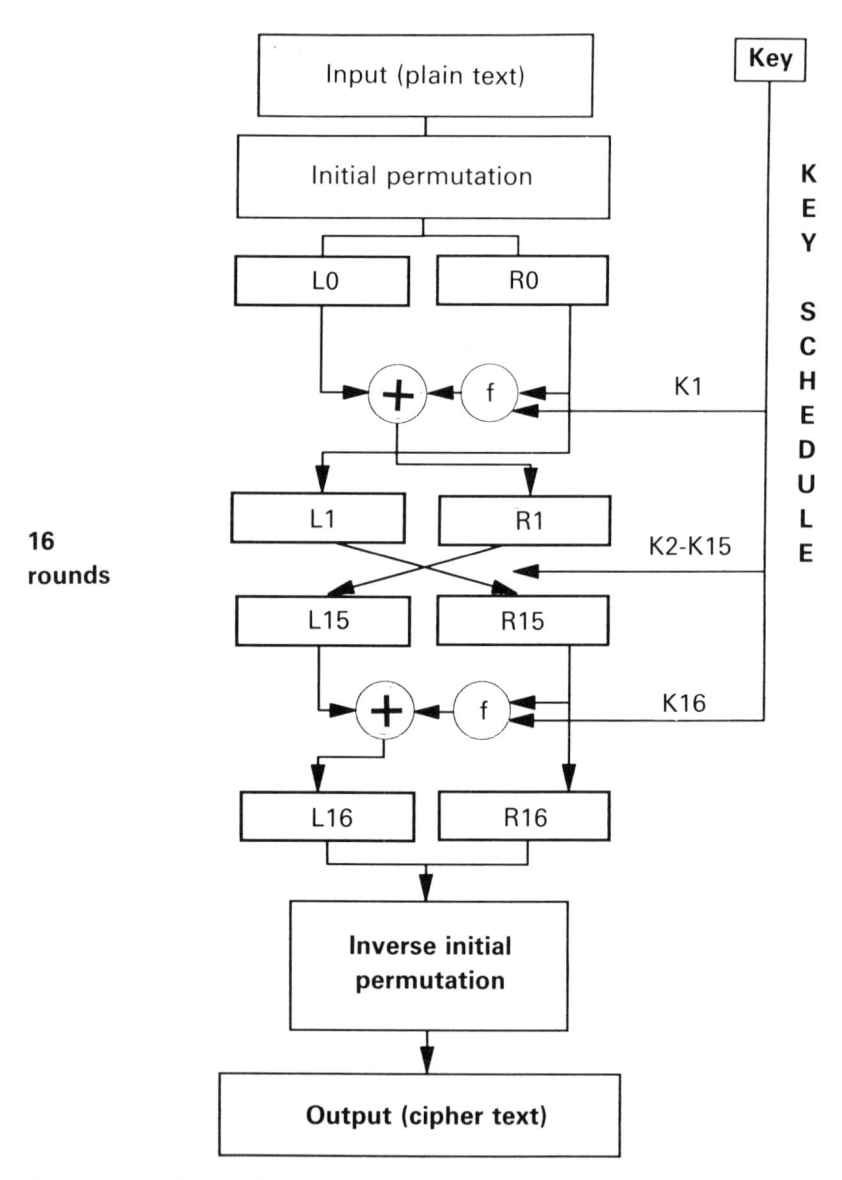

*Figure 11.1   The data encryption algorithm*

initial permutation of the bits of the input block. This is followed by an iterative process of 16 rounds, each of which uses a different 48-bit selection, K1–K16, from 56 bits of the secret 64-bit key K. The process of deriving K1–K16 from K is called the *key schedule*.

For each round of the iterative process, the 64-bit input block is divided into a left half $L_n$ and a right half $R_n$. $R_n$ and $K_{n+1}$ are processed by a function (f) and then exclusive ORed with $L_n$ to form the right half for the next round n + 1. The left half for n + 1 is just the right half from n, unchanged. This interchange of left and right halves follows each round except the last. A final permutation completes the process. This final permutation is the inverse of the initial permutation, which means that if a block is subject to the initial permutation, immediately followed by the final permutation, the original block is recovered.

Different methods of producing cipher text from plain text may be divided into three classes: *transposition (permutation) ciphers* change the order of the symbols in the plain text; *substitution ciphers* replace symbols with other symbols without changing the order in which they appear; *product ciphers* combine transposition *and* substitution. The relationship between cipher text and plain text may be studied in terms of two characteristics. The complexity of the relationship between the plain text, the key and the cipher text is called *confusion*. An algorithm with good confusion properties is difficult for a cryptanalyst to break.

A further desirable property is that a change in the plain text should result in changes throughout the cipher text. This is called *diffusion* and good diffusion characteristics means that the cryptanalyst needs large amounts of cipher text in order to attempt to deduce the algorithm, or, the key. In general, substitution results in confusion and transposition results in diffusion. Strong encryption algorithms result from combining the two in a product cipher. Much of the information theory foundation of modern cryptography was laid in a famous paper by Shannon in 1949.

The DEA is based on a product cipher. The function, which operates on a 32-bit R and a 48-bit K to produce a 32-bit output, consists of four operations. An expansion permutation of R into 48 bits, an exclusive OR with K, a substitution on the 48-bit result that reduces it to 32 bits and a final permutation. The strength of the algorithm lies in the careful choice of the various permutations and substitutions to achieve good confusion and diffusion and the fact that the basic enciphering operation is repeated a number of times.

An important property of the DEA is that the same algorithm is used for both encryption and decryption. The only difference is that the key schedule is reversed so that $K_{16}$ is used in round 1, $K_{15}$ in round 2 and so on until $K_1$ is used in round 16.

The DES algorithm is a block cipher. It takes as its input a fixed length block of text and produces a fixed length block of output. In the case of DES, both blocks are 64 bits long. The algorithm may be used in several modes of operation. The simplest mode is to use the algorithm to encrypt a message by dividing the message into blocks of 64 bits and encrypting each block. If the message is not an integral multiple of 64 bits, the last block is padded with random bits before encryption. This mode of operation is called Electronic Codebook (ECB) mode.

In ECB mode, a given input block and a given key always result in the same output block. If an attacker knows the format of a message, for example that a particular word which never changes always appears in the same position, he or she is in the advantageous position of having known plain text *and* cipher text. Such risks can be avoided by making each cipher text block dependent not only on the corresponding plain text block but also on all previous cipher text blocks. This may be achieved by adding (exclusive OR) each block of plain text to the cipher text of the previous block before input to the algorithm. The mode is called Cipher Block Chaining (CBC).

A block cipher is suitable for data that conveniently divides into blocks of 64 bits, padding the last block if necessary. A stream cipher enables a bit string of arbitrary length to be encrypted. A stream cipher encrypts a string of bits by adding it (exclusive OR) to a secret bit stream generated by a cryptographic process. The DES algorithm may be used as this process. The initial bit stream is generated by using an initialization vector to provide the DES input block. Thereafter, either cipher text from the previous encryption or the previously generated bit stream are fed back into the algorithm to produce the next secret bit stream. These modes of DES are called respectively *Cipher Feedback (CFB)* and *Output Feedback (OFB)*. The modes of operation of DES are described, with examples, in FIPS publication 81.

The DES requires that the algorithm be implemented in hardware to fully conform to the standard, although many software implementations exist.

Throughout its existence, DES has been under attack, sometimes for legitimate cryptanalytical reasons and sometimes as a result of scepticism about its origins and the role played by the National Security Agency. Despite these attacks, the algorithm has never knowingly been broken. There remains, however, a strong belief that it can be broken by means of methods that rely on its limited key length of 56 bits and on the increasing power of parallel processors.

## Asymmetric cryptographic algorithms and RSA

DES is a public algorithm that relies entirely on the secrecy of the key. It is a symmetric algorithm that provides a secure channel between two parties in both directions. Keeping the key secret is a major disadvantage, particularly if the algorithm is used to provide secure channels though a network. DES shares this disadvantage with similar algorithms that rely on a secret key. Distributing keys to network users ultimately relies on trusted personnel rather than on cryptography.

The problem of key distribution could be resolved if a system were devised in which a key had two parts, such that data encrypted using one part could be decrypted only by having the other part. Indeed, in such a system, the encryption key would not need to be kept secret but could, instead, be publicly available. Anyone could use this public key to encrypt a message in the knowledge that it could only be decrypted by a holder of the corresponding, and obviously secret, key. Such systems, relying on a public/secret key pair, have been developed. They introduce a degree of asymmetry in that two pairs are needed to provide a secure two-way channel. In addition to easing the key distribution problem, they turn out to have other advantages over symmetric systems.

Public key systems, and their underlying algorithms, are increasingly used either to replace or in combination with purely secret key systems. An obvious example is the use of a public key to encrypt a DES key for distribution to the holder of the corresponding secret key. Couriers are no longer needed.

Public key systems were first proposed by Diffie and Hellman in 1976. For hundreds of years, up to that point, encryption was thought to depend on the secrecy of the key. Several public key algorithms have subsequently been developed, of which the one most commonly in use was proposed by Rivest, Shamir and Adleman in 1978 and is thus known as the RSA algorithm. It is described in this section as an example of a public key system. The mathematical basis of public key cryptography, although not unduly complicated, is sufficiently specialized to be beyond the scope of this book. Instead the focus here is on statements of the principles of the technique without mathematical justification.

Many problems in mathematics are known to be difficult to solve. Some mathematicians spend their time trying to solve them; others spend time trying to show that they are difficult and evaluate their degree of complexity. Problems that are difficult to solve form the basis for cryptographic algorithms where breaking the algorithm is equivalent to solving the underlying mathematical problem.

The encryption function in RSA is very simple—it is the power function. A block of plain text, P, when encoded in binary form is a (large) number. Cipher text, C, is produced by the process:

$$C = P^e \bmod n$$

where e and n are two numbers that constitute the public key. That is, the number C is produced by raising the number P to the power e in modular arithmetic with modulus n. Typically, n has 200 decimal digits.

It must, of course, be possible to reproduce P from C using the secret decryption key d. That is:

$$P = C^d \bmod n$$
$$\text{or } P = (P^e)^d \bmod n$$
$$\text{or } P = P^{e \times d} \bmod n$$

This suggests that if a special relationship can be found between the numbers e, d and n that enables a number P to be unchanged when raised to the power e × d under the modulus n, then this is the basis of an encryption system. This relationship is derived from some results from the theory of numbers.

The number n is first chosen as the product of two large prime numbers, p and q. Thus:

$$n = p \times q$$

This is done by generating random large numbers and testing them for primality using well-established mathematical techniques.

Next e is chosen so that it is relatively prime to the number $(p - 1) \times (q - 1)$. Two numbers are relatively prime if they have no factors in common. The numbers e and $(p - 1) \times (q - 1)$ are not themselves necessarily prime but their greatest common divisor (gcd) is 1. For example, 9 and 14 are relatively prime. Again, well-established techniques exist for determining the gcd of two numbers and hence demonstrating relative primality.

Finally, d is calculated, such that:

$$e \times d = 1 \bmod (p - 1) \times (q - 1)$$

The numbers e and n are made public while d is kept secret, but note that it can be calculated if p and q are known. Therefore p and q are not revealed and can be calculated from n only if the problem of factoring a large number can be solved.

In practice, the algorithm works as follows. A machine wishing to receive and decrypt secret information generates a set of numbers n, e and d by virtue of the process outlined above. The pair (n, e) are released by the machine, as its public key. Any other machine can now encrypt a message that only the original machine, which has retained the secret key d, can decrypt.

The RSA algorithm has interesting and useful properties. Either of the numbers e and d can be used as the public key and the other retained as the secret key. Furthermore, encryption followed by decryption is the same as decryption followed by encryption as:

$$(P^e)^d = (P^d)^e = P$$

This latter property is important in the generation of digital signatures, ensuring non-repudiation of messages by the sender.

## 11.4 Cryptography and security functions

In the previous section some of the attacks that may be made on a network or on the data it carries were mentioned. The provision of access control by user or device authentication and the protection of the

*Network security*

content and integrity of messages depends on secrets. The best way to keep information secret is to encrypt it. Hence cryptography plays an important role in network security. In this section the uses of cryptography are examined to provide the functions necessary for network security.

**Data secrecy**

In earlier chapters the need for networks to deliver messages without error, without loss, without reordering and without duplication was described, as were some of the protocols that have been designed to meet this need. They are intended to allow for the accidental malfunction of some network component. The interest in this chapter is in protecting messages against malicious damage, designed to breach the security of the network.

It is possible and, in many cases, even easy, to introduce a machine into a network for the purpose of monitoring network messages, changing them, removing them or adding false messages. The use of encryption techniques guards against some of these attacks.

An encrypted message can be read only after decryption using the appropriate secret key. In a symmetric cryptosystem, it can be encrypted only by a machine holding the same secret key. In an asymmetric system, it can be encrypted by any machine as the encryption key is public. In both cases, the secret key is needed to read the message.

**Authentication**

A frequent need in data processing systems is to ensure that somebody or something is authentic. The system needs to ensure that a user's identity is verified, that a device connected to the system is legitimate, that data has not been modified in transit or in storage and that it originated at the claimed source. The reputation of a business can depend on the measures it takes to ensure authenticity. Cryptography plays a vital role in these measures.

**Personal authentication**

Proof of identity depends on a person possessing something that only this person is expected to have. This may be some physical object (usually a token), some knowledge or a unique personal characteristic. It is referred to as a *Personal Authentication Value (PAV)*. One or more PAVs are offered to the system, as proof of identity, and the system compares each with a copy of the PAV that it holds. Obviously the PAV should not be transferred to another person. Protection outside the system relies on the person holding the token or knowledge. Protection inside the system relies on encryption.

Many types of PAV are used by a data processing system to identify and authenticate users. The most common is the combination of *user identifiers (userids)* and *passwords*. When these are entered at some terminal, this information is sent to a point in the system where copies of valid userids and passwords are held. This information is encrypted in transit and may also be encrypted in storage at the point of verification. The method is inherently weak because people tend to disclose their passwords to others, either intentionally or unintentionally. Another common PAV is a combination of a token and knowledge, such as an ATM card and a PIN. An attacker needs to possess both to gain access. Again, the knowledge (the PIN) is protected by encryption in transit to the point of verification.

Strong personal authentication relies on a non-transferable PAV, such as a unique physical characteristic of the person. Several such characteristics may be quantified and recorded so as to make them suitable for processing by a machine. The most popular method is based on the dynamic characteristics of a person's signature.

Signatures have long been accepted as a means of personal authentication by visual comparison with a copy, but the appearance of a signature may easily be reproduced by a forger. A much more reliable method checks the dynamics of the signature—the speed of writing, the pressure, the points at which the pen is lifted and so on. These parameters are not consciously controlled by a person and so are far more difficult for a forger to reproduce as for that person it is a conscious process. These factors can be measured and reduced to a digital pattern that can be compared with a copy supplied by the person on enrolment and held by the system. The copy is normally held on a token (such as a smart card) carried by the person and inserted into a reader when personal authentication is requested.

Other physical characteristics, such as voice, fingerprint, handprint and retinal patterns, are used, too, although most of them have undesirable social connotations or are not user-friendly.

**Device authentication**

It has been stressed several times so far that network communication between machines, with little or no human intervention, is increasingly used to support business transactions. It is important, in such circumstances, for each machine to be confident that it is communicating with a genuine partner. Such confidence may be established by each machine demonstrating to the other that it has secret knowledge. Clearly, this knowledge should not be transmitted between the machines. Rather, it is used to generate messages that the machines exchange to establish mutual authenticity. The process is known as *handshaking*.

A typical handshake works as follows. Two machines, A and B, share a secret key. Machine A generates a random number, encrypts it using the secret key and sends it to B. B decrypts the number and subjects it to some simple known operation, such as adding one or changing particular bits. B encrypts the result and returns the modified number to A, which decrypts it, reverses the operation and should recover the original number. If so, A knows that B is genuine. B may authenticate A in the same manner. Possessing the secret key is taken as authentication.

**Message authentication and non-repudiation**

Even when a message is fully encrypted, it may be intercepted and changed. The change, at best, makes nonsense of the contents and, at worst, produces a different but valid message. A means of detecting changes is needed so that a changed message can be discarded. Information that can be shown to be unchanged since its creation is said to have *integrity*.

*Message integrity* is achieved by creating, and attaching to the message, further information that is uniquely related to the contents of the message. If the contents are changed without there being a corresponding change in the attached information, this relationship is destroyed and the message loses its integrity. The additional information, attached to a message and used to authenticate it, is called an *Authentication Code* or *Message Authentication Code (MAC)*. Cryptography provides an ideal mechanism for generating a MAC.

Several methods, based on cryptographic processing, are used to produce the MAC. The first such method described below uses the DES algorithm in CBC mode. This mode of operation has particularly good diffusion properties so that a change in the plain text results in changes throughout the cipher text. This suggests that the cipher text may form the basis of a MAC.

To generate the MAC, the message is encrypted using DES/CBC. The key used as input to the algorithm is generally different to that used to encipher data for transmission. When the last cipher text block has been produced, the most significant m bits of this block are extracted and attached to the plain text message before it is transmitted. The rest of the cipher text is discarded. Typically, m is 32, resulting in a 4-byte MAC. The receiver of the message regenerates the MAC from the plain text and compares the regenerated value with the received value. If they are equal, the message may be assumed with very high probability to be unchanged.

Although a DES MAC ensures the integrity of a message itself, it does not validate the *source* of the message. The message may have been generated by any entity knowing the MAC generation key. In particular, it may have been manufactured by the receiver. An asymmetric system may be used to ensure that changes to a message are detected and also to ensure that the sender can be identified. Our second example uses the RSA system.

An RSA cryptosystem encrypts data using the public key of a key pair. The data can be decrypted only by the holder of the matching secret key. We pointed out earlier that either the public key or the secret key may be used for encryption and the matching key used for decryption. If data is encrypted using the secret key, although it may be decrypted using the public key, it could have originated only from the holder of the secret key. Therein lies a means both of message authentication and non-repudiation. The term *digital signature* is used to denote information attached to a message that ensures both its integrity and its source.

The method, discussed above, of generating a MAC using a DES system produces an m-bit authentication code that is independent of the length of the message. In an RSA system, the message to be signed is first reduced to a number of fixed binary length by passing it through a publicly available hashing algorithm. Hashing is a technique for reducing an arbitrary string of symbols to a number, called the hash value. The hash value is then encrypted by (raised to the power of) the sender's secret key and attached to the plain text as a signature. The hashing process may be repeated by the receiver and the resulting hash value compared with the signature decrypted using the sender's public key. If they are equal, the message has not changed and, furthermore, it genuinely came from the sender. The signature is somewhat analogous to the use of a medieval seal to detect both the opening of a message and to guarantee its source.

## 11.5 Key management

Previous sections of this chapter have shown that the security of a data processing system and of the data it carries depends on certain information being kept secret. Authentication of people depends on the secrecy, or non-transferability, of the PAV. Authentication of devices and the protection of data depend on the secrecy of a cryptographic key. Protection of a transferable PAV is a human responsibility. The subject of this section is the protection of keys.

Ultimately, of course, the protection of keys is also a human responsibility. A cryptographic device needs to be initialized by a human operator. This process includes the entry, in plain form, of high-level keys that are subsequently used to protect lower level keys generated by the device itself. The human responsibility may be shared, and the risk of a compromise reduced, by requiring that the initialization process be performed by two or more people, none of whom knows, for example, a complete key.

Most general-purpose cryptosystems use published algorithms and, consequently, rely for their integrity on the secrecy of keys. The generation, protection, distribution and destruction of keys, together with the relationships between them, forms the subject matter of key management, to which much effort has been devoted.

Cryptographic processing of data, at source or destination, is performed by a hardware or software device that implements some cryptographic algorithm. In addition to performing basic encryption/decryption functions to protect and/or authenticate data, the device may be required to generate keys for various purposes and store them or release them to the outside world in enciphered form. These keys may be used to encrypt other keys, to encrypt data or to generate authenticators.

The set of keys used by a cryptographic device generally have a hierarchical relationship. At the highest level of a simple hierarchy is a local master key, used by the device to protect its own stored data. At the next level are *Key Encrypting Keys (KEKs)*, which are used to protect lower level data keys or authentication keys when generated and released for transport to a remote device. These lower level keys, in turn, are used to protect data for a limited period (such as a day or a session) before being changed and redistributed under the protection of a KEK. More complicated hierarchies are common.

In a symmetric system, in which sender and receiver share a common, secret key, the distribution of these keys to all points that need them and the synchronization of changes are problems that increase rapidly in proportion to the number of end points. The key management problem is considerably eased by adding asymmetric cryptographic functions to the symmetric system to form a hybrid system. For example, cryptographic devices are used that implement both the DES and RSA algorithms. DES, with its greater efficiency, is used for session encryption and authentication; RSA is used to protect the session keys for distribution to their users.

## 11.6 The practical use of cryptography

In earlier sections of this chapter it was seen that security is closely identified with cryptography as the recognized means of protecting data in storage or transit. We turn now to the practical use of cryptography in networks and, in particular, to the level within the communication system at which cryptographic processing is applied.

A message transmitted through a network from one user to another consists of user data, to which are attached a number of headers containing protocol control information. This information is added by successive layers of communication function in the end systems and used to ensure the delivery of the message to its destination. Some of it is relevant to *all* nodes through which the message passes; some of it is relevant only in the end nodes.

The user is concerned with protecting the data that is transmitted to prevent it from being read or altered during its passage through the network. From the point of view of the user, the sooner the message is protected, the better. If necessary, the user could encrypt or authenticate the data before passing it to the communication system for transmission. This, however, requires security functions to be available to an application programmer as network users are increasingly application programs. In an application-level security system, the part of the message that is protected is the user data.

There is a case to be made for including security as a service provided (automatically or at the user's request) by the communication system. Indeed, this is the most common way in which secure dialogues are provided in a network. The layer in which encryption occurs then becomes important. The protocol control information associated with the lower layers is needed at every node. If it is encrypted, decryption is required at each node before the information can be used. For example, addresses must be available at each node to control the routeing process. Decryption at each node exposes the message to attack while it is being processed by the node.

Despite this, the most common use of encryption in networks is through the use of *line encryptors*—devices that encipher each message (including all its headers) at the data link level immediately before it is transmitted on the link. The message is deciphered at the other end of the link before being processed by the communication system. Some more intelligent encryption devices exclude from the encryption process those lower layer headers that are needed on the way to the destination. A message is enciphered on leaving the source and is deciphered only when it reaches its destination.

The use of line encryption devices gives the user no control over the security process: *all* outgoing messages are enciphered and *all* incoming messages must be deciphered. Enciphering a message introduces a processing overhead that the user may want to exclude for non-sensitive messages. Moving the interface to the encipherment process to a higher layer of the communications system enables the user to exercise control on a 'per message' basis. Providing security services directly to an application provides the greatest degree of control and enables services other than encipherment to be provided, such as access control.

To illustrate the inclusion of data protection functions in a communications architecture, let us return briefly to SNA. The architecture allows for the establishment of a secure session between two LUs. This calls for encipher/decipher functions in each LU and a key that is shared between them for the duration of the session. Cryptographic processing is included as an optional function in the transmission control layer of the LU (more precisely in the *Connection Point Manager*, which handles all incoming and outgoing requests and responses). The algorithm used is, as might be expected, the DEA.

The session key is sent to each LU during the session establishment process (see Section 7.5). Each LU has a master key, known to the SSCP. When a request for a secure session is made, the SSCP generates a random number to be used as a session key. This number is sent to the primary LU enciphered under the master key of the primary LU and also under the master key of the secondary LU. The primary LU retrieves the key, using its own master key. It also forwards the key to the secondary LU, still encrypted using the secondary LU master key, in the bind request. The secondary LU may now also retrieve the session key. Finally, a cryptographic handshake occurs between the two LUs to ensure that each has successfully retrieved the session key. All subsequent messages on the session are enciphered. *LU6.2* provides a more flexible method, enabling the using application to request encipherment of selected messages.

There is considerable activity in the various standards organizations relating to security. At the time of writing, this work is not in a sufficiently coherent state to allow anything more than a brief indication of the types of activity being pursued to be given here.

The joint technical committee of ISO and IEC, *JTC1*, through its *Standards Committee SC21*, has developed an extension to the OSI reference model. This is *ISO 7498 Part 2*, the *OSI Security Architecture*, and forms the basis of most other standards' activity. It defines the terminology of security and describes security services and mechanisms in a general manner. It then indicates in which layers of the reference model these services and mechanisms may be provided and gives a justification for this. The document concludes with some fundamental work in the area of security management. *ISO 7498-2* is required reading when studying international security standards.

JTC1 has a number of other committees concerned with different aspects of OSI security. A separate ISO technical committee (*TC68*) works on standards related to wholesale and retail banking. *CCITT Study Group VII (SG VII)* is also an important arena for security standards activity, particularly for message handling and EDI systems. Particularly important standards that form a framework for these various activities are the multipart *IS 10181*, which expands the general discussion of security services given in 9498-2, and the multipart *IS 10164*, which covers aspects of security management.

## 11.7 Summary

Network security is a subject that is a little obscure to many people. This is partly because of the very nature of the subject, partly because of its strong link with cryptography and its mathematical framework. Providing a secure network costs money and introduces performance, usability and management overheads that network providers are often reluctant to accept. The cost of lack of security is difficult to quantify as it involves loss of reputation as well as loss of money. Furthermore, it is not in the network provider's interest to publicize breaches of security.

Early data networks were not as reliable as those to which today's users have become accustomed. Reliability has been improved by increasing attention to network management. Security will continue to be something of a Cinderella area in networking until it is given the same attention as network management, the subject of the next chapter.

*A bank's reputation relies on protecting its customers' deposits. Means of protecting cash in storage or in transit are familiar. Banks are also concerned with the transfer of the ownership of money, the ubiquitous cheque being the common means of achieving this. The ownership of large sums of money, however, is more often transferred by means of a network message between computers. Cheques that have been interfered* with, such as alterations made to the amount to be deducted from the account or a forged signature, should be rejected by the bank. An electronic message with an altered amount or the equivalent of a forged signature, therefore, should also be rejected, but such changes are not so easy to detect. In addition to protecting customers' money, a bank is required to protect information 'deposited' by customers. Banks are major users of security systems, particularly those based on cryptography.

The WNB uses a range of data security techniques: network lines carrying sensitive data are fitted with line encryptors; messages having monetary value need to be authenticated; high-level personal authentication is required in order to gain access to sensitive applications, coupled with dual control to reduce the threat from hostile employees (even the admirable WNB has hostile employees); network access controls and closed user groups provide a general level of security that is applied to all the bank's staff.

Banks, including the WNB, have traditionally used DES as the basis of their cryptographic security. The benefits of public key systems in the areas of key management, message authentication and non-repudiation are beginning to be recognized. The WNB will, in future, have a hybrid approach to security.

# CHAPTER 12  Network management

## 12.1 Introduction

The user of a network—a person or an application program—produces information and expects it to be conveyed to a remote user without error, often quickly and sometimes securely. The user further expects the network to be able to provide a connection with the required quality every time it is needed and to maintain the connection while the user needs it. The users are prepared to pay for this service in proportion to the use made of it and expect to receive a bill in a format that they can understand. In the event of the network failing to meet this level of service, the user expects the provider to be able to give the reason, to keep the user informed and to restore service quickly.

This presents the provider with a demanding task. The network may span the world and consist of many complicated components, not all of which are controlled by the provider. Failure of any component potentially affects the service to some user. Failure of a component shared by many users affects all of them. The network topology may change frequently to accommodate new users or increased demand. The provider is expected to take advantage of new technology.

The hardware and software components from which networks are built are inherently highly reliable and increasingly so. They do, nevertheless, fail from time to unpredictable time. Complicated communication architectures are used to detect and recover from some failures, but these are not designed to cope with permanent failure of a component. The secret of maintaining service levels lies in knowing that a component has failed, knowing which one, being able to evaluate the impact on users and being able to do something about it. Possession of this knowledge gives the provider control over the network. When it is coupled with an efficient administrative system that is used to record the network topology and changes to it, to record the status of network faults, to analyse network performance and the use of the network, the result is a managed network.

One way to approach the problem of managing a network would be to have each component continuously monitored by a human operator. On the questionable assumption that such an operator could always tell when a component was functioning improperly, this would provide some knowledge. Such knowledge, though, is of little value if it is held only by these individual component monitors. They need to tell someone who can assess whether the apparent failure is real or a result of failure in some other component, determine the impact on users and perhaps effect a repair. In order to tell someone, they need a means of communication.

Such a system is clearly not a practical way to run a network. Within it, however, lie many of the fundamental concepts of network management. Instead of having *people* monitor components and report problems, the machines monitor and report on themselves. Reports are fed to some point that accumulates reports from a number of components and exercises control over these components. A hierarchical tree of such focal points may be established to provide an ever-widening view of the network. A view of the whole network is available at the root of the tree and may be combined with supporting knowledge of the network structure and its users to assess the impact of a failure and determine a means of restoring service to affected users. Information is exchanged between components and management points through a network that is usually, but not necessarily, the network being managed.

One of the difficulties in network management is determining where exactly the demarcation line between network and users lies and, hence, the scope of network management. Architecturally, the division is clear: the network starts at the boundary of the uppermost layer of the communication system. In an OSI system this is at the service boundary of the uppermost layer in the protocol stack; in an X.25 network, at the interface to the packet layer; in an SNA network, the interface between the LU and the end-user (not very apparent except in LU6.2). A network management system should, ideally, be able to monitor and control all components within the network boundary.

In order for a network component (such as a switch, a multiplexer, a modem or a line encryption device) to monitor its status, report that status and react to commands from the manager, it must include functions other than communication functions. These functions do various things. They monitor and record the operation and performance of the component. On detecting an abnormal situation, they become users of a communication system to report the situation to the management point. They may also report status when requested by the manager or accept and react to other management requests, such as performing a local test or reloading some software.

We now begin to see the emergence of a logically separate management system, consisting of interconnected users who are local agents, within each component, of a central management application. The provision of an interface to this management application enables the network to be controlled by a human, or possibly a programmed, operator. The network that carries messages between the manager and its agents is the management network, usually but not always the network being managed.

Reference was made above to the topological scope of a management system. Its functional scope is also a subject that provokes some discussion. Some functions are more clearly network management functions than others. They tend to be those functions, exercised while the network is running and with operator intervention, that monitor the state of network components and change that state if necessary. They can be termed network control functions.

Other functions that come under the heading of network management are of a more administrative nature and can be termed network administration functions. They may be distinguished from network control functions by the fact that they are performed off-line from the network. They include the analysis of performance, fault and usage statistics gathered by network control functions so that reports and bills can be produced. They generally incorporate database management functions to record the network configuration or to manage the process of repairing faults. The dividing line between these network administration functions and the general administration of the business is rather vague. This chapter will focus on network control and begin with the recent, far from complete, work on management under the umbrella of the OSI model.

## 12.2 The OSI management framework

The OSI standards makers are, as always, attempting to take a rigorous and complete, but abstract, view of managing the OSI environment. The resulting standards are, inevitably, difficult to read and to apply to real networks. Nevertheless, the OSI management framework is a valuable aid to understanding the basic principles of network management. The framework is described in part 4 of the reference model standard (ISO 7498-4) which forms part of a growing body of standards relating to specific management areas.

A real network consists of a set of physical entities—*boxes* and *wires*. The boxes are terminals, hosts, intermediate switches, multiplexers and modems. The wires are those media capable of carrying electrical signals. When a network is in use, other (logical) things exist, such as connections (sessions, calls, dialogues, conversations) between users. These things, both physical and logical, may be described as having certain attributes and being in certain states. A physical circuit has a particular bit rate and may be available or not. A counter of messages has a value and may be enabled or not. A connection has throughput and security attributes and may be operational or not. A complete description of a network may be achieved by recording the values of the attributes and the states of all the things that make up the network, both physical and logical.

Of course, the standards bodies will not allow us to use a word like 'thing'. They usually substitute the word *entity*. In the management framework, the term used is *managed object*. A managed object is something that can be managed, if it exists!

A managed object is an abstract description of a physical or logical component of a network. It exists when it is created, at which point it describes an actual component of the network. It ceases to exist when it is deleted, although the abstract definition is still available for use. While a managed object exists, it has attributes, is in a particular state and may be related to other existing managed objects.

Each managed object that exists in an OSI system is represented by an entry in a database—the *Management Information Base (MIB)*. The MIB is the complete description of the instantaneous state of the network referred to above. It is constantly changing as managed objects are created and deleted or their attributes, states and relationships change. It is a *distributed database* as information is recorded in many components of the network.

The concept of managed objects recorded in the MIB is the basis of OSI network management. If the managed objects—and their relationship to real network components—are properly defined, all the information that is needed to control the network is recorded in the MIB. If network managers can retrieve this information they know the state of all network components and hence the overall state of the network. If they can change the state of a component, they can control the network.

Reading and writing in a distributed database clearly implies an exchange of management messages between local and remote elements of the management system. This exchange occurs between management application processes in each open system. As was seen in Chapter 6, Section 6.5, application-to-application communication requires a set of functions in the application layer that support the particular needs of that communication. The set of functions is an *Application Service Element (ASE)* and the support that it provides is a *service*. Management applications are supported by a *Common Management Information Service Element (CMISE)*, which provides the *Common Management Information Service (CMIS)* and uses the *Common Management Information Protocol (CMIP)*.

The primitives of the CMIS define the requests that a management application can convey to a peer application. The basic operations are:

- get—to retrieve information from the MIB
- set—to modify information in the MIB
- event report—to report an event
- action—to request some action
- create—to create a managed object
- delete—to delete a managed object.

The OSI framework divides network control functions into five areas that together are called *Specific Management Functional Areas (SMFA)*, formerly called *Specific Management Information Services (SMIS)*, and their protocols, *(SMIP)*. Each functional area makes use of some of the CMIS primitives.

**Fault management**

*Fault management* is a set of functions that enables abnormal operation of a component to be detected and isolated. It includes the generation of unsolicited reports when a particular event occurs or a preset threshold is exceeded. It also includes facilities for remote diagnostics. It does not include error recovery, which is seen as a configuration management facility and may be outside the scope of the management framework.

**Configuration management**

*Configuration management* consists of functions to change the way in which a component operates, such as changing routeing tables or reconfiguring a component.

**Accounting management**

*Accounting management* enables usage information, needed to produce bills for users, to be accumulated by network components and reported for subsequent analysis by an administrative function.

**Performance management**

*Performance management* functions enable the performance of components to be monitored and recorded for future analysis and prediction. Whether notification of performance degradation lies in this area or in fault management is debatable. Restoration of acceptable performance, if indeed it is possible as a control function, is likely to be a configuration management function. This emphasizes the fact that this division into functional areas should not be applied too rigidly.

**Security management**

This is the least well-defined management area, reflecting the late appearance of security matters in the OSI environment. It is intended to provide functions with a security emphasis, such as the reporting of multiple unsuccessful logon attempts or the recording of an audit trail. Most, if not all, of the required functions would seem to be provided by fault management.

The OSI management framework has been described in some detail, despite its abstract approach. The value of the architecture, as in other aspects of the OSI environment, lies in the fact that it provides a framework in which more pragmatic approaches to the subject may be placed.

## 12.3 Management in the TCP/IP environment

The management structure of a TCP/IP internet is based on three fundamental standards. These are *RFC 1155 (Structure and Identification of Management Information* for TCP/IP-based internets), *RFC 1156 (Management Information Base for Network Management* of TCP/IP-based internets) and *RFC 1157 (Simple Network Management Protocol)*. These will be referred to respectively as SMI, MIB and SNMP. The titles of these documents give some indication of the framework for TCP/IP management.

## The Structure and Identification of Management Information (SMI)

SMI defines the structure of managed objects in an internet. Managed objects are abstract descriptions of real things; the real things are *instances* of managed objects that are manipulated using a management protocol. Managed objects have *names* while instances of managed objects have *instance identifiers*. Managed objects conform to one of a number of data types. Simple types are *integer, octet string, object identifier* and *null*. The first two are self explanatory.

An object identifier is a data type that denotes an object to which a value has been assigned by international agreement. It consists of a set of non-negative numbers that may be represented as a tree, with the allocation of values to the nodes of the tree being assigned to different authorities. For example, root nodes are defined for the CCITT (value 0), ISO (value 1) and joint CCITT/ISO objects (value 2). The ISO assigns numbers to subordinate nodes that represent, for example, member bodies or organizations with which it is otherwise associated. The latter organizations are collectively assigned the number 3 in the tree structure. One such organization is the US Department of Defense, which is assigned the number 6, and one of the Department's responsibilities is (or was) the Internet, assigned the number 1.

Any object defined by the internet is formally prefixed by 1.3.6.1, which is a concise way of identifying a tree that represents the object's antecedents. The *Internet Assigned Numbers Authority (IANA)* may now assign values to its own object identifiers within its own sub-tree. It has assigned the value 2 to the node in this sub-tree representing management matters and the value 1 to the MIB in which the managed objects reside. The formal syntax used to define the SMI is ASN.1. The object management, representing the sub-tree of internet managed objects, is formally written

        mgmt OBJECT IDENTIFIER::-internet 2

meaning that the thing Internet has chosen to call 'mgmt' is an object identifier whose value is internet 2, where 'internet' is defined as

        internet OBJECT IDENTIFIER::-iso org(3) dod(6) 1

In addition to the simple types, the SMI defines some data types for its own use. These include *Address, NetworkAddress, Counter* and *TimeTicks* (a counter counting in hundredths of a second). Finally, the structure allows for lists and tables of different data types.

Each managed object has a defined level of access, chosen from *Read-Only, Read-Write, Write-Only* and *Not-Accessible*. The final attribute of a managed object is its status—*mandatory* (managed nodes are required to implement the object), *optional* or *obsolete*.

Armed with this formal structure, the MIB describes those objects the instances of which constitute the real world of a managed node and a managed network.

## The Management Information Base (MIB)

The MIB divides managed objects into groups, each of which is assigned a number in the MIB sub-tree. The groups, with a brief description of their functions, are shown below. They are defined by MIB II, a development of the original standard known as MIB I:

- *system*: the managed node as a whole
- *interfaces*: a description of the node's network interfaces
- *AT*: IP address translation
- *IP*: the internet protocol
- *ICMP*: the internet control message protocol
- *TCP*: the transmission control protocol
- *UDP*: the user datagram protocol
- *EGP*: the exterior gateway protocol
- *transmission*: specific interface types
- *SNMP*: the simple network management protocol.

A description of some of the objects in some of the groups now follows.

The *system group* contains objects that describe attributes of the node itself. They include the objects *sysDescr*, a 256-character displayable string that describes the node, *sysObjectID*, which describes the management software (known as the agent) and *sysContact*, which contains the name of a person to be contacted for operations on the device.

The *interfaces group* describes the network interfaces that a node supports. The object *ifType* identifies the type of interface (such as *iso88025*, token ring or FDDI). The object *ifInOctets* is a counter for octets that the interface has received from the physical medium (obviously with a read-only access level). The object *ifAdminStatus* is an integer, with read-write access, that records the state of the interface (up/down/testing).

The *address translation group* contains the address translation table, for each interface, between IP addresses and physical media addresses. The *internet protocol group* consists of objects related to the internet protocol, such as the default time to live for IP datagrams (read-write access), and various counters for datagrams handled or discarded and fragments needing reassembly (all read only). Similarly, the *transmission control protocol group* consists of counters for TCP segments, for the number of current connections or the number of active/passive opens.

## Simple Network Management Protocol (SNMP)

A network MIB consists of information—held, in instances of objects, in the various groups outlined above—and distributed across the nodes of the network. The contents of the MIB, at any one time, provide both a static description of network components and a dynamic snapshot of the state of the network. Network management, essentially, involves being able to retrieve this picture and, for some objects, to change it. This is achieved by sending messages to the agents in the managed nodes. This in turn requires a protocol to define the messages. The protocol associated with the TCP/IP suite is SNMP. It could hardly be simpler.

Four functions are supported by the protocol. The *get* function enables management information to be retrieved from a remote node. *Get-next* retrieves a list of instances of an object. *Set* sends management information to a node. *Trap* enables a node to report unusual events.

Before describing the messages, some security aspects of network management need to be considered. Management information is generally sensitive and should be accessible only to authorized managers. In particular, setting a value when there is an instance of an object can alter the behaviour of a node. Two aspects of gaining access to management information need to be considered, both of which depend on the concepts of a *community* and a *view*.

A community is a relationship between an agent and one or more managers. To get, set or trap management information at a node, a manager needs to be in a community relationship with the node's agent.

A view is the subset of objects visible to a community. Each object in view may have read-only access or read-write access for members of the community. In addition, each object has its own access level defined in the MIB. The operations that may be performed by a manager, via the agent, when there is an instance of an object are determined by the access privilege of the community and the access level of the object. The possibilities, divided into four classes of community profile, are shown in Figure 12.1.

Communities are named. When SNMP messages are sent between managers and agents, they contain a community name that is used by the receiver to authenticate the sender. The authentication mechanism is not sophisticated in that names are not protected by encryption—if

| Community access mode | MIB access level | | | |
|---|---|---|---|---|
| | Read-only | Read-write | Write-only | No access |
| Read-only | 3 | 3 | 1 | 1 |
| Read-write | 3 | 2 | 4 | 1 |

| Class | Operations allowed |
|---|---|
| 1 | None |
| 2 | Get, get-next, set, trap |
| 3 | Get, get-next, trap |
| 4 | Get, get-next, set, trap |

*Figure 12.1  SNMP access classes*

the name is recognized, the sender is deemed to be authentic. The operations that may be performed are determined by the class of community profile defined by Figure 12.1.

An SNMP message consists of a version number (indicating the level of SNMP in use by the sender), a community name and one of five message types. These are get request, get response, get-next request, set request and trap and each have associated data fields. One of these fields is a list of MIB variables and their values. The value of a variable is retrieved by including its name in the list of a get request. The value is returned in a get response. Get-next enables a sub-tree of the MIB to be traversed and all values retrieved. A value is written to a variable with a set request and the success or otherwise returned in a get response. Various error codes are defined, such as attempting to write to a read-only variable or referencing an unrecognized variable.

The trap operation results in an unsolicited message from a managed node to the manager of its community. The node's agent identifies itself with the value of its sysObjectID variable and its network address. Several generic traps are defined by the protocol, including *link-down*, *link-up* and *authentication-failure*. Others may be defined by the user. A list of variables, containing information related to the trap, is included in the trap message. The fields of SNMP messages are encoded (converted to strings of octets) using the *Basic Encoding Rules for ASN.1*.

The transport of SNMP messages between a network management station and a managed node is as simple as the protocol. The preferred method, and the one specified in *RFC 1157*, is to use the *User Datagram (UDP)* protocol from the TCP/IP suite (see Chapter 9, Section 9.4). Other options are a direct mapping to an Ethernet frame and a mapping to the OSI transport service, in either connectionless or connection-oriented mode. Almost anything that will transfer messages from one place to another may be used, although some are more suitable than others.

The power of SNMP lies in the SMI and the MIB on which the protocol operates. Although closely associated with the TCP/IP suite, its use is by no means confined to networks using this suite. The protocol does not offer the range of operations defined by the OSI CMIP and a hybrid system is sometimes used in a TCP/IP environment. This is *Common Management Protocol and Services Over TCP/IP (CMOT)*, which means that OSI services are provided over a TCP/IP stack. It uses a minimal layer 5/6 protocol called the *Lightweight Presentation Protocol (LPP)*. So far, its use has been limited.

SNMP is the most widely implemented non-proprietary management protocol. The simplicity of the protocol encourages its implementation and enables management agents to be incorporated in many networking products from different manufacturers.

## 12.4 Management of an SNA network

In the introduction to this chapter it was suggested that management of a network requires a focal point to which management information is directed and from which management control commands can be issued. The architectural structure of an SNA control domain, with a unique NAU permanently connected to all other NAUs in the domain, immediately lends itself to this centralized approach to management. The SSCP is a natural focal point for management activity and a natural home for an operator-controlled management application.

SNA NAUs have always had built-in management functions and the SNA protocol has always included a number of control RUs of either type. The management functions are concentrated in the network services component of the function management layer of a NAU. They consist of *session services*, which enable a NAU to initiate a session and to report progress to the SSCP, *configuration services*, which are concerned with establishing and changing the network configuration and *management services*, which support most of the control functions that have been covered in this chapter. Originally, a small number of RUs were defined in the protocol to provide these functions, but the number has grown over the years and so they were rationalized into, effectively, a single RU—the ill-named *Network Management Control Vector (NMVT)*.

Network control messages flow on the SSCP-PU and SSCP-LU sessions that are established when the network is activated and exist for the lifetime of that activation. Consequently, a permanent management network is established that shares the network links with user messages. Management messages originate in or are destined for the management services component of the SSCP, which also provides an operator interface. The SNA management system was originally called *Communications Network Management (CNM)*, but is now frequently called the *Network Management Architecture (NMA)*.

As SNA networks grew in size and complexity, applications were developed to assist the network operator in monitoring and controlling the network. These, being Virtual Telecommunication Access Method (VTAM) applications, were host based. In 1986, these applications were consolidated into a single, strategic management application called *NetView*. NetView has subsequently been developed to enable some control functions to be exercised from a PC (*NetView/PC*) and forms the basis of a wider management system called *SystemView*.

The NMA recognizes three types of management point—*focal point*, *entry point* and *service point*. A focal point is the single point, within a network or domain, that provides a complete view of the state of the network and at which operator commands are issued. It is implemented via an application such as NetView. An entry point is a node in the network that makes management services available to itself and to

## Network management

devices connected to it. For example, a communications controller or a cluster controller provides an entry point. A service point provides a gateway between the SNA management network and non-SNA devices, enabling the scope of the management system to include non-IBM and non-SNA devices. NetView/PC may be used to provide a service point.

In summary, the modern view of SNA management is a hierarchy of focal, entry and service points, each containing management services, with an operator interface provided by NetView. Communication within this structure uses SSCP-PU/LU sessions carrying *management services RUs*.

Management services RUs are messages, in defined format, exchanged between management services components in the SSCP and its domain of PUs and LUs. They enable the SSCP to request a PU to carry out tests and to report the result, to dump its memory contents and return them to the SSCP as well as to report various types of management statistics. A PU may send an unsolicited alert and an LU may request an echo test from the SSCP. A relatively new RU has been added to the list. This is the *Network Management Vector Transport (NMVT) RU* on which all future development of the network management protocol will be based.

An NMVT RU consists of a number of fields, forming a major vector, and containing a 2-byte length field, a 2-byte type field and a variable length data field. The data field consists of one or more subvectors, each also with the length-type-data format. Some of these subvectors, such as the date/time subvectors, are common to all major vectors; others are related to a particular type of major vector. Major vectors currently defined include *alerts, trace data, problem determination statistics* and *response time statistics*, each with its own subvectors.

## SNA management and OSI

There are substantial differences (and some similarities) between the OSI management framework and the SNA Network Management Architecture. The OSI framework (as discussed in the previous section) relies on communications between applications using CMIS and CMIP. SNA, on the other hand, includes management functions and communication *within* the communications architecture. It relies on applications to provide the interface between the management system and the operator. It should be noted, however, that some aspects of OSI management, layer management and protocol management are closer to the SNA approach.

There have been, in recent years, welcome signs of convergence in certain areas of SNA and OSI. One of these is the management area. IBM offers, in its *OSI Communications Subsystem (OSI/CS)* product, a gateway between SNA and OSI systems. The product provides support for the CMIS and will handle CMIP messages. It also communicates via LU6.2 sessions with NetView that includes a command processor to convert messages between SNA and OSI protocols. It is thus possible for a NetView operator to manage a hybrid SNA/OSI network.

## 12.5 Integrated network management systems

The users of data processing equipment generally like to adopt a multivendor purchasing policy to give them the freedom to choose products from different vendors that satisfy their particular needs and budgets. They have a reasonable expectation that products from different manufacturers will work together. If this interworking is not provided by manufacturers, customers look to the standards bodies—hence the growing popularity of TCP/IP with its related upper-layer protocols and the increasing convergence of proprietary architectures and OSI. These trends towards interworking are welcome but far from complete. In the meantime, customers are expanding their networks and building new ones from an ever-increasing choice of components. Both public and private network providers need to be able to manage these multivendor networks.

A manufacturer of a particular type of component generally incorporates facilities for remote management from a central point. The management systems are likely to be as different as the types of component with which they are associated. The user is forced to install them all to achieve comprehensive network management. Each is likely to have its own control terminal and network control centres become filled with subnetwork control terminals, each requiring different knowledge to operate it. None of them give a complete view of the state of the network.

This situation has led to the development of integrated network management systems. Such systems provide a single point of control to which the different management systems pass information and from which they receive commands. The single point is the *general manager*; separate points of control for different types of component are *element managers*. The structure is illustrated in Figure 12.2.

Such a structure requires a common protocol—a common language for communication between the general manager and the element managers. CMIP and SNMP are obvious candidates for this protocol and manufacturers are increasingly providing element management systems that conform to one or other of these standards. Many of the older ones do not and so development is required to convert their proprietary protocol into a standard for communication with the general manager. As networks grow and internets are built, it becomes increasingly challenging to implement a management system that will provide a view of the complete internet. The solution lies in integrated systems based on a common management framework and a common management protocol. The OSI framework and CMIP are most likely to provide this solution.

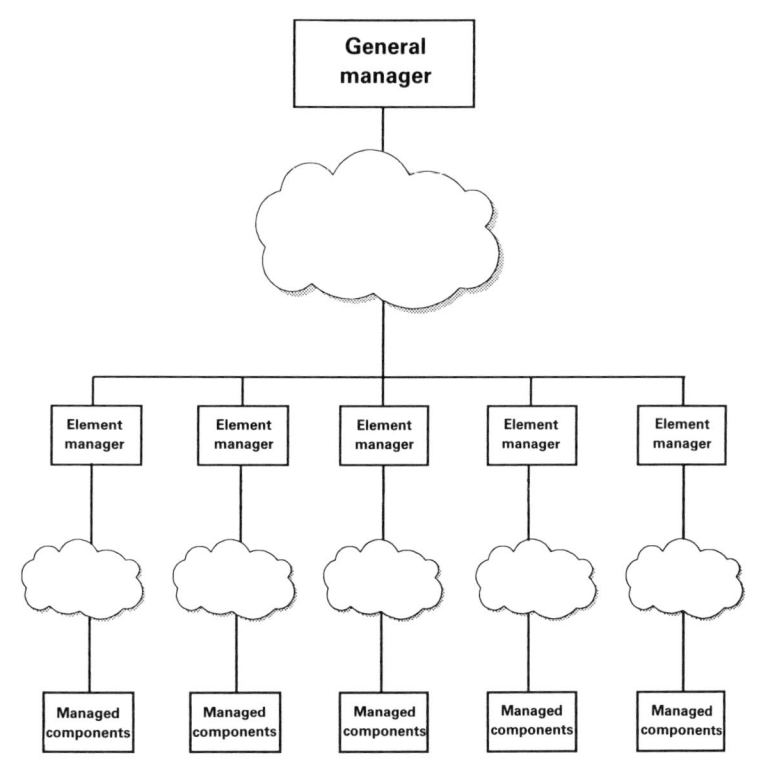

*Figure 12.2    Integrated network management*

## 12.6 Summary

*The WNB believes in open architectures, and its approach to network management reinforces this belief. The bank's network is built with components from many sources, many of which have proprietary management systems offering some or all of the facilities that have been discussed in this chapter. These systems are element managers for the WNB integrated management system, which is based on the OSI network management framework.*

*One of the WNB's basic requirements (outlined in Section 1.2) was that the voice and data services within the branch be managed centrally. In the WNB's design, this has been achieved by means of management control of the PABXs and an integrated network management centre, which controls element management systems for the various components of the LANs and WANs. The integrated network management centre accepts signals from the element management systems and draws management conclusions that are presented to operators. The operators are able to communicate directly with the element management systems in order to investigate faults and provide recovery.*

*The integrated network management system is connected to a single help desk that serves the branches. Information provided by the management system about faults on the network, in the data centre or in the branch equipment is passed to the help desk where operators are able to explain the problem to the branch staff and give an indication of the nature and timescale of the recovery processes.*

# CHAPTER 13 Conclusion

The intention in this book has been to provide a wide-ranging survey of communication techniques and their applications in a typical large business. The treatment of many topics is necessarily superficial, while others have been omitted altogether in the interests of simplicity and manageability. The material is intended to provide an introduction to information networking and enable readers with a need for more detailed knowledge to identify their specific interests.

The remaining years of the twentieth century promise exciting developments in information transfer. For many, this has hitherto been limited to the post and telephone systems, together with public broadcasting. The provision of integrated digital services over optical networks will revolutionize the distribution of information. Whether all this information is wanted—or needed—remains to be seen.

*WNB believes that standards and open architectures are the best way of developing its business and serving its customers. This belief is reflected in its use of many of the standard approaches to networking that have been discussed in this book. The bank depends heavily on its computers and the network that provides access to them. The customers of the WNB's IT department are the bank's business units. Providing a quality service to these units helps the bank to provide a quality service to its customers.*

*This concludes the survey of communication in the Wessex and Northern Bank. WNB's open systems strategy is not completely implemented and its network has a hybrid architecture and components from many sources. The authors believe that the bank is on the right lines in its journey towards a truly open, managed and secure communications system. Our readers may care to pop into a WNB branch and see for themselves!*

# Bibliography

The following list is confined to books published in or after 1988.

Black, Uyless D., *Data Networks: Concepts, Theory and Practice*, (Prentice-Hall, 1989)

Black, Uyless D., *The X Series Recommendations*, (McGraw-Hill, 1991)

Comer, Douglas E., *Internetworking with TCP/IP* (2 volumes), (Prentice-Hall, 1991)

Currie, W. Scott, *LANs Explained*, (Ellis Horwood, 1988)

Cypser, R. J., *Communications for Cooperating Systems*, (Addison-Wesley, 1991)

Davidson, John, *An Introduction to TCP/IP*, (Springer-Verlag, 1988)

Easington, R. J., *X.25 Explained*, (Ellis Horwood, 1988)

Griffiths, John M. et al, *ISDN Explained*, (Wiley, 1990)

Halsall, Fred, *Data Communications, Computer Networks and Open Systems*, (Addison-Wesley, 1992)

Henshall, John and Sandy Shaw, *OSI Explained*, (Ellis Horwood, 1988)

Jain, Bijendra N. and Ashok K. Agrawala, *Open Systems Interconnection*, (Elsevier, 1990)

Kapoor, Atul, *SNA: Architecture, Protocols and Implementation*, (McGraw-Hill, 1992)

Kauffels, F.-J., *Network Management*, (Addison-Wesley, 1992)

Marsden, Brian W., *Communication Network Protocols*, (Chartwell-Bratt, 1991)

Nutt, Gary J., *Open Systems*, (Prentice-Hall, 1992)

Pfleeger, Charles P., *Security in Computing*, (Prentice-Hall, 1989)

Rose, Marshall T., *The Open Book: A Practical Perspective on OSI*, (Prentice-Hall, 1990)

Rose, Marshall T., *The Simple Book: An Introduction to Management of TCP/IP-based Internets*, (Prentice-Hall, 1991)

Rose, Marshall T., *The Little Black Book: Mail Bonding with OSI Directory Services*, (Prentice-Hall, 1992)

Stallings, William, *Local Networks*, (Macmillan, 1990)

Stamper, David A., *Business Data Communications*, (Benjamin/Cummings, 1991)

# Index

Abstract syntax, 108
Abstract Syntax Notation (ASN.1), 108, 210
Accounting management, 209
Active attack, 189
Address Resolution Protocol (ARP), 163, 168
Advanced Peer-to-peer Networking (APPN), 138
Architecture, 43, 76
    development of, 46
    layers, 43
    primitives, 92
    protocol, 92
    services, 92
    stack, 44
    subsets, 43
ARPANET, 159
ASCII, 13
Association Control Service Element (ACSE), 109
Asymmetric algorithm, 195
Asynchronous Balanced Mode (ABM), 77
Asynchronous Response Mode (ARM), 77
Asynchronous Transfer Mode (ATM), 184
Asynchronous Transmission, 17
Attacks, 186
Authentication, 187, 197

B-channel, 174
Bar incoming calls, 71
Baseband LAN, 146
Basic information unit (BIU), 125
Basic rate ISDN, 174
Baud, 19
Baudot code, 13
Bearer, 174
Bearer service, 174, 176
Binary Coded Decimal (BCD), 14
Bind image, 118
Binding, 118
Bit stuffing, 77
Block ciphers, 193
Block synchronization, 19
Boundary node, 120
Bracket, 132, 136
Bridge, 33, 155
Broadband ISDN, 181
Broadband LAN, 146

Call accepted packet, 69
Call connected packet, 69
Call redirection, 71
Call request packet, 69

Carrier Sense Multiple Access/Collision Detection (CSMA/CD), 60, 146, 178
CCITT, 48, 64, 76, 174, 210
CCITT No. 7 system, 181
Cell relay, 184
Chain, 131
Challenge and response, 187–188
Character synchronization, 19
Checkpoint, 105
Cipher, 190
Cipher text, 190
Clear indication packet, 69
Clear request packet, 69
Clear text, 190
Clearing House Automated Payment System (CHAPS), 5
Closed user group, 71
Code, 190
Collision, 59, 142, 146
Commitment, Concurrency and Recovery (CCR), 110
Common Application Service Element (CASE), 109
Common Management Information Protocol (CMIP), 208, 216
Common Management Information Service (CMIS), 208
Common Management Protocol and Services Over TCP/IP (CMOT), 213
Communications media, 24
Compression, 21, 23, 108
Configuration management, 209
Confirmed service, 93
Connection orientated, 66, 96, 167
Connectionless, 66, 96, 164, 167
Countermeasures, 187
Cryptography, 190
Customer Information Control System (CICS), 117
Cyclic redundancy check, 80

D-channel, 174
Data Circuit-terminating Equipment (DCE), 67
Data Encryption Algorithm (DEA), 191
Data Encryption Standard (DES), 191
Data flow control, 131
Data integrity, 199
Data packet, 72
Data secrecy, 197
Data stream, 134
Data Terminal Equipment (DTE), 67
Data token, 106
Diagnostic packet, 75

Dialogue control, 104
Document Content Architecture (DCA), 137
Document Interchange Architecture (DIA), 137
Document Transfer and Manipulation (DTAM), 177
Domain, 114
Domain Name System (DNS), 171

EBCDIC, 14
Echo cancellation, 175
Element address, 121
Element manager, 216
Encryption, 108, 129, 130, 190
Error correction, 21
Error detection, 21, 80
Error recovery, 42
Ethernet, 146, 164, 213
Explicit route, 121
Explicit route control, 124
Extended sequence numbering, 71

Facilities field, 71
Facilities request packet, 72
Facility registration packet, 71
Facility request block, 87
Fast packet switching, 182
Fast select, 71
Fault management, 209
Fibre Distributed Data Interface (FDDI), 148
File Transfer Access and Management (FTAM), 111
File Transfer Protocol (FTP), 169
Final form text, 138
Flow control, 42, 45, 74, 87, 124, 166
Format identifier (FID), 125
Frame, 77, 124, 143, 177
Frame check sequence, 80, 145
Frame relay, 183
Frequency division duplex, 175
Frequency Division Multiplexing (FDM), 20
Frequency Shift Keying (FSK), 17
Function management, 132
Function Management Header (FMH), 134
Functional units, 106

Gateway, 33, 157
General Format Identifier (GFID), 68, 74
Generating polynomial, 81
Graphical user interface, 12
Group 4 fax, 176

H-channel, 181
Hamming code, 21
Handshake, 198
Huffman compression, 23

I-frame, 78
I.430/I.431, 177
Incoming call packet, 69–70

Information coding, 13
Information Management System (IMS), 117
Information Technology, 12–13
Institute of Electrical and Electronics Engineers (IEEE), 143
Integrated Digital Network (IDN), 173
Integrated network management, 216
Integrated Services Digital Network (ISDN), 17
Intermediate node, 120
International Alphabet, 13
International Standards Organization (ISO), 47–48, 91
Internet, 159, 210
internet, 159–160
Internet Activities Board (IAB), 172
Internet Control Message Protocol (ICMP), 163, 168
Internet Engineering Task Force (IETF), 172
Internet Protocol (IP), 160
Internet Research Task Force (IRTF), 172
Interrupt packet, 73
IP addresses, 162
ISO 646, 13
ISO 7498, 47, 50, 203
ISO 8802, 143
ISO 9314, 148
ISO 9594, 171
ISO 10021, 111
ISO 10164, 203
ISO 10181, 203

Key, 190
Key encrypting keys, 201
Key management, 191, 200
Key schedule, 193

Line encryptors, 202
Link Access Protocol Balanced (LAPB), 79, 176
Link Access Protocol for the D-channel (LAPD), 178, 183
Local Area Network (LAN), 58, 141
Logical Channel Identifier (LCI), 67–68, 71
Logical Link Control (LLC), 143, 152
Logical Unit (LU), 55–56, 114, 116
   LU2, 55, 117
   LU6.2, 116–117, 132, 135, 206
   LU6.2 verbs, 136
   LU type, 135

Managed object, 208–210
Management information base, 208, 211
Manchester encoding, 18
Masquerade, 187
Medium access control (MAC), 60, 143, 151
Message authentication code, 199
Message Handling System (MHS), 111
Message Orientated Text Interchange System (MOTIS), 111

# Index

Message transfer agent, 111
Metropolitan area network, 141, 149, 185
Modem, 17, 33
Monitor station, 144
Multiplexer, 20, 33

NetView, 214
Network, 27, 95, 160
   addressing, 31
   circuit switched, 33
   links, 32, 95
   local area, 34
   metropolitan area, 34
   nodes, 28, 95
   packet switched, 33
   structure, 49
   topologies, 29
   type A/B/C, 103
   wide area, 34
Network Addressable Unit (NAU), 55, 57, 114–115
Network administration, 207
Network control, 207
Network Management Vector Transport (NMVT), 133, 214–215
Network security, 186
Network Service Access Point (NSAP), 109
Network Virtual Terminal (NVT), 170
Non-repudiation, 199
Normal Response Mode (NRM), 77, 143
Numbering plan identification, 70

Object identifier, 210
One-way function, 190
Open Document Architecture (ODA), 177
Open Systems Interconnection (OSI), 47, 50, 159, 206
Optical fibre, 24, 173, 182
OSI management, 207

Pacing, 124, 126, 130
Packet, 66
Packet assembler/disassembler (PAD), 84
Packet type identifier, 69
Passive attack, 189
Path control network, 55, 57–58, 114, 121
Path Information Unit (PIU), 121, 125
Pels, 14
Performance management, 209
Peripheral node, 120
Permanent Virtual Circuit (PVC), 67
Permutation ciphers, 193
Personal authentication, 187, 197, 204
Personal Authentication Value (PAV), 197
Phase Shift Keying (PSK), 17
Physical Unit (PU), 55, 114
Presentation Service Access Point (PSAP), 109
Primary rate ISDN, 174
Primary station, 77

Product ciphers, 193
Profiles, 134
Protocol Control Information (PCI), 94
Protocol Data Unit (PDU), 94
Pseudo-header, 168
PU type, 120, 135
Public key, 195
Pulse Code Modulation (PCM), 15, 173, 176

Q.921/Q.922, 183
Q.931, 180
Quality of Service (QOS), 96, 100–101

Receive not ready packet, 75
Receive ready packet, 75
Reject packet, 75
Release token, 106
Reliable Transfer Service Element (RTSE), 110
Remote Operations Service Element (ROSE), 110
Request for Comment (RFC), 172
Request/Response Header (RH), 58, 125, 129
Request/Response Unit (RU), 125, 129
Reset packet, 75
Residual errors, 102
Restart packet, 75
Reverse Address Resolution Protocol (RARP), 163, 168
Reverse charging, 71
Revisable Form Text (RFT), 137
Rivest, Shamir and Adleman (RSA), 195
Router, 33, 156
RSA algorithm, 195, 199

S-frame, 78
Secondary station, 77
Security management, 209
Sequence number, 75, 79, 130, 165
Service Data Unit (SDU), 93
Session, 55, 114
   control sessions, 117
   cross-domain, 114, 119–120
   LU-LU, 55
   SSCP-LU, 55, 118, 131
   SSCP-PU, 118, 131
Session establishment, 118
Session key, 202
Session types, 116
SETUP message (ISDN), 180
Signalled errors, 103
Signature dynamics, 188, 198
Simple mail transfer protocol (SMTP), 169
Simple network management protocol (SNMP), 171, 209, 211, 216
SNA distribution services (SNADS), 138
SNA Network Interconnect (SNI), 161
SNA node, 113

223

Society of World-wide International Financial Transactions (SWIFT), 5
Socket, 165
Specific Application Service Element (SASE), 110
Stack, 91
Start/stop, 18, 85
State variables, 74
Stream ciphers, 194
Sub-area, 120–121
Substitution ciphers, 193
Supplementary service, 174
Switched Virtual Circuit (SVC), 67
Symmetric algorithm, 191
Sync-major token, 106
Sync-minor token, 106
Synchronous Data Link Control (SDLC), 123, 125
Synchronous transmission, 18
System Services Control Point (SSCP), 56, 114, 214
Systems Network Architecture (SNA), 46, 53, 113

TCP protocol port, 165
TCP segment, 164
Teleservice, 174, 176
TELNET, 170
Time division duplex, 175
Time Division Multiplexing (TDM), 20, 177
Time to live, 162
Title, 109
Token, 60, 106, 143
Token ring, 60, 143
Transfer syntax, 108
Transmission control, 129
Transmission Control Protocol (TCP), 164
Transmission group, 124
Transmission group control, 124
Transmission Header (TH), 58, 122, 125
Transport class, 101, 103, 164
Triple X, 85
Trivial File Transfer Protocol (TFTP), 169
Type of Address (TOA), 70

U-frame, 79
Unconfirmed service, 93
Upper Layer Protocol (ULP), 168
User agent, 111

User datagram protocol (UDP), 167, 169

Virtual circuit, 67
Virtual route, 121
Virtual route control, 124
Virtual Telecommunication Access Method (VTAM), 214
Voice, 184

Well-known port, 165, 169
Wessex and Northern Bank (WNB), 25, 39, 62
  as a clearing bank, 1
  Branch Accounting System, 4
  branches, 1–8, 62
  constituents, 1
  corporate database, 5
  employees, 1
  foreign exchange, 8
  information flows, 3, 9
  international business, 8
  investment bank, 9
  IT group, 1–2
  LANs, 158
  network, 9, 37–38, 62, 89, 139, 172, 185
  network management, 217
  network security, 11, 204
  office automation, 7
  profit, 1
  special services, 6
  structure, 1
  treasury division, 8
  use of open systems, 62, 112
Window, 67, 74, 125, 166

X.3, 85
X.21, 82
X.25, 54, 57, 62, 64, 99, 111, 128
  optional facilities, 71
X.28, 85
X.29, 85
X.75, 161
X.121, 70
X.400, 63, 111, 165
X.500, 171